Contents at a Gl[ance]

Golden Retrievers

Golden Retrievers

2nd Edition

by Nona Kilgore Bauer

A Wiley Brand

Golden Retrievers For Dummies®

Published by
John Wiley & Sons, Inc.
111 River Street
Hoboken, NJ 07030
www.wiley.com

Table of Contents

Introduction

Whether you're thinking about making a run for the gold or you already own one or a dozen Golden Retrievers, you've come to the right book. Through these pages, I explore all the elements of your Golden Retriever's life (present and future company included), from the joyous days of puppyhood to the sweet serenity of the senior years.

Before you turn to the next page, I must warn you in advance. I will occasionally nag a bit. That's because certain dog facts and rules are important enough to bear extra emphasis, and I will lose sleep if you don't understand them. If you notice it, I'm proud of you, because it means that you remember what I said.

How to Use This Book

This book is intended for busy 21st-century dog owners who don't have time to sit down and read through 300 pages at a crack. This is a reference you can jump in and out of as dog questions rear their furry heads. Just flip to the Table of Contents or the index to find the pertinent pages on that topic.

That's not to say you *shouldn't* read this entire book! Every chapter offers important nuggets of information that I believe every Golden owner needs to know. But you don't need the details on senior dog food if your Golden's just a pup, so that's the real beauty of the For Dummies formula. You can go directly to the information you need at the time.

In case you're wondering about those little gray boxes you see throughout the book, these sidebars contain bonus information — kind of like puppy treats. These goodies are not essential to the overall content of each chapter, so don't feel guilty if you skip past one or two!

Foolish Assumptions

I made a few assumptions when I wrote this book:

>> You are hooked on Golden Retrievers and either own one or you're thinking about taking the plunge.

>> You want to find out the best way to raise and train your Golden, as a loving family dog and well-behaved canine citizen.

>> You want your Golden to not just survive, but thrive, and you bought this book to help you make that happen.

Icons Used in This Book

Throughout this book, various icons appear in the margin to highlight different types of information.

These icons help you discover ways to make your life (and your dog's life) easier.

The Warning icon means just that!

Remember icons are memory boosters so that you won't forget important doggie details.

This icon marks pure canine pleasantries that dog folks like to know.

Where to Go from Here

Where you start in this book depends on what you want at any particular moment. If your Golden just dug into the trash for the umpteenth time and you're counting to ten, then check out Part 2. Other needs and questions will point you to other sections of the book. It's all just the flip of a page away. So go ahead, indulge yourself and explore everything this book has to offer!

My goal in writing this book was to make you the smartest Golden owner in your neighborhood — heck, even the entire town! If I succeed, everyone will be richer for it — you, your Golden, and, of course, I'll sleep a whole lot better, too.

1

Finding Your Soul Mate

Golden Retrievers are great dogs. But they also shed, chew, and need lots of exercise. Are you ready for that?

In this part you learn the importance of becoming a Golden Retriever expert and researching this special breed before you decide to add one to your family.

Find out how and where to look for a healthy Golden who will be compatible with your family. (Skip the Internet and newspaper. Good breeders don't advertise!)

Learn how to choose the pup who's right for you. Hunting buddy? Family camping companion? Snuggle bunny? Your breeder can help you decide which puppy fits your Golden dreams.

Chapter **1**

Are You Meant for Each Other?

I f you live in a typical neighborhood, then you're probably neighbors with at least one Golden Retriever. Goldens seem to be everywhere — down the block, on television, and in every magazine. These big, beautiful furries are the most popular advertising gimmick of the 21st century. Not only are they huggable, they're trainable as well. What other dog can leap so high or smile so wide into that camera lens? As one of the five most popular dog breeds of the American Kennel Club (AKC), Goldens are no doubt one of the most photographed subjects in the media. Of course, Golden fanatics don't see anything strange about this, and love every doggie moment. Heck, even nondog people will admit (under their breath) that those Golden Retrievers are kinda cute.

This chapter gives you the inside scoop on this special breed. If you haven't fallen in love with your neighbor's Golden already, you will by the time you're done browsing this book.

But — and this is a big *but* — although Golden Retrievers are great dogs, they're not for everyone. This chapter also tells you how to determine whether you're one of those lucky people who is perfect for the breed.

The Name Game

The Golden Retriever is aptly named — especially the "golden" part. What began as a description of this dog's yellow coat more appropriately describes his sunny disposition and his 14-karat value to his owner and to society. Goldens are great family dogs and all-around good sports who think they were created purely to please their person. This happy, funny, friendly fetcher of anything not nailed down has captured a permanent corner of the American heart, home, and marketplace. Give them a spot with a human on it (as you can see in Figure 1-1, this Golden will gladly join you on the couch!), a puddle to play in, and a stick or tennis ball to fetch and carry (maybe not in that order), and you've made their day. As a bonus, throw in an occasional duck or pheasant — after all, retriever is 50 percent of this dog's name!

FIGURE 1-1: There is no better place to lounge than with a Golden at your side!

© Getty Images.

ARE ALL GOLDEN RETRIEVERS GOLDEN?

The color of that lush Golden Retriever coat dates back to the breed's four original yellow ancestors crossed with a few selected hunting breeds sprinkled here and there during the late 19th century. Today, the breed color can range from very pale blond to reddish gold to deep Irish Setter red.

Keep in mind that the color of the Golden's coat has nothing to do with his intelligence or equally golden temperament. Color matters occasionally in the conformation ring. Some show judges seem to prefer a blonde or lighter coat, which only means they probably spent too much time watching reruns of old Marilyn Monroe movies.

More than Beauty

The Golden Retriever's personality is as golden as his outer coat. This dog was bred to please, and please he does. He started out as a hunting partner who delivered birds to hand, and has evolved into modern times delivering whatever suits his owner's fancy. He's always happy to oblige.

Because they were originally bred to work in tandem with humans, Goldens are also highly trainable and eager to please. These dogs are a breath of fresh air in an era of too many wild and crazy dogs who sometimes drive their owners nuts.

WARNING

Trainable doesn't mean that Golden Retrievers are born already trained. It just means they're very willing fellows who like to work as a team, and if you're the captain of the team, your Golden will be delighted to do your bidding. Remember the part about the captain; it's important! (See Chapter 7 for more on training.)

FORGIVE AND FORGET

Goldens have the dog world's most forgiving disposition and will blithely dismiss all those dumb mistakes you're bound to make. Whether you come home 2 hours late, forget his dinner bowl, or accidentally step on his tail, he'll forget it ever happened once you smile at him. (A hefty scratch behind his ears, and he's your slave forever.) That does not imply that you have his permission to do stupid things. It just means he understands you're only human.

Likewise, you should follow his good example and forgive your dog his trespasses. In dog terms, they're not mistakes because he's just a dog and is the product of his instincts and your training, good or bad.

The Do-It-All Golden Retriever

If the Golden Retriever were a human, you'd be envious. Not only are Goldens beautiful, intelligent, and friendly, they're also natural athletes who have dipped their paws into every canine sporting discipline. These dogs are joyful companions who are willing to try anything as long as they can enjoy it with someone fun to be with.

Beyond sportsmanship, that famous Golden nose has nudged its way into almost every other facet of the human-animal connection. Today, Golden Retrievers serve as assistance dogs for the physically disabled, guide dogs for the blind, and hearing dogs for the deaf. And that Golden nose keeps on sniffing, working for law enforcement as drug and arson detectives, and as search and rescue dogs who find victims buried under snow and earthquake rubble. Beyond that, with their sweet demeanors, they also excel as therapy dogs in hospitals and nursing homes where, unlike the average hourly employee, they love their jobs. And they work for free, unless you count dog biscuits as a paycheck.

Why Not a Golden Retriever?

Of course, you want a Golden Retriever. What person in his right mind wouldn't? And you firmly believe you and the dog would be a golden combination. Right?

Well, maybe. Despite their high-profile status in the media, Goldens aren't for everyone. This is a sporting breed, folks. These high-energy dogs require training. On the other hand, Goldens are easily trained and love to learn, so training could and should be a fun but very busy experience.

With no offense intended to my favorite breed, the following sections outline some reasons that you may want to think twice about life with a Golden Retriever.

Hair, hair, everywhere

The Golden Retriever has what's called a *double coat*, which means that he has a soft downy undercoat to insulate him from the cold and heat and a longer outer coat of guard hairs. These hairy critters shed their downy undercoat in huge quantities every spring and leave a little dog hair all over the house all year long. The resulting clouds of dog down all over the house can make you tear out your hair as well.

DO YOU REALLY WANT A PUPPY?

Golden Retriever puppy fever isn't a dog disease; it's a people condition that most often occurs in spring when some humans become infected with an uncontrollable urge to add a puppy to the family. It can lead to dog heaven or, heaven forbid, a nervous breakdown if the affected person thinks all Goldens are like the ones they see on television. The cure — getting that cute puppy immediately — can be worse than the disease.

If you're serious about getting a Golden puppy (or *any* puppy) and not just caving in to the kids or some other wild and crazy impulse, follow the advice of responsible dog owners and breeders. Look deep into your dog-loving soul and check out the big picture. Love alone is not enough. This is a commitment that hopefully will last 12 or more years!

TIP

Brushing will help keep that nuisance dog hair to a minimum. Daily brushing is best — twice weekly is a must. If you use a professional groomer, expect to pay $50 to $75 per grooming session. Pretty is seldom cheap. (For more on grooming, see Chapter 13.)

Move over!

If you want to live with a Golden Retriever, make sure you have room for one. These big sprawling fellows easily occupy at least one couch cushion or easy chair. Everything's big, including their muddy paw prints on your kitchen floor and their nose prints on the window. That happy Golden tail can easily clear your coffee table. (Sorry, move your Waterford.)

REMEMBER

In short, Goldens need space, and lots of it, both in-house and out. A yard is a must, and good fencing is the best way to keep him safe and out of trouble. (Yes, given the opportunity, he will try to wander off in search of squirrels, bunnies, and other varmints.)

BORN TO RETRIEVE

The Golden Retriever is a Scotsman, a hunting dog born and bred in Scotland over 150 years ago. To the Golden's credit, he has surpassed Scottish tweeds and kilts in popularity, and today performs well beyond the duck blind he was born for. Overdosed with talent and versatility, the 21st-century Golden consistently outperforms other breeds in almost every discipline in dog sports, including more mundane activities like sock and shoe theft. (Just ask my personal Golden Retriever crew about that!)

Daily dose of exercise

A normal Golden usually creates a little happy chaos, which is part of his universal appeal. These spirited dogs have an inbred desire to retrieve, play, chase, and chew. They need daily exercise to expend all that sporting energy, or they will entertain themselves in the usual canine fashion. (Think destruction!)

A typical Golden Retriever household usually has a few ragged chew marks on the chair legs, dog toys strewn about the living room, piles of shredded sticks in the backyard, and one or two large sticks at the front or back door, the ones he delivered to you as his special prize.

REMEMBER

Your Golden will not exercise without you. *You* are his incentive to romp and play. Daily walks and jogs (a favorite Golden activity, as shown in Figure 1-2), Frisbee games, and bumper chasing (those large, hot-dog-shaped canvas or plastic retrieving objects sold in pet stores for retrieve-a-holic dogs) can help keep your Golden tired and content. For more on exercising with your dog, see Chapters 10 and 17.

FIGURE 1-2:
A good run is great for *both* of you!

© Getty Images.

Just like people, you can't stereotype Goldens. If you're discouraged about all this talk about active, high-energy Golden Retrievers, don't worry. You can still find a quiet(er) Golden companion who won't totally disrupt your household. Some lines (or families) of show-type Goldens produce a more laid-back animal who doesn't act like Robo Cop. See Chapters 3 and 4 for more details.

Get up and go!

WARNING

If you're on the go and never home and your Golden's alone most of the day, he will be stressed and unhappy. That's not fair to the dog and may be disastrous for you. Goldens need to be with people, and an isolated and lonely Golden can easily suffer from separation anxiety, which will lead to destructive behavior. It's a natural canine stress reliever.

On the other hand, if you're an active family that loves the outdoor life and plan to take your Golden to soccer practice and baseball games, then the two of you are probably a good match.

Train, train, train

Smart as he is, a Golden Retriever will not train himself. Good manners are not included in his pedigree. It's up to you, the team captain, to teach your dog acceptable behavior — what he may and may not do at home and in the neighborhood. Obedience training is the only way to accomplish that. Few pet owners have the know-how, expertise, or motivation to do it solo, so training classes must be part of your agenda. That also means practicing every day with your dog, or your once-a-week classes will be wasted.

WARNING

Don't be misled by the over-used 10-minutes-a-day obedience slogan. Training is an ongoing process whenever you're with your dog and he's awake. If you can't or won't commit to raising your Golden as you would an infant or toddler, don't blame your Golden if he's wild or disobedient. See Chapter 9 for more on teaching your Golden obedient behavior and good manners.

Love-'em-all

If you're looking for a guard dog, get rid of this book and investigate another breed. Most Goldens are complete love sponges who would happily lick the boots of an intruder. You can encourage them to bark at people who approach your house, but you can't — and shouldn't — teach them to intimidate or bite. Their very size may deter a home invader, but anyone familiar with a Golden's love-'em-all attitude knows that a scratch behind Golden ears means instant friendship.

That said, I firmly believe that my Golden family would sense any danger to me personally and would defend me to the death. Stories abound about Golden Retriever heroes who have protected children and adults who were in danger or threatened by some adversary.

Kids or dogs?

If you have kids under age 3 or 4 and you get a puppy, you will now have the equivalent of two or three kids under 3! Double your pleasure, and — you got it — twice the work. And a major communication problem.

Because neither pup nor child has learned the house rules yet, almost everything they hear will be a no-no, which creates a negative learning environment for both kid and dog. Puppies nip and chew, and kids pull tails and sit on furry bodies. Both require 24-hour attention. And face it, when you have to prioritize, the puppy naturally loses. That's not fair for the dog. Some breeders may recommend that you wait until your child is older before they let you have one of their prize packages. My personal age limit for kids is 4 years old.

A Golden Price Tag

Dogs are not a bargain if you think long term. Even if you find a pup for free (*never* a bargain!), you still have to pay for food, veterinary care, training, equipment, toys, and possibly doggie day care. And there are no laters or maybes. A sick dog, like a sick child, needs attention now, not when you have the money. In both the short term and the long haul, dogs, especially large ones, add up to mega bucks. So, before you fall in love with some cute fuzzy puppy, consider these figures provided by the AKC:

>> **Veterinary expenses:** Initial veterinary care (shots, worming, and other healthy stuff) runs at least $150 to $200, with lifetime vet care totaling well over $2,500. That's without the cost of spay/neuter surgery (typically at least $200) and the possibility of other surgery due to accident or illness. Factor in preventive medications for typical canine illnesses, and the total medical care can run well over $4,000 during the lifetime of your dog. (For more on preventive care, see Chapter 11.)

THE MIDAS PUPPY

Some breeders who raise competition Goldens may have "pet-quality" pups from certain litters. Pet-quality pups are those who don't make the cut for competition in the field or show ring, but still possess all the other important Golden qualities and thus may be less expensive. But that $200 Golden pup from a newspaper ad is not a bargain and may end up costing a fortune in medical bills, not to mention heartbreak. Obtaining your Golden pup from a reputable breeder is your best bet. (For more on choosing a breeder, see Chapter 3.)

» **Obedience classes:** Training fees for puppy classes and early obedience instruction start at $50 to $100, the same for the additional classes you'll need to make your dog bomb-proof, and will run well into the hundreds if you continue formal training. (For more on training, see Chapter 9.)

» **Food:** Good-quality dog food for an average-size Golden can cost up to $500 a year. That's $5,500 over an 11-year period. (Imagine feeding a Great Dane!)

» **Miscellaneous costs:** Dog supplies, grooming equipment, leashes, collars, and toys carry an initial cost of $250, with a lifetime estimate of $2,500 if you take good care of your dog. (And, of course, you would!) Registration fees vary by state and county, and there's usually flea and tick control, which every Golden owner faces every year.

The grand total comes in at $10,000 to $15,000, the approximate 10- to 13-year lifetime cost for the privilege and pleasure of living with a Golden Retriever. And don't forget the initial purchase of the dog, which can range from a $100 donation to an animal shelter to up to $1,200 for a decent to competition-quality Golden with health guarantees.

WARNING

If your Golden damages or destroys your possessions (bet on it!) or a neighbor's (probably), you can add hundreds more to annual living expenses.

Chapter 2

What to Look for in the Breed

All breeds must have what the American Kennel Club (AKC) calls a "standard"; that is, what a properly bred Golden or other breed should look and act like. After all, that's what makes a "breed" a breed. Without a standard, you could breed a dog with big black or white spots to another spotted dog, and a few generations down the road you'd have a leopard-spotted Golden. That's also what genetics are all about.

Note: In the official publication, "An Introduction to the Golden Retriever" by the Golden Retriever Club of America, it includes the Standard for the breed, which is outlined in this chapter. It states, "The Board of Directors of the American Kennel Club has approved the revised Standard for the Golden Retriever submitted by the Golden Retriever Club of America, effective January 1, 1982."

It's the job and purpose of every breed's parent club (in our case, the Golden Retriever Club of America or GRCA) to decide how to preserve the purity of its chosen breed. Goldens were originally hunting dogs, and the standard says so. The standard also dictates other characteristics of the Golden, such as his color, coat type, size, and temperament. In this chapter, I present the complete Golden Retriever standard as approved by AKC.

Officially Golden

The AKC first recognized the Golden Retriever in 1925. By 1938, the breed had gained enough popularity that Golden fanciers formed a national breed club. Thus was born the Golden Retriever Club of America to help direct the future of the breed in the United States. Today, the GRCA has almost 60 member clubs across the country.

Those local Golden Retriever clubs are a major resource for Golden Retriever owners. You don't have to be a canine expert or good at anything doggie to join a dog breed club. Just loving your dog like crazy is reason enough. You can get lots of good dog advice and information from more experienced club members, and it's a great place to share dog tales and boasts about your Golden that your other friends may be sick of hearing.

AKC Standards

The AKC has different standards for each breed of dog. The following sections describe the ideal Golden Retriever. This provides a guideline for judges and breeders to follow when assessing Goldens in the show ring, as well as their personal dogs, and their breeding potential. Please keep in mind that the language is like a canine legal document and can be difficult for the layperson to understand.

BEAUTY, BRAINS, AND BIRD DOGS

Always great showmen and competitors, Goldens trip the light fantastic in the conformation ring, beguiling the judges and the spectators with their beauty and performance (see figure). Goldens consistently outshine all other breeds in the obedience ring, winning trials and wowing the audience with their high-stepping strut. And a lucky minority still pursue their birthright in the field: in hunting tests, field trials, and doing the real thing with their hunter-owners. Beyond even that, Goldens also steal the show at agility events and flyball competitions. With all those fun activities, no wonder these Golden dogs are always smiling!

It was inevitable that a dog this versatile and talented would be embraced by sporting specialists and bred for specific qualities for various canine competitions. Today, the conformation crowd breeds Goldens for their grand good looks. The obedience enthusiasts prefer high-stepping Goldens who love teamwork, and the bird dog division looks for Goldens who still love birds and water.

As a result, there are often huge differences in how each type of Golden looks and acts. They're all Golden Retrievers, but consider those differences when you consider a particular litter of pups. While each type should have a heart of gold, remember there are several varieties of the breed.

Mary Bloom/AKC Stock Images.

TIP

Few Goldens meet every requirement in the standard. Some have minor faults, and some have faults that disqualify them from the breed ring. However, dogs who are not perfect physical specimens still make wonderful companions and competitors. A reputable breeder will explain the differences between his or her "show quality" and "pet quality" puppies.

General appearance

Figure 2-1 is a good representative profile of a typical Golden Retriever. A symmetrical, powerful, active dog, sound and well put together, not clumsy nor long in leg, displaying a kindly expression and possessing a personality that is eager, alert, and self-confident. Primarily a hunting dog, he should be shown in hard-working condition. Overall appearance, balance, gait, and purpose to be given more emphasis than any of his component parts.

Faults: Any departure from the described ideal shall be considered faulty to the degree to which it interferes with the breed's purpose or is contrary to breed character.

REMEMBER

The Faults definition is intended primarily to guide those who judge the dogs in the conformation ring.

Size, proportion, substance

Males 23–24 inches in height at withers; females 21½–22½ inches. Dogs up to 1 inch above or below standard size should be proportionately penalized. Deviation in height of more than 1 inch from standard shall disqualify.

Length from breastbone to point of buttocks slightly greater than height at *withers* (top of shoulder) in ratio of 12:11. Weight for dogs (males) 65–75 pounds; bitches 55–65 pounds.

Head

Broad in skull, slightly arched laterally and longitudinally without prominence of *frontal bones* (forehead) or *occipital bones* (top back point of the skull). *Stop* (between the eyes, where the top of the nose and forehead meet) well defined but not abrupt. *Foreface* (front of face) deep and wide; nearly as long as skull. Muzzle straight in profile, blending smoothly and strongly into skull; when viewed in profile or from above, slightly deeper and wider at stop than at tip. No heaviness in *flews* (the skin that hangs from the dog's muzzle or his lip). Removal of whiskers is permitted but not preferred.

SNOW NOSE

Don't worry if your Golden's nose turns a little pink in winter. It's called a snow nose and will turn black or brownish-black again in spring. Some dogs get it, and some don't. Others get it later in life, and some never do.

Eyes friendly and intelligent in expression, medium large with dark, close fitting rims, set well apart and reasonably deep in sockets. Color preferably dark brown; medium brown acceptable. Slant eyes and narrow, triangular eyes detract from correct expression and are to be faulted. No white or *haw* (lining inside the lower eyelid) visible when looking straight ahead. Dogs showing evidence of functional abnormality of eyelids or eyelashes (such as, but not limited to, trichiasis, entropion, ectropion, or distichiasis) are to be excused from the ring. (See Chapter 15 for a discussion on eye problems and hereditary eye disease.)

Ears rather short with front edge attached well behind and just above the eye and falling close to cheek. When pulled forward, tip of ear should just cover the eye. Low, hound-like ear set to be faulted.

Nose black or brownish-black, though fading to a lighter shade in cold weather not serious. Pink nose or one seriously lacking in pigmentation to be faulted.

Teeth scissors bite, in which the outer side of the lower incisors touches the inner side of the upper incisors. *Undershot* (the lower front teeth protrude beyond the front upper teeth in bite or closed position) or *overshot* (just the opposite; the lower jaw is shorter, so the upper front teeth bite down over the lower teeth) is a disqualification. *Misalignment of teeth* (irregular placement of incisors) or a *level bite* (incisors meet each other edge to edge) is undesirable, but not to be confused with undershot or overshot. Full dentition. Obvious gaps are serious faults.

Neck, topline, body

Neck medium long, merging gradually into well-laid back shoulders, giving sturdy, muscular appearance. No throatiness.

Back line strong and level from *withers* (top of the shoulders, just behind the neck) to slightly sloping *croup* (the lower back, from the front of the pelvis to the base of the tail), whether standing or moving. Sloping back line, *roach* (humped up) or sway back, flat or steep croup to be faulted.

Body well balanced, short coupled (not an excessively long body), deep through the chest. Chest between forelegs at least as wide as a man's closed hand including thumb, with well-developed *forechest* (top of the chest). *Brisket* (lower chest under the breast bone extending to between the front legs) extends to elbow. Ribs long and well sprung but not barrel shaped, extending well toward hindquarters. *Loin* (from the rib cage to the pelvis) short, muscular, wide and deep, with very little tuck-up. *Slabsidedness* (a flat or caved-in chest), narrow chest, lack of depth in brisket, excessive *tuck-up* (underneath the rear part of the body) to be faulted.

Tail well set on, thick and muscular at the base, following the natural line of the croup. Tail bones extend to, but not below, the point of *hock* (the joint between the lower thigh and rear *pastern* (sort of the rear elbow). Carried with merry action, level or with some moderate upward curve; never curled over back nor between the legs.

Forequarters

Muscular, well-coordinated with hindquarters, and capable of free movement. Shoulder blades long and well laid back with upper tips fairly close together at withers. Upper arms appear about the same length as the blades, setting the elbows back beneath the upper tip of the blades, close to the ribs without loose-ness. Legs, viewed from the front, straight with good bone, but not to the point of coarseness. *Pasterns* (on the leg, just above the foot, where the foot or wrist/carpus bends into the leg; metacarpus in front, metatarsus in rear) short and strong, sloping slightly with no suggestion of weakness. *Dewclaws* (a nail on the small fifth toe on the inside of the front leg above the rest of the toes) on forelegs may be removed, but are normally left on.

Feet medium size, round, compact, and well knuckled, with thick pads. Excess hair may be trimmed to show natural size and contour. *Splayed* (the toes or digits are split apart or separated) or *hare feet* (center toes are more than a hair longer than the outer toes) to be faulted.

Hindquarters

Broad and strongly muscled. Profile of croup slopes slightly; the pelvic bone slopes at a slightly greater angle (approximately 30 degrees from horizontal). In a natural stance, the femur (thigh bone, rear leg) joins the pelvis at approximately a 90-degree angle; *stifles* (a joint in the thigh, sometimes called the knee) well bent; *hocks* (tarsus — the joint between the lower thigh and rear pastern) well let down with short, strong rear pasterns. Feet as in front. Legs straight when viewed from rear. *Cow hocks* (hind legs that bend in), *spread hocks* (just the opposite), and *sickle hocks* (hocks with angulation in sickle shape) to be faulted.

Coat

Dense and water repellent with good undercoat. Outer coat firm and water resilient, neither coarse nor silky, lying close to the body; may be straight or wavy. Untrimmed natural ruff; moderate feathering on back of forelegs and on underbody; heavier feathering on front of neck, back of thighs, and underside of tail. Coat on head, paws, and front of legs is short and even. Excessive length, open coats, and limp, soft coats are very undesirable. Feet may be trimmed and stray hairs neatened, but the natural appearance of coat or outline should not be altered by cutting or clipping.

GOLDEN MYTHS AND HISTORY

A charming tale existed years ago about a group of Russian circus dogs who evolved into the very talented Golden Retriever.

Okay, so maybe not. The truth is you can thank a Scotsman for your lovely breed. Sir Dudley Marjoriebanks — later elevated to Lord Tweedmouth and so named because his estate rested on the Tweed River in the hills of Inverness, Scotland — was an avid sportsman with a special passion for water fowling. Apparently, collecting the ducks he shot over those rough coastal waters wasn't easy, because he longed for a canine hunting companion who would not only swim out to retrieve his birds, but also deliver them to hand. And he had a yen for a yellow dog to do the job. (Sounds like a good idea to me, too.)

So in 1868, Tweedmouth launched his first experimental yellow breeding, mating a liver-colored Tweed Water Spaniel (the name begs no explanation) named Belle to a yellow Wavy-Coated Retriever named Nous, which in Greek means "wisdom." See anything prophetic in that name? Nous was the only yellow pup, in those days called a "sport," out of a litter of all blacks, which was the standard color for the Wavy-Coat.

Surprise! Nous and Belle produced four yellow furries, which Tweedmouth promptly named Cowslip, Ada, Crocus, and Primrose. He kept Cowslip for himself and gave the other pups to good friends who shared his passion for breeding a yellow sporting dog.

Tweedmouth's kennel records show a detailed history of Color-Me-Yellow canine marriages dating back to Cowslip and his littermates. Linebreeding of this nature was pretty radical in those days, so Tweedmouth was a true vanguard of his time.

(continued)

(continued)

So where did red-gold and rust-colored Goldens come from? Okay, carry that a little further. Who were the parents that produced so many other shades of gold? Surely not just the yellow dogs that Tweedmouth was so avidly promoting.

Enter the Irish Setter (sorry, Scotland), the Bloodhound, and the yellow Labrador. Breeding reliable retrieving dogs also meant improving and preserving essential sporting qualities like scenting ability and other important hunting talents. So along the way these retriever pioneers occasionally outcrossed their yellow dogs to other popular hunting breeds. It's often said the Golden's nose is one of its most famous parts, and you can thank the Bloodhound cross for that.

The Golden's destiny eventually took them across the Atlantic into the United States and Canada. In the early 1900s, British military officers and other professionals often traveled with their hunting dogs so that they could do a little shooting on their business trips. (Sort of like today's political junkets.) Eventually, the dogs merged into the U.S. population, growing especially popular in the bird-rich areas of the northern states and coastal areas. The breed is still abundant in those states where pheasant stock is plentiful and that Golden nose can track them down.

Tweedmouth really did his homework. His yellow retrievers had such sweet and winning personalities they just naturally wiggled their way into the house after a hard day of hunting. Always smiling, great with kids, and eager to please, the Golden was as good in the house as he was afield. By 1950, the breed was becoming well known as a dual-purpose dog.

Color

Rich, lustrous golden of various shades. Feathering may be lighter than rest of coat. With the exception of graying or whitening on face or body due to age, any white marking, other than a few white hairs on the chest, should be penalized according to its extent. Allowable light shadings are not to be confused with white markings. Predominant body color that is extremely pale or extremely dark is undesirable. Some latitude should be given to the light puppy whose coloring shows promise of deepening with maturity. Any noticeable area of black or other off-color hair is a serious fault.

Gait

When trotting, gait is free, smooth, powerful, and well-coordinated, showing good reach. Viewed from any position, legs turn neither in nor out, nor do feet cross or interfere with each other. As speed increases, feet tend to converge toward center line of balance. It is recommended that dogs be shown on a loose lead to reflect true gait.

Temperament

Friendly, reliable, and trustworthy. Quarrelsomeness or hostility toward other dogs or people in normal situations, or an unwarranted show of timidity or nervousness, is not in keeping with Golden Retriever characteristics. Such actions should be penalized according to their significance.

(For more information on a Golden Retriever's temperament, see Chapter 1.)

Disqualifications

Deviation in height of more than 1 inch from standard either way. Undershot or overshot bite.

IN THIS CHAPTER

» **Interviewing breeders**

» **Considering puppy alternatives —
older puppies and adult Goldens**

» **Understanding pedigrees**

» **Analyzing health clearances**

Chapter **3**

Finding a Golden Breeder

Ever take a look at your family tree? Just as humans have family trees, dogs have pedigrees. And just as your ancestry can reflect bank robbers or other unsavory people, so, too, can a dog's pedigree reveal some very common, even crummy, parents, grandparents, aunts, or uncles. And their genetic influence will determine what kind of dog your Golden will grow up to be. Good breeders avoid those questionable ancestors and look for qualities like temperament, talent, health, even longevity, when they build that canine family tree or pedigree. Thus, experienced Golden owners and competitors always research pedigrees when looking for their next super dog. So, follow their example when you're looking for a Golden puppy; pedigree is the first order of the day. In this chapter, we'll plan your breeder/puppy search.

Finding a Reputable Breeder

References are the first and most obvious way to find a reputable breeder (with *reputable* being the most important factor). Talk to people who own Goldens you admire and ask them where they got their dog. If they found their wonder dog through a newspaper ad, take a pass and keep looking. With all due respect to the dog's owner, reputable breeders seldom advertise. They usually have reservations in advance and depend on referrals from other dog friends or previous puppy clients. They also don't want to sort through all the riffraff to find proper homes for their babies, and they will keep puppies past the normal 7- to 8-week placement age until the right dog person comes along.

Here are a few other ways to get referrals to a good breeder:

>> **Ask your veterinarian.** If you don't have a veterinarian, ask a friend or family member's vet.

>> **Spend the day at a dog show, an obedience trial, or field event.** You'll see a wide variety of Goldens and can get up close and personal with the ones you like. Most dog owners who show their dogs in the various dog activities enjoy nothing more than talking about their special Goldens and where they got them. You'll be introduced to the Golden world and learn often valuable information about the breed and its many talents.

>> **Contact the Golden Retriever Club of America (GRCA) on their website (https://www.grca.org).** You'll find all sorts of good information on the breed as well as breeders in your geographical area. It will even tell you what questions to ask the breeder (in case you forget what you read in this book!).

TIP

When you're visiting a breeder, don't hesitate to ask about previous litters and where you could meet other dogs she's bred and the people who own them. Reputable breeders should be more than willing to offer references.

What should you expect from a breeder you plan to visit? He or she . . .

>> **Understands the genetics behind the mating of a particular sire (father) and dam (mother).** A reputable breeder plans a litter for specific reasons and has reasonable expectations for what the breeding will produce. She never does it just because her Golden is sweet or beautiful and her neighbor's Golden is a handsome guy and they'd have such pretty babies, and so on. That's the stuff unhealthy and unsound dogs are made of.

>> **Has a written puppy contract that specifies health guarantees.** If the pup fails to meet the health guarantees in the contract, the breeder will agree to take the puppy back, replace the puppy with one of equal value, or refund your purchase price. The contract may include a spay/neuter clause and indicate whether the pup is being sold on a limited registration. See "Do you require that your puppies be spayed or neutered?" later in this chapter for details on limited registrations.

>> **Usually breeds no more than one or two litters a year.** A reputable breeder does not have several litters at the same time or keep several different breeds of dogs on the premises. Nor do her dogs or puppies spend their entire lives in pens, cages, or kennels, popping out puppies every year. Golden breeders are devoted to their breed. Their dogs are members of the

family and usually live in the house (at least most of the time) and enjoy the same privileges as the kids. (Okay, maybe they don't all sleep on the bed like mine do.) The puppies shown in Figure 3-1 are comfy in their breeder's yard. Make sure that any breeder you consider fits that description.

You may have to travel to find a good quality litter. If the breeder is too far away to visit, ask her to send a video of the puppies and her other dogs.

FIGURE 3-1:
Litters of 6 or more puppies are not unusual, and even litters of 10 or 11 pups are not uncommon.

Close Encounters of the Furry Kind.

Visiting a Breeder

The puppy environment is one important indicator of the breeder's level of care and expertise. You should check out not only where the puppies are raised, but how they are raised. The puppies should be in the house or an adjoining room, not isolated down in a basement, outdoor kennel or kennel building, or dark corner of the garage. (The key word here is *isolated*.) They need to be near family areas where they can be raised and socialized with people every day. Puppies need to be exposed to a variety of sights, sounds, and surfaces in order to become stable and confident when they leave their pack. The greater their exposure, the easier the transition from canine family to human.

The puppy area should be reasonably clean, but do consider the nonstop food chain in a litter of healthy pups. What goes in keeps coming out all day long, so scrupulously clean is pretty tough, but your overall impression of "clean" is a good clue.

The puppies themselves should have clean, thick coats and feel solid and muscular. There should be no crusted or runny discharge from their eyes, ears, or nose, or watery or bloody stools. Their dewclaws should have been removed soon after birth, and they should have had one or two wormings, and a parvo-distemper shot before they are released to their new owners. The breeder should provide paperwork supporting those and any other medical issues. If your breeder passes these initial tests, it's time for "the interview." Following are some questions you should ask.

How long have you been breeding Golden Retrievers?

Experienced breeders are more knowledgeable than a novice who is breeding for the first or second time. If it's a first-timer, she should have an experienced mentor who has counseled her through the breeding process.

Do you belong to a breed or kennel club?

TIP

Breeders who are truly involved in Golden Retrievers usually belong to one or more dog clubs; ideally, a Golden Retriever breed club.

Do you screen your breeding dogs for genetic defects?

Both the sire and dam of every litter should have hip, elbow, eye, and heart clearances. (See Chapter 15 for an explanation of hereditary diseases.) These clearances will appear on the pedigree.

The Golden Retriever Club of America (GRCA) states that "Reputable breeders are expected to conduct screening examinations for these diseases on the parents of a litter, and to disclose the results to prospective buyers."

Are you involved in any dog activities or events with your Goldens?

Most breeders of quality Goldens show or train their dogs for some type of performance event or dog-related activity, such as conformation, obedience, agility, hunting, or other field activity. Therapy Goldens are also active in hospitals and nursing homes.

Have your Goldens earned any titles?

Breeders who earn titles in various canine competitions prove their experience and their love and commitment to the breed.

When do you allow your puppies to go to homes?

A breeder who releases puppies under 7 weeks of age does not have the best inter-est of the puppy in mind (or the buyer, for that matter). A good breeder will wait until the puppies are 7 to 10 weeks old before allowing them to go to a home.

What do you require of prospective puppy buyers?

Good breeders have certain requirements about *who* will raise their puppy, *how*, and *where*. If they ask these personal questions, it's because they care about the future of their babies. These are their "grandpups," and members of their dog family!

TURNING THE TABLES: BREEDER INTERROGATION

As you visit or contact breeders, you'll discover that the good ones not only give you scads of information about the breed in general and, more specifically, their puppies, but they quiz *you* as well! That's great, because it means she knows her dog facts and wants to make you dog-smart, too, especially if you're going to raise one of her puppies. She cares not just about her pups, but also about the families who take them home. She may ask questions about your dog history, such as whether you've ever owned a dog, what kind he was, and what became of him.

She'll also want to know about your family, the ages of your kids, and who will be home to raise the puppy. Some insist on meeting all family members before sending a puppy home. (I do.) Don't be offended; she's not being nosy. It's just your typical job interview. How else can she determine whether or not you qualify as a good puppy parent? If she doesn't ask you any questions, find another breeder. A good breeder is very protective of the puppies she brings into the world.

Do you give any guarantees with your pups, and are those guarantees in a written contract?

Reputable (there's that word again!) breeders offer health guarantees and reasonable return policies in a written contract and will explain the specifics of that contract.

Do you require that your puppies be spayed or neutered?

Reputable breeders sometimes sell their pet-quality puppies on spay/neuter agreements or on a limited registration basis, meaning the dog is ineligible to be entered in a breed competition in a licensed dog show (conformation). However, the dog is eligible, to be entered in any other AKC-licensed event, such as Obedience, Agility, Field Trials, and other performance events. If the dog is bred, its offspring will not be eligible for registration. These restrictions will depend on your future goals for the puppy.

Most breeders will tell you what it's like to live with a Golden Retriever — the good and the bad. No breed of dog is perfect, and she should volunteer the disadvantages of Golden ownership along with all the happy news. (See Chapter 2 for more on the cons of Golden ownership.)

REMEMBER

The puppies can't go home until they're 7 to 10 weeks old, depending on the breeder's policy. Most breeders release their puppies at about 7 or 8 weeks of age, while a few keep their puppies longer. (If the breeder lets them go at 5 or 6 weeks, say good-bye and leave.) Breeders usually allow visitors after the pups are 3 or 4 weeks old, but you can't tell much about individual personality until they're at least 5 weeks of age. You can visit them; however, to spend time watching the puppies in action, get better acquainted with the breeder and the Momma Golden, before deciding if you want to join her Golden family.

Adopting an Older Golden

If the thought of struggling through housetraining and canine puberty doesn't appeal to you, consider the joys of adopting an older Golden Retriever. When you adopt a dog who has grown past the cute bouncy puppy stage, what you see is what you get. (Figure 3-2 shows a typical grown-up Golden who would *love* to join your family.)

Close Encounters of the Furry Kind.

With an adult dog, you don't have to guess about its coat type or adult size or its personality. An older or more mature Golden is often already housebroken and has some degree of basic house manners or training. Of course, puppies are great fun, but they're also work, and you can eliminate those challenges if you bypass adolescence and go directly to adulthood.

If you worry that an older Golden will not bond or relate to you because you didn't nurture him from infancy, forget it. An almost unfortunate fact about this breed is that they will love just about anyone who loves them back. As much as I hate to think about it, I know that my beloved Goldens would be just as happy with someone else who loved and cared for them the way I do. That's just the nature of this sweet beast.

You can often find adult Goldens and older Golden puppies through breeders, Golden Retriever rescue services, or animal shelters, as discussed in the following sections. Having adopted a few senior Goldens myself, I can happily attest that they are the "lovingest" and sweetest dogs ever! Rescue Goldens at 10 or 11 years of age are understandably harder to place because of their limited life expectancy. However, they deserve a happy, loving home in which to enjoy their last few years.

Breeders

Occasionally, a breeder will keep more than one puppy from a litter to evaluate his potential as a future show dog or field prospect. If and when the pup doesn't fulfill her expectations, she places him in a pet home. These dogs are usually excellent companions, sometimes even fine competitors, for a novice Golden owner. If they have been well socialized and cared for, they will bond easily with a loving human being.

Once in a while, a breeder also gets a puppy or older Golden back from a previous litter for some unfortunate reason. (Some reasons are legitimate, like divorce or allergies, while some are inexcusable, such as he barked too much, jumped on the kids, got hair in the pool, don't have time, and so on.) The breeder will evaluate the dog *and* you before placing him in second home to prevent another life change for the dog. If you work with a breeder, make your preferences known so that she can arrange a perfect match.

Rescue groups

Golden Retriever rescue services work with animal shelters, animal control agencies, and dog owners to assist in relocating and rehabilitating abandoned, abused, and confiscated (from puppy mills and brokers) Goldens into healthy, loving homes. Over 100 rescue services are affiliated with Golden Retriever clubs across the country. They rescue and rehome thousands of Goldens every year. (While local Golden clubs are supportive of these rescue groups, they do not set policy, and the rescues operate independently of the affiliate clubs. You can find names and locations of Golden rescue groups by visiting the GRCA website at https://www.grca.org.)

The GRCA also awards a variety of titles that are GRCA titles, and not recognized by AKC and will not appear on an AKC pedigree. If the sire or dam has earned any GRCA title, the breeder may add him or her to her copy of the pedigree or inform the client of the dog's achievements. Complete information on those titles can be found on the GRCA website.

The rescue process can range from very simple to extremely complicated, depending on the geographical area and the number of people and dogs involved in each rescue operation. Rescue volunteers provide health care and foster care, and do personality and temperament evaluations before each placement. They want permanent loving homes for these Golden victims, so they look for lifetime commitments from adoptive families.

If you work with a Golden rescue group to find an older puppy or adult (puppies come along infrequently), you can usually rely on their evaluation of the dog, their choice for you, and their help in the dog's adjustment to his new environment. The last thing the rescue group wants is for this dog to be uprooted once again. Expect them to be firm and possibly intimidating to make sure that you're the right person for this dog. They already know the dog. They *don't* know you!

On a personal note: For years I worked independently with local agencies and area veterinarians as a Golden Retriever rescue committee of one. Now I act as an interim liaison between those sources and my Golden club's official Golden rescue group, which is 200 miles away. In years past, I averaged two or three Golden strays a year from this rural community, and I am absolutely thrilled to tell you that every single Golden who came into my home from who-knows-where was an absolute peach who I would have kept in a heartbeat if I wasn't already over-dogged. Each one went on to a good home with a family who swears this was the best dog they ever saw. I rest my case!

Animal shelters

Many animal shelters work with area breed rescue groups when a purebred dog arrives. If no Golden Retriever organization or dedicated volunteer is available to assist with the adoption, the dog goes into the general shelter population. Shelters in smaller communities of under 100,000 often work with a few reliable individuals who raise certain breeds and are willing to assist or act as an adoption agent on their own. The vast majority of shelters have the dog's best interests at heart and do their best to screen and evaluate their animals to determine whether they are adoptable, and to ensure a good match with the adoptive person.

TIP

When you visit a shelter, bring a prepared checklist, just as if you were adopting a puppy. Don't be shy. Ask lots of questions and spend time alone with a dog before you agree to take him home. Your best choice is that middle-of-the-road guy we always talk about. Not too timid or too pushy, and never aggressive in any way. Don't cave in or feel sorry for a dog who isn't right for you or who could present more problems than you're prepared to handle. The awful truth is that you and I can't save them all.

There will be paperwork with each adoption agency, whether shelter or rescue organization, which is for the dog's protection as well as yours. They will charge an adoption fee, which may include certain health services for the dog. Almost all require that every adopted Golden must be spayed or neutered.

If you adopt or purchase an adult Golden or older puppy, bring him home during a vacation period or at least over a weekend when you can spend 2 or 3 days helping him adjust to his new home (see Chapter 5). All dogs, regardless of age, need reassurance and attention to make them feel safe and comfortable in a new environment.

After a reasonable adjustment period, take your new Golden to obedience school. Like all Goldens, he'll love doing something with his person, he'll enjoy learning new things, and he'll especially like knowing you're in charge, which is the main benefit of the obedience experience.

The Paper Trail: Pedigree and AKC Registration Papers

You've all heard those famous dog words, "Of course, he's a good dog; he's AKC." Or "He's a good dog, he has all his papers," or "He's purebred, his parents were AKC."

Don't buy into that! "Papers" and "AKC-registered" have absolutely nothing to do with a dog's quality or worth. They mean one thing only: that the dog's parents were recognized by AKC as being of the same breed. What it does not prove or guarantee is that those parents, or their offspring, were healthy, sound, stable, or even decent animals.

Registering your dog

If you want the official paperwork from the AKC, you must first complete the registration form you received from the breeder. You simply fill in the dog's name (50 letters or less), write in your name as the new owner, and sign and send to the AKC at their Raleigh, NC, location (8051 Arco Corporate Drive, Raleigh, NC 27617) along with the stipulated registration fee. You can also register online (easier!) by visiting the registration site on the AKC website (https://www.akc.org/register). Your confirmation usually arrives in 4 to 6 weeks.

AKC also offers an Indefinite Listing Privilege (ILP) for dogs who are purebred but have no proof of parentage. You can show ILP-registered dogs in AKC-licensed performance events, but they're not eligible to be shown in conformation. To obtain an ILP number, send good-quality photographs of the dog, including frontal view and both sides, along with a spay-neuter certificate from a veterinarian, to the same Raleigh address as above. Contact the AKC for more details on how to present the necessary information.

Analyzing a pedigree

An AKC registration form and a pedigree are two different documents. The *registration* is simply the AKC's confirmation of a puppy's sire and dam, and certifies you as the owner of that pup. It is *not* the dog's *pedigree*, which is a three-to-five-generation list of all of the dog's ancestors.

The *sire* and *dam* are your dog's father and mother. In the next generation, you have two *grandsires* and *granddams*, and so on up the pedigree ladder. Your pedigree will list any titles and may include certain health clearances as well. (See the sections "Healthy Parents, Healthy Pups" and "Gold Links: Mom and Dad," later in this chapter, for more.)

WARNING

Steer clear of the breeder who tells you her dog doesn't need a hip clearance because he can jump a 6-foot fence in one great leap. Or one who tells you the pups are from "championship lines" when in fact you see only one solitary Ch. title (see Table 3-1) from three generations back.

Looking at titles

Titles may appear before and/or after a dog's name, indicating some great or small accomplishment in a particular area of the dog world.

Titles in a pedigree prove that a dog is as smart, beautiful or handsome, and talented as a breeder claims. Table 3-1 gives you a list of some common titles and what they mean.

If a pedigree lacks titles (or clearances), it doesn't mean that the puppies have no potential as competitors or pets. But unless the breeder is very experienced and knows what she's doing, a nondescript pedigree offers little assurance that the pups are top-quality Goldens, especially in the health department.

REMEMBER

In Table 3-1, the hunt test dog is judged against a standard of performance and is not eliminated because another dog had better work. Hunt test titles appear after the dog's name.

TABLE 3-1   **AKC Pedigree Titles**

Title	Meaning
Ch.	Bench (Show) Champion. This title appears in front of the dog's name, indicating the dog has been declared a quality and breedable specimen of the breed by judges who are licensed to evaluate that breed. Dogs earn points toward their championship in accordance with the number of dogs defeated in the show ring. They must earn a total of 15 points, including two "major" wins of three or more points, with a maximum of five points awarded at any one show.

Obedience titles

Title	Meaning
OTCh.	Obedience Trial Champion. This is the ultimate title in competitive obedience. The title appears in front of the dog's name. To become an OTCh, a dog must earn a total of 100 points, including one first place in both the Open B and Utility classes, another first place in either class, with three first places under three different judges.
CD	Companion Dog. An obedience title that appears after a dog's name. To earn a CD, the dog must qualify in the Novice class three times under three different judges, performing exercises such as heel on- and off-leash, stand for a brief hands-on exam by the judge, come into the front and heel position when called (recall), and sit and lie down in place during a group exercise with other dogs. (*Note:* A qualifying score requires a minimum of 170 points out of the maximum 200.)
CDX	Companion Dog Excellent. The CDX dog competes in the Open class and must qualify three times under three different judges. He must perform more difficult exercises such as heel off-leash (heel-free), retrieve a dumbbell thrown across the ring (retrieve on flat) as well as over a high jump, drop into a down position on command during the recall, jump over a broad jump on command, and sit and lie down in place during a group exercise with the owner/handler out of sight.
UD	Utility Dog. The highest level of difficulty. In the Utility exercises (three qualifying scores, three different judges), the dog must respond to hand signals, do scent discrimination, a directed retrieve, directed jump, and a group examination.
UDX	Utility Dog Excellent. Awarded to the UD dog who obtains qualifying scores in both Open and Utility classes at the same trial, at ten different trails.

Tracking titles

Title	Meaning
TD	Tracking Dog. All tracking titles appear after a dog's name. To earn the TD, a dog must follow a 440- to 500-yard track, which includes at least two right-angle turns on a track that is 30 minutes to 2 hours old, and retrieve the glove or wallet dropped at the track's end.
TDX	Tracking Dog Excellent. This title is earned by following an "older" track (3 to 5 hours) that is also longer (800 to 1,000 yards) and that has five to seven directional changes with the additional challenge of human cross tracks.
VST	Variable Surface Tracker. In the real world, dogs track through urban settings as well as through wilderness. A VST dog must follow a 3-to-5-hour-old track down streets, through a building, and in other areas devoid of vegetation.

Field titles

Title	Meaning
FC	Field Champion. This prefix title is earned in an all-breed (meaning all retriever breeds) field trial "Open" competition, a stake that is open to professional handlers as well as amateur handlers. Untitled dogs also compete against dogs who have already earned their championship, making the field extremely hard to beat. The dogs are tested in four series, two on land and two in the water, under a wide variety of difficult conditions. Points are awarded for first through fourth place, with one win and 10 points required for the title.

Title	Meaning
AFC	Amateur Field Champion. In the Amateur stake, only amateur handlers are allowed to compete. As in the Open stake above, dogs compete against both titled and untitled dogs, making the competition equally tough. The dogs are tested on land and in water under similar arduous conditions. An AFC must earn a total of 15 points, including one win, to title.
Hunt test titles	
JH	Junior Hunter. A suffix title requiring four qualifying scores or "legs." Dogs must complete two single retrieves on land and two in water at a maximum of 100 yards.
SH	Senior Hunter. A title requiring five legs, four if the dog already has a JH. Senior dogs complete longer and more difficult double retrieves on land and in water, do a single land and water blind (birds the dog has not seen shot), and honor another working dog (remain steady while the other dog retrieves).
MH	Master Hunter. The highest hunt test title offered. The MH dog needs six legs, five if he has an SH. He must complete multiple land, water, and combined land-water retrieves, do multiple blinds on land and in water, and work under more difficult and complex conditions.

Healthy Parents, Healthy Pups

The sire and dam of any Golden litter you consider should carry the standard health clearances for hips, elbows, eyes, and heart. All these dog parts can be defective. If either parent has *hip or elbow dysplasia* (poor development of those joints), cataracts, or heart disease, it's a good bet they could pass that condition along to their offspring. (See Chapter 15 for complete information on hereditary disease.)

WARNING

Avoid pups from parents who have chronic allergies or who are on thyroid medication.

Listed below are four health clearances that should be included in a pedigree.

> **Hips and Elbows:** An updated or current AKC registration will show an *OFA rating* after a dog's name, indicating the dog has been declared free of hip dysplasia (HD) and elbow dysplasia (ED) by the Orthopedic Foundation for Animals (OFA), which is the official hip clearinghouse for dogs.
>
> Example: Dam: Chances R Gingersnap, SF123456 (AKC registration number) (8-98) (date of evaluation) OFA24E (OFA rating).
>
> In the above OFA number OFA24E, the *24* indicates the dog's age in months (it cannot be cleared by OFA until it is 2 years of age), and the letter *E* following that number indicates a rating of Excellent. *G* means Good and *F* means Fair. Dysplastic ratings of Mild, Moderate, or Severe indicate the degree of hip dysplasia and will not appear on the registration.

OFA ratings were not recorded with AKC prior to the 1990s, so the breeder could produce OFA certificates if the dog's AKC registration certificate lacks that information. Clearances are now a standard requirement.

» **Eyes:** Eye clearances are also registered with OFA. Until 2014, the Canine Eye Registry Foundation (CERF), provided its own numbered certificate of clearance. That organization has been incorporated into OFA as CAER, the OFA eye certification registry. Because eye clearances are only valid for 1 year, they do not appear on a pedigree. But the breeder should have Board-certified ophthalmologist certificates stating that both parents' eyes have been examined and found to be free of hereditary cataracts.

» **Heart:** Even the dog's heart needs another letter of approval. This time, the letter should be from a Board-certified cardiologist stating that both parents' hearts were tested and found to be free of a heart disease called *Subvalvular Aortic Stenosis* (SAS). This horrible disease involves a stricture in the left ventricle of the heart, which restricts the blood flow out of the heart, leading to sudden and unexpected death after normal activity or exercise. (For more on SAS, see Chapter 15.)

TIP

Look for health clearances on the puppy's grandparents and other ancestors. The stronger the gene pool, the healthier the offspring.

CANCER CONCERNS

Sadly, the Golden Retriever is one of the breeds at highest risk of developing cancer. Currently, about 60 percent of Goldens will die from cancer, with lymphoma and hemgiosarcoma being the two most common types of cancer affecting the breed. Researchers studying cancer in the breed have identified genetic mutations in Goldens diagnosed with those and other cancers. Thus, the Golden Retriever Lifetime Study was born in 2012, funded by the Morris Animal Foundation and the Golden Retriever Foundation (part of the GRCA). Three thousand privately owned Goldens ranging in age from 6 months to 2 years of age have signed on to the project. The study will run for 10 to 14 years, and will track the dogs throughout their lives. The owners and their veterinarians are providing detailed records of the dogs' health, nutrition, and environment. Since Goldens wear so many hats — as show dogs, hunting dogs, search and rescue dogs, assistance and therapy dogs, and family pets — they are exposed to a wide variety of environmental conditions. The Lifetime Study website states, "As the years progress, we are gathering millions of data points that will lead us to a better understanding of how genetics, lifestyle, and environment impact our study dogs' health and well-being." That, hopefully, will provide a path on how to prevent cancer through better breeding practices. Learn more at https://www.morrisanimalfoundation.org/golden-retriever-lifetime-study.

Gold Links: Mom and Dad

It's important to meet your potential puppy's parents. Good temperament is also inherited. (Okay, face it. Just about everything is inherited.) If the sire or dam or other close relative is aggressive with other dogs or people, it's a good bet that some of the puppies will reflect those qualities. When you visit a litter of pups, interact with one or both parents if you can. Quite frequently the sire lives elsewhere, but the dam should always be present.

WARNING

If the breeder won't let you meet the mom, or either the mom or dad is surly, growly, overly shy, or slinky, look elsewhere for a pup.

Chapter **4**

Selecting Your Special Puppy

There's more to finding the right puppy than just finding a good breeder (see Chapter 3). Golden Retrievers have as many personalities and talents as they do coat colors. This chapter explores the different types of Goldens and helps you decide which one is the perfect match for you. That way, you won't just fall in love with the first pretty face you see (we hope!).

A Golden Partnership

When you think about life with a Golden Retriever, what picture comes to mind? Is your Golden athlete flushing dove or pheasant from the field? Are you and your Golden chasing tennis balls and Frisbees on the beach? Or are the two of you nestled in front of the fireplace, snoozing the weekend away? (As you can see in Figure 4-1, Golden Retrievers are the perfect snuggling partners.)

FIGURE 4-1:
Goldens are the
best snugglers
ever!

Before you begin your search, you should have some idea of your future life together. Ask yourself the following questions:

>> **Do you hunt, or would you like to?** If so, you'll need to research field and hunting lines to find a Golden who can share your duck blind and shag those pheasants from the field and hedgerows.

>> **Are you a sports nut, a camping enthusiast, or a dedicated jogger?** You'll probably want a typical spirited Golden who would enjoy your outdoor activities.

>> **Are you a sedentary person who spends most of your leisure time curled up with a good book, or a senior citizen who wants a Golden mostly for its huggability?** You don't need a high-powered Golden who craves action and would be bouncing off the walls from boredom. Better to look for a laid-back animal, possibly from show lines, where the breeder's priorities lean more toward looks than athletics.

TIP

Be specific when looking for your ideal Golden. If the breeder raises field-type Goldens and you want a career in conformation, be honest with her and look elsewhere for your pup. The reverse is also true. Don't purchase a show dog if you want to hunt, run field trials, or excel in the obedience competition. Pretty dog, yes. Hunting partner, rarely.

REMEMBER

Forewarned is forearmed! Those little yellow fuzzballs will steal your heart with one sweet puppy kiss, and suddenly you own one. Unless you are absolutely positive this is *the* litter, don't fall in love with the first pup who licks your cheek (yeah, right!) and try to visit more than one litter. That's the only way to learn the differences in Golden personalities and how each breeder raises them. Remember, all Goldens are not created equal.

Male or Female?

Both males and females make excellent pets, and any differences depend more on individual personality than on gender. Males, of course, are about 10 to 15 pounds bigger, and therefore stronger, and may display more male dominance, especially with "woosy" people (that is, people who can be big softies or pushovers). And they do lift their leg when urinating, putting your prize shrubs and flower beds at risk. Most males also take a little longer to mature, stretching their teenage rowdiness well into their second year.

Females, on the other hand, mature more quickly and tend to become lady-like before they're 2. (They squat to urinate, which saves your bushes but kills your grass.) They are usually about 10 pounds smaller and thus might be a bit easier to handle. While some females may be more sensitive and easier to discipline, others tend to sort of wilt when disciplined. Personally, I've raised plenty of both — wild and wooly females, and soft, tender males — and it all depends on personality.

TIP

If you already have an adult dog of any breed, consider getting the opposite sex from your present dog. Males tend to get into dominance wars at certain life stages, and dogs of opposite sexes usually cohabit better.

Breeders often use some form of identification when each pup is born: colored rickrack, elastic pot holder rings, a touch of nail polish on a toe. Newborn pups resemble a pile of skinny wriggling . . . and adorable! . . . nameless critters, The breeder needs some way to tell at a glance which pup always finds the best end of Mom's dinner table, and which one does something first or last. I prefer colored elastic ribbons, and when I have a litter, my usual puppy conversation is always about what Pink or Blue or Orange did today.

Eenie, Meenie, Miney . . . YOU!

Who's the fairest of them all? How do you know which one is THE one, the pup who will fit into your family activities and routines? Listen to your breeder. Her observations are often a good criterion in evaluating puppies. After all, she has spent the last 7 weeks living 24 hours a day with her furry charges and can point out the alpha pup, the middle-of-the-road guys, and a shy, quiet wallflower, if there is one. She can help you match a puppy to your goals and lifestyle. (If you don't have a breeder, check out Chapter 3.)

Testing for Golden Personalities

Many people still rely on puppy tests. Puppy testing is certainly not a science and is a questionable art at best. Test results are objective and influenced by who performs the test, where the test occurs, the time of day, and whether the pups are hungry or tired. And puppies mature at different rates, with one pup precocious at 5 or 6 weeks, while a littermate may not blossom until several days later. Many experts discount test results and point out that some of the great dogs of the past have been leftover pups the breeder either gave away or kept because no one wanted them.

A testing process offers no guarantees. It's just one more way of trying to beat the odds. Still, some testing can't hurt and often just confirms what a dedicated breeder already knows about her pups. Many breeders and trainers have their favorite testing methods, using similar tests labeled with their own different names.

Ideally, testing should be performed when the pup is almost 7 weeks old, by an experienced Golden Retriever owner or breeder who has some knowledge of canine behavior and testing procedure, and who has had little or no exposure to the litter.

The prospective owner can assist the tester in this process. Testing should also be conducted in an area that is unfamiliar to the pups.

TIP

You and the tester should record a detailed description of each pup's reactions (tail up, body crouched down, and so on) as well as apply a numerical grade. These notes will help you remember why you gave a particular score, and are especially helpful when testing a large litter. It's easy to forget how puppy No. 2 reacted an hour earlier. Be familiar with the stated reactions before you begin to score the pups.

The following sections discuss the different kinds of puppy testing and how they are scored.

Behavioral tests

Remember, puppy testing is subjective, not a science or even an art. But it can't hurt . . . and it might help you narrow down your choices! These first series of tests are a composite of tests developed by well-known canine behaviorists and are the most widely used among hobby breeders. These tests should be performed by a stranger. Here's how they work:

>> **Attraction:** The breeder takes the puppy to a quiet testing area and sets him down about 10 feet from the tester. The tester squats down and claps her hands while bending toward the pup, saying nothing. Observe how the puppy comes to her, and score according to the chart below.

>> **Handling:** The tester strokes the puppy from head to tail for about 30 seconds. Again, record the pup's response and assign a score.

>> **Holding or cradling test:** The tester picks up the pup and cradles it upside down with all four legs skyward, in her arms for about 20 to 30 seconds and scores accordingly.

>> **Following:** The tester releases the puppy, stands up, and then walks away without a word. If the pup follows, the tester chats with him to see whether he will come along. If he doesn't follow at all, the tester keeps walking for a few more feet to see whether he'll finally come along. Allow about 1 minute for this test and score accordingly.

Table 4-1 explains how to score each reaction.

Scores of mostly 1s indicate an extremely dominant and aggressive pup with a strong and willful personality. He will require an experienced owner who must be prepared for frequent challenges to authority. This puppy will not be good with children and will need expert socialization by a very dominant owner. Not recommended for the average pet or companion home.

TABLE 4-1

Puppy Test Scores

Category	Reaction	Score
Attraction	Comes at once, bites or nips at your hands or feet	1
	Comes quickly, licks but does not nip or bite	2
	Comes slowly but without hesitation or shyness	3
	Comes reluctantly or not at all, sits and observes instead	4
	Does not come, turns and goes the other way	5
Handling	Nips, growls, becomes agitated or excited	1
	Jumps up happily, paws up, no nipping or biting	2
	Wiggles around, licks at your hand	3
	Rolls over on his back	4
	Slinks away or walks away	5
Holding/Cradling	Struggles fiercely, nips, bites, or growls	1
	Struggles, then settles down or wiggles happily	2
	Settles down first, then wiggles or struggles	3
	Does not resist or struggle at all	4
	Wiggles a little the entire time	5
Following	Chases your feet, jumps on you or your feet, nips or bites	1
	Follows happily, stays with you	2
	Follows willingly, but slowly	3
	Does not follow, sits and watches	4
	Does not follow, walks away	5

A puppy with mostly 2s is also a dominant pup who will require a strong leader with experience, and will need consistent training to become a reliable family companion.

Bless the puppy who scores mostly 3s! He is a middle-of-the-road guy, friendly and outgoing, who will respond well to people and children. He will need more praise for confidence.

A puppy who scores mostly 4s is quite submissive and will need a gentle hand to build long-term confidence. He may not socialize too easily and is probably not a good choice for children.

A puppy who scores mostly 5s is terribly shy and would resist training. Pups with too many 5s could be potential "fear biters" — pups who might bite suddenly without provocation — and seldom make good family dogs. They need to live with owners who understand their special needs and who will work to build the puppy's confidence.

REMEMBER

These numerical categories are merely guidelines. Most pups will end up with combination scores. Dogs who score 2s and 3s or 3s and 4s usually make good family dogs. And remember, tests do not always reflect many aspects of the puppy's character.

Competition pup tests

This next set of exercises is sometimes used by obedience competitors. They should also be conducted by a stranger.

>> **Confidence and courage:** Set up a large nonskid-surface table in a quiet area or a room that is completely new and foreign to the pup. The tester should carry the pup and place him on the table without a word. Gauge the pup's reaction according to Table 4-2.

Pups who score 1 or 2 are bold, courageous, and outgoing and will accept challenges and training with enthusiasm. These puppies are good choices for competition or a busy, active family.

Scorers of 3 or 4 are less confident puppies who would make good companions but will need more careful socializing and confidence building in their training. They will require a gentler, more patient hand in training.

Scores of 5 indicate puppies who are insecure and will require lots of extra TLC and training to become happy willing workers and family members. These puppies may not be good with young children.

» **Desire to retrieve:** This test is obviously more important to those who plan to hunt or field trial with their Golden. The tester takes the puppy to an unfamiliar area and sets him down without a word. The area has been cleared of all distractions, toys, paper, or anything that may attract his attention. The tester then teases the puppy with a dead pigeon or some highly visible retrieving object like a stuffed white sock. When the puppy is all excited, the tester tosses the sock (at the pup's eye level) about 6 to 8 feet in front of the puppy. A good place to perform this test is down a hallway with any doors closed so the puppy has nowhere else to go.

Grade the pup's reaction on a scale of 1 to 3 as described in Table 4-3. After the retrieve, the tester can call the puppy to return with the object, but the return does not affect the test results. Coming back is a response that is taught as the puppy matures, but the desire to retrieve is built into the pup genetically.

TABLE 4-2   ## Confidence and Courage Responses

Reaction	Score
Happy and fearless, tries to run around or jump off table	1
Tail high and wagging, investigates table, shows no fear	2
Tail wags slowly, curious but apprehensive, may crouch a bit, sniffs to investigate	3
Tail down or tucked under but wagging slightly, slinky, rather fearful, sniffs or investigates with much caution	4
Tail between hind legs, freezes and won't move, does not sniff or investigate	5

TABLE 4-3   ## Retrieving Scores

Reaction	Score
Goes wild at the sight of the bird or stuffed sock and strains madly to retrieve it when it's thrown	1
Shows enthusiasm for the bird or stuffed sock and runs out happily to retrieve it	2
Shows little interest in the retrieve object and merely wanders out to get it or fails to go at all	3

Puppies who score a 1 should make good hunters and good performers in field or obedience competition.

Puppies with scores of 2 should be adequate performers and with proper training and encouragement can reach competent levels of performance.

If you want a puppy who can do any type of hunting or retrieving activities other than a Frisbee game, do not consider a puppy who scores a 3. While some pups' hunting ability develops slowly with maturity, if you're hoping to enjoy hunt tests, hunting, or field trials, you need to narrow the field as early as possible. A promising puppy increases your odds of success in adventurous activities.

REMEMBER

Realize that by the time you test puppy No. 9, the testing area will have been compromised with lots of puppy scent, and the early pups tested may be more wide awake and energetic than the last. The test results should be only one part of your puppy selection process. And since puppies mature at different rates, their test results might differ in a few days.

Your observations also factor into your choice of puppies. Observe their behavior within the pack to see who's the boss pup, who seems precocious, who is the most inquisitive, and so on. If your breeder is involved in any type of performance competition, rely also on her evaluation of each pup.

If You Can't Decide . . .

If you can't decide between two equally adorable pups, don't even think about taking both. Puppies will always prefer the company of another pup to their human companion (in Figure 4-2, these puppies are enjoying playtime together). It's species selection, and your personal charisma is not involved. However, the more dominant puppy will assert himself over the submissive one and may even develop a bully personality. These patterns of behavior can magnify over time, and by spending so much time together, each pup will be harder to train. Naturally, your puppy must learn how to behave around other dogs, but the two-puppy household is not the way to accomplish that. You're after that special human-canine bond.

FIGURE 4-2:
Puppies
instinctively
prefer to play
with other pups.

Close Encounters of the Furry Kind.

If you still crave two Goldens, don't despair. Wait until your dog is 2 years old before getting a second pup. By then Golden No. 1 will be your soul mate. However, raising that second pup will present different challenges, because you'll have to separate him from your older Golden for periods of time to prevent that canine species selection instinct and maximize the human bond. In my own dog family, I keep a puppy with me almost exclusively until he's at least 6 months old.

2

Welcome Home!

Your puppy's homecoming should be a safe and happy time — for you and your family as well as for the pup!

In this part you learn how to make sure your home and yard are safe spaces for him to explore, play, and thrive. "Dog-proof" your kids so they understand the best way to live with their new family member.

Provide a safe, comfortable place for him to sleep. Establish a crate routine so he can enjoy nap and quiet time in his own personal space. Discover the many stages of puppy growth and how that affects his behavior.

Learn how to speak "dog" so you can communicate with your puppy in terms he will understand. And because the best way to prevent problem behavior is before it starts, begin training your puppy right away, before he learns bad habits.

Chapter **5**

Setting Out the Welcome Mat

S electing your puppy is merely the first rung on your life-with-a-Golden ladder. Once you have found the perfect pup, you can't just plunk him in the car and head for home. Nope, not yet! Before you make that exciting journey, you must puppy-proof your entire premises from the ground up, and give your kids a short course in canine safety. In this chapter, we'll delve into all the important (and fun!) things you need to know about laying the proper groundwork for your new family member.

Outfitting Your Puppy

Just like outfitting a newborn baby, your puppy will need his own layette of canine goodies — some necessary and others just plain fun. But hang on to your purse strings; shopping for puppies is a grand adventure that can easily spin out of control — and stretch your budget. Make a list of essentials and the extra goodies so you know where to draw the line.

Puppy food

Lay in a supply of a quality large-breed growth/puppy food (see Chapter 10). Ask the breeder what she has been feeding the puppy and what she recommends. If you plan to feed something different, take home a small bag of her food to mix with your new food so your puppy can adjust gradually to the change in diet. Be sure to ask your breeder how much your puppy has been eating, although calculating that can be difficult if eight or nine puppies are sharing one large food pan. Start with a 20-pound bag. Does that sound like a lot? It won't last long!

Food and water bowls

Stainless-steel food and water bowls are good choices for big guys like Goldens. They're indestructible and easy to sanitize. Buy the two-quart size right off the bat and don't bother with those cute tiny puppy pans; they'll outgrow them in a blink. (Figure 5-1 is a good example of how *not* to feed your pup. Too much food!)

WARNING

If you crave those neat stoneware bowls, think about your back and how often you'll have to pick up those heavy dishes. Plastic bowls are too flimsy and do not sanitize as well.

FIGURE 5-1:
Chow time!

© Getty Images.

Collars and ID tags

For immediate daily use, purchase a narrow adjustable nylon webbed collar with a plastic quick-release buckle. This collar will expand 2 to 3 inches in length as the puppy grows. The 8- to 12-inch size will fit your little guy, but not for long. Your Golden puppy will grow faster than your crabgrass. You'll replace this collar at least twice during his first year.

If you prefer a leather collar, note that some leather dyes can stain the puppy's fur, especially if he plays in water (that includes big puddles!). It's a waste of money at this early age.

WARNING

Never use a chain (or choke) collar on your puppy. Those collars are for older, bigger dogs, are intended for training purposes only, and should never be worn beyond a training session. Tales abound about dogs who have hanged or choked themselves to death when their chain collars tangled on furniture or a fence post. Your pup may graduate to a training collar (*during training sessions only* — see Chapter 9) at 5 or 6 months of age, depending on his size and temperament.

Always attach identification to your puppy's collar from day one. (Perish the thought, but what if he gets lost?) Never include his name (a stranger could too easily call him) — just use your own name and telephone number. After he is fully grown and can wear a collar he won't outgrow, purchase a fabric adjustable collar. My personal choice is a collar with the ID information woven into it (you can find these on the Internet). I also use "Reward" and my phone number on the woven collars (woven information is permanent). I do not attach the standard S-hook dangle tag. Dangle tags can get caught on carpeting and come off easily, and there goes your ID.

I have also used a brass plate with my name and phone number riveted to the collar, and a line that reads "Dog needs medication" (whether that's true or not). If the dog is stolen, a thief might think twice about the value of a dog who has some sickness or disease. If he's lost, that "health" information may motivate whoever finds the dog to return him promptly or take him to a vet. Can't hurt, might help!

TIP

Some breeders microchip their pups before sending them to a home. If your breeder did not, you should have your pup chipped during your first vet visit. It's a simple and painless process that provides permanent identification. You must, however, register your personal information with the manufacturer. All shelters and veterinarians check for microchips when dealing with a lost dog.

SAVE YOUR PET IN CASE OF FIRE AND OTHER EMERGENCIES

Attach fire alert stickers on all the entry doors to your home to alert emergency personnel that you have pets in the house. You can find these stickers at most pet shops or make your own. Be sure to include the number of pets in the house and their names on the stickers.

Leashes and harnesses

You probably thought a leash was just a leash, right? Hey, dog life just isn't that simple! For training purposes and control, you'll need an entire wardrobe of "lines" with which to lead and train your dog:

» **A 4- to 6-foot nylon or lightweight leather leash:** You will use this shorter lead in the house, for tethering and teaching household manners.

» **Collar tab:** You can make a collar tab or purchase one. This 6- to 10-inch length of leash or lightweight cord clips to your puppy's collar to wear around the house. This tab will enable you to grab and control your pup when necessary. He'll graduate into this short tab shortly after coming home. You may end up using the collar tab on your Golden throughout his first year.

» **A narrow 6-foot leather lead:** This is lightweight and easy to fold in your hand while walking. You'll need this size for obedience class in a few weeks. Get it before you bring your puppy home.

» **A 20- to 30-foot long line plus a 50-foot long line:** You won't need this one for the first month or two, but once your Golden gains confidence in his new surroundings (it happens in a heartbeat!), you'll need long line, which is a fabric leash available in pet stores or pet supply catalogs (as are most of the items in this chapter), or you can make your own as I do from a length of soft nylon or poly rope and a clip (for his collar), both available at hardware or discount stores. I frequently use both sizes (not at the same time, of course).

WARNING

» **A 16- to 20-foot extendible flexi lead:** Flexis are controversial in that they can easily lead to accidents, where the dog runs away or into the street and is injured, because the flexi is too loose. Once considered a convenient way to allow the dog to walk or roam away from you, they have lost favor. If you elect to use a flexi lead, do so with extreme caution.

TIP

In addition to the standard leash and collar, a dog harness provides an extra measure of control. A harness fits under the dog's chest and across his back. It is very simple to use and puppies and adult dogs rarely object to them. Therapy groups routinely use a harness on their dogs.

You can also use head gear worn with the leash to help control a puppy who adamantly resists a buckle collar when on leash. The Halti, the Come-Along, and the Gentle Leader-Promise Head Collar are different versions of the same type of head collar. Made from a webbed nylon material, the head gear goes over the bridge of the nose and the leash attaches to an O ring under the dog's chin. It's really more of an emergency measure. Your obedience instructor can show you proper leash work with a harness or a head collar. See Chapter 9 for more on obedience training.

Bedding

It's easy to go overboard on bedding because bed choices are unlimited and oh-so-tempting. Plush cushions, fluffy beds, and covered foam mattresses, all with patterns and colors galore to match your dog or your decor. My preference always runs to ducks and geese. After all, my dogs are working retrievers, Golden variety!

TIP

A bed, plain or fancy, is not a canine necessity. Some pups will make confetti out of their designer beds. Test your pup first with an old blanket to curl up on before you invest in expensive sleeping gear. Cutesy beds, if you so desire, can come later, when your Golden has outgrown the chewing stage.

THE SCOOP ON RAWHIDES

Rawhide chews of various sizes and shapes are made from processed beef hide, so carnivorous dogs naturally love them. Ask your vet for advice on rawhides. Puppies and adult dogs have been known to choke on rawhide chews of all types . . . pressed strips as well as knotted bones. Rawhides also have been known to produce loose stools, and some meat-flavored rawhides can stain your carpet. Pig's ears cause upset stomachs, and cow hooves create a most unpleasant odor. None are healthy for your Golden. When purchasing any edible or chewable product, buy only those made in the U.S.A. In the U.S., rawhide is considered a food by-product, and the processing is government-controlled. That's not the case in other countries, where the chemical processing of rawhide materials is not regulated, and the preservatives may contain formaldehyde, arsenic, and other toxic chemicals.

Toys and chewies

Golden Retriever puppies are really miniature chewing machines disguised as dogs. As a breed, Goldens tend to be very oral and possess a manic desire to have something in their mouth. If they don't have toys to satisfy their chewing instincts, you can guess what will happen to your shoes and furniture. My own Goldens recommend these toys:

>> **Nylabones and Gumabones:** These hard, bone-shaped chew toys are great chewcifiers, and they come in shapes and sizes to fit every age and breed. They won't splinter, but examine them frequently for spiky ends. When the ends get spindly, just discard them.

  Avoid giving your dog any "people" bones to chew on, such as any cooked bones, or chicken, turkey, pork, or steak bones. These can splinter and get caught in your dog's throat.

>> **Hard sterilized bones:** These bones, found in pet supply stores, are another retriever favorite. Like the Nylabone, these thick, hollow bones won't fragment or splinter. Because I live with adult power-chewers, almost every room in my house is usually littered with Nylabones and hard bones.

>> **Kong toys:** Those hard rubber objects come in puppy and adult sizes and are almost indestructible.

  Woolly toys: Puppies love 'em! Your pup will shake them and toss them around, and later snuggle up with them. (Just make sure none have tiny button-type eyes, fuzzy noses, squeakers, or other small parts that can be pulled off, shredded, and/or swallowed.) My own puppies always shredded these toys once they got bored with them. Other pups keep their stuffies forever.

>> **Empty, clean gallon and half-gallon milk jugs:** These make excellent puppy toys that bounce around easily and make lots of noise. Puppies love to bat them about with their paws and will get crazy when they play with them. Replace as needed because they'll get chewed up in a hurry.

Of course, you're bound to go overboard with toys because they're all so doggone cute. Buy as many as your heart desires, but offer your puppy only two or three items at a time. Give him too many choices, and, just like a child, he'll get bored with all of them. Keep a couple of favorite chew toys in his crate, and rotate a few others in his toy bucket. Incidentally, show him his toy bucket once or twice. That's one place he will not forget!

Here are some toys you will want to use with caution or under supervision, or avoid altogether:

- » **Braided rope toys:** These have major shredding potential and should be used with caution, and always with supervision. If your pup or adult dog starts pulling them apart, or worse, ingests some of the threads, it can become a life-threatening surgical nightmare. They should never be used for tug-of-war. (See Chapters 8 and 16.) Remove and discard chew ropes the minute they get even a little stringy. If parts of the rope toy disappear and do not reappear in the dog's stool, suspect the worst and see your vet.
- » **Squeaky toys:** The squeakers can be pulled out and swallowed.
- » **Squishy rubber toys:** Although small pieces of shredded rubber toys can survive the digestive process, a whole rubber ducky would never make it through. If your pup's a bonafide chomping champ and one of his favorite toys disappears, suspect the worst and take him for a checkup.

WARNING

It probably goes without saying that you should not give your puppy any shoes or socks as toys. And *never* toss your old or discarded tennis shoes or slippers into the toy bucket. Of course, puppies can't distinguish between old and new, and will eventually chew up any and every shoe he finds. No socks either, even knotted ones. They shred, and if your pup swallows one, he will end up in surgery. (My oldest son's very sweet yellow Labrador did just that. A $2,500 price tag!)

CHEW PREVENTION

Get your chew deterrent before your puppy comes home and starts "remodeling" your furniture. You can spray furniture legs and leashes with a product called Bitter Apple (or Bitter Grape), both available in pet supply stores. Test it before using it on fine wood furniture. Bitter Apple cream lasts longer, but is less convenient to use than the spray. Although Bitter Apple is really nasty tasting, a few puppies actually seem to like it and chew right over it.

You also try using a loud rattle can to deter your little chewer. Fill an empty aluminum soup or soda can with a half-dozen pennies and tape the opening shut. Use it only as directed (in Chapter 8) and only when your verbal corrections or other methods fail. When you shake the can, the loud rattle will startle your puppy to stop what he's doing.

Grooming tools

You don't need many grooming tools to start, but you should have a slicker brush to get your puppy used to the grooming process early on. A mild shampoo is also a good idea, just in case your puppy gets into something smelly, which is a favorite Golden trick. For more on grooming, see Chapter 13.

Great crates

A crate is your most important puppy purchase. Every puppy deserves his own private space, a place where he can escape from the hectic pace of human life. A crate is not a cage your puppy can't get out of. He thinks it's a place where humans can't get in, his very own safe house where he feels secure. Canines are natural den creatures, an instinct passed down from their wolf ancestors. Contrary to human perception, your puppy will not think he's looking at the world through a jailhouse window. In his dog's-eye view, it's a personal haven of security.

A pet crate is also good for child-proofing; this is not a playhouse the kids can share with him. (At least for a while. After the kids and puppy are better acquainted, they may end up together in the crate — but only after your puppy has fully adjusted to the kids and his new dwelling.)

WARNING

Children should never stick their hands into your dog's crate or poke any object at the pup. Whether he is sleeping or awake, children need to respect his space and privacy.

Crates come in wire mesh or plastic, like the airline travel crate. Some wire crates conveniently fold up suitcase style to fit into the trunk of your car for traveling. My personal choice is the wire crate. I think my dogs feel less isolated and closer to their human family. Wire crates also are better ventilated, which is a bonus in warm weather. For privacy and at bedtime for puppies, I just drape a large towel or light-weight blanket over the top and sides. Make sure the covering is draped away from the sides to prevent the pup from snagging the fabric to chew or swallow (surgery!).

Purchase an adult-size crate; your puppy will soon grow into it. A 22-inch by 36-inch wire crate or a large-size airline crate will be comfy for the average adult Golden. He only needs to lie down comfortably; he doesn't need a dance hall.

Baby gates

Believe it or not, most puppy families can't survive without baby gates. Baby gates confine a puppy to his playroom (usually the kitchen or utility room) and keep him out of rooms where he could get in trouble or make mischief. They are very handy in all stages of dog life.

BE AWARE OF OPEN WINDOWS

Dogs can and do jump out of open screened windows for reasons known only to the dog. Never leave a dog or puppy where he can climb up and push through an open window. Install safety grills on house windows or open them from the top. Open car windows are also dangerous.

Puppy-Proofing Your House and Yard

Before you bring your puppy home, you should take a dog tour of your property. Your home, garage, and yard may be — and probably are — littered with hazards that can harm or endanger your new puppy. To change it into a pet-friendly domicile, check it out from your puppy's point of view. Complete an eye-level inspection, and then get down on your hands and knees and see what your puppy might find intriguing from his vantage point. Then hide it or get rid of it! If your neighbor shows up as you're crawling around on all fours, just ask him to join the fun.

To puppy-proof your house, follow these tips:

>> **Keep medication bottles and cleaning supplies locked up or out of reach.** The sound of pills rattling in a plastic bottle can intrigue a puppy, who can easily chew the bottle open.

>> **Don't toss dental floss where your puppy can get into it.** Dental floss will not digest and can become tangled in a pup's intestines. It's a surgical nightmare.

>> **Unplug electrical cords.** You can also attach them inconspicuously to the wall or press them under baseboards. Puppies are especially attracted to loose cords. (I can't tell you how many computer or telephone cords I've replaced in my office because I trusted a rogue puppy as I worked right beside the pup!) Chewed cords are a common cause of household fires and electrical burns in canines. Think injuries and dollar signs.

TIP

There is an electrical extension cord on the market that automatically shuts off the power when chewed to prevent animal (and child) injuries. Cost: about $10 each.

>> **Beware of coins, socks, needles, and tinsel.** Actually, beware of any miscellaneous objects small enough for a puppy to pick up and chew or swallow. Any veterinarian will gladly tell you horror stories about impossible trinkets they removed during surgery. (Dangerous, expensive, and unnecessary!) The common theme in these events is the owners never thought their puppy or dog would ingest such ridiculous objects.

>> **Watch out for stringy stuff like yarn and sewing gear.** I know of one dog who died from swallowed twine that tangled in his intestines. If the worst happens and your Golden eats a no-no, immediately call your vet. (See Chapter 11 for more on first aid.)

>> **Do not use roach or rodent poison or other pesticides in areas accessible to your puppy.** You can't be too careful. And remember, puppies can wiggle into impossible-to-reach places.

Keep cigarettes out of reach. Ingested cigarettes can lead to nicotine poisoning. Keep any packs of cigarettes out of reach, and keep those ashtrays clean. Better yet, give up smoking. Second-hand smoke is bad for your dog's health.

>> **Keep the toilet lid down, and never use toilet bowl cleaners that attach to the side of the tank or bowl.** All puppies are born with toilet sonar and quickly discover the coldest water is in the toilet bowl. In my 40 years of Golden companions, only one has never attempted to slurp from an open toilet bowl.

>> **Keep the diaper pail lid shut tight.** Is there a baby in the house? There's not a dog afoot who doesn't love to ruminate in soiled diapers. It's not only disgusting, it's dangerous. Dogs have actually died from ingesting soiled diapers. They may vomit up part of the material, but the remaining toxins can send his body into a prolonged death spiral. Don't let diaper duty distract you from your dog's behavior.

>> **Secure all trash.** Most Golden puppies are natural garbage explorers and will dig out chicken bones and other rotten stuff with serious potential for choking or tearing up your dog's intestines. My first Golden was a classic garbage dog who would empty our upright kitchen trash container every time we stayed out past the curfew she imposed on us. She would poke her head under the tilt-lid and make dozens of trips in order to carry every little-bitty piece out onto the family room couch.

>> **Hide your underwear.** Puppies — and some adult dogs, too — love to chew up and swallow socks and other clothing items with your body scent that they find lying on the floor. Most puppies are underwear aficionados and will gobble up things like jockey shorts and pantyhose, especially unlaundered ones. And remember, ingested undies warrant an expensive trip to the vet! If you value your Calvin Kleins, stash them in the hamper after wearing.

>> **Hide the cat litter boxes.** Pups — in fact, all dogs — love to snack on kitty droppings. (It's not technically dangerous, just gross.)

WARNING

Be careful with flea control products on your carpet and on your dog (see Chapter 12). Most are toxic and should be used with extreme caution. Always secure your dog away from the treated areas. Double-check with your vet for recommendations.

Outdoor hazards

Some uncommon chemicals for use outdoors are canine hazards. For example, the treated lumber used in decks and landscaping has been preserved with chemicals that are toxic and can be fatal for a dog who chews or ingests the wood. Check with the manufacturer and installer before purchasing and using such materials.

Certain varieties of acorns are so toxic to dogs that just one nut can cause death within a few hours. Ask your area nursery or landscaper to identify your trees. (The Internet is a great resource for such information.) Outdoor birdbaths are also risky. (Come to think of it, who ever heard of an indoor birdbath?) The water contaminated from bird droppings can be dangerous or fatal to dogs. Clean them daily; your birds will love you for it!

You'll also want to dispose of or secure these dangers that may be stored in your garage:

» **Antifreeze:** Everyone knows (or should know!) the dangers of antifreeze. This bright green liquid has a sweet taste that attracts dogs and cats. Even a few drops can kill a large animal. Keep antifreeze containers tightly closed and out of reach and clean up spills immediately. Watch for leaks on your driveway or at the curb.

» **Weed killers, pesticides, and herbicides:** If you store these kinds of products in your garage, keep them well secured and out of reach. (Better yet, dispose of them — see the following sidebar.) Make sure that rodent traps or poisons are completely inaccessible. A curious puppy can be amazingly creative. He can dig into surprising places, and then chew apart and swallow last week's paint roller plus your turpentine brush.

Botanical dangers

Many years ago, I was surprised to learn how many plants could cause anything from diarrhea to death if my Goldens ate them. Yikes! I had to do some rapid replanting in my yard and garden. Lily of the Valley, Oleander, Rhododendron, Japanese Yews, and Poinsettia are just a few of more than 80 varieties of common house and yard plants that are toxic if ingested. (You can find a complete list of toxic plants on the Internet.) Put house plants up high or move them where your puppy can't get into them. Always do a thorough greenery check inside and out before you bring your pup home.

HERBICIDE HAZARDS

According to a recent study conducted over a 6-year period at Tufts University's School of Veterinary Medicine, exposure to lawn chemicals, specifically those applied by professional lawn care companies, raised the risk of canine malignant lymphoma (CML) by as much as *70 percent*. Dogs at highest risk for CML were over 50 pounds and lived where professionals applied both herbicides and pesticides, as well as insect growth regulators (IGRs). Other studies showed that dogs exposed to those treated lawns had detectable amounts of the chemical in their urine, and that absorption of the herbicide through their skin occurred for several days after it has been used on your lawn.

If you absolutely must use the weed killer 2,4-D, or any glyphosate (sold commercially as Roundup) or IGR product, prohibit dog activity on treated areas for at least several days or until after the next cutting. For even better safety measures, don't use those products at all. And don't allow your dog access to any grassy area (along public highways, parks, schoolyards, or nature preserves) unless you can confirm no chemicals have been used. Keep him on a leash and stay on the sidewalk instead. (Sorry, I know that limits your walking places!) Cancer is a huge threat to the Golden Retriever breed, so let your puppy play in the dandelions instead. He'll love it!

If the worst happens and your dog or puppy chomps on some forbidden plant or flower, call your veterinarian for instant help and then rush the animal to the clinic. If possible, take along a sample of the ingested plant or product. The bottom line here is to never underestimate your pet. (See Chapter 11 for more information about poisoning and how to recognize the signs.)

IN THIS CHAPTER

» **Introducing puppy to his new world**

» **Feeding your puppy**

» **Treating your puppy to pedicures and body rubs**

» **Socializing your puppy**

» **Creating golden bonds**

Chapter **6**

Welcoming Your Puppy Home

The "how" of welcome home is just as important as the "when." This is a tough time for your pup. Just think about it from his perspective. He has no idea who you are or that you're going to love and care for him forever. He just knows he's leaving the only home he's ever known, not to mention saying good-bye to his mom and siblings. Don't let that wagging fuzzy tail deceive you. Beneath his furry chest, there beats an anxious heart that's wondering, "Where's Mom?" In this chapter, you discover what you need to know to make his welcome home as calm as possible, and also encourage all the good habits you want your adult Golden to have.

Bringing Your Puppy Home

To help your puppy with this major life change, arrange to pick him up over a long weekend or during your vacation so that you'll have several days to devote just to him. Arrive at the breeder's early in the day so that he will have more "awake" time to adjust to his new world. If possible, bring another person; one of you will have to drive, and the other can tend to the puppy. If you do this solo, put a crate or carrier in your car. Driving and holding a puppy is a recipe for an accident!

TIP

If possible, leave the kids at home. Their excitement and happy, squeaky voices will only add to the puppy's stress and make his departure still more difficult. If they do come along, make *sure* that they stay quiet and don't fondle or pester the puppy. (Oh yes, they will!)

The breeder should give you some type of puppy packet with your pup's AKC registration (which you both must sign), his pedigree, a health record of shots (there should be only one shot: a distemper/parvo vaccine or a 5/way distemper/parvo/adenovirus/hepatitis/parainfluenza vaccine) and wormings, and a list of instructions about food and general care.

You should also have your own list of prepared questions. In your excitement, you're bound to forget to ask about a few important details. Ask about feeding and sleeping schedules, and what kind of food he's been eating and how much.

TIP

Bring an empty gallon jug and fill it with water from the breeder. Mix that water gradually with yours at home. A change in water (for example, well water to city water) can cause loose stools. Why take chances?

Bring along a couple of large towels. Toss one towel in with your puppy's littermates and let them drag it around to fully impregnate it with their special puppy scent. That towel will be your puppy's personal security blanket in his crate at home. Use the other towel to hold the puppy (not if you're driving!). A big towel will be snuggly, and you'll also have a safety net if puppy urinates or throws up during the ride. It may not happen, but you'll be sorry if you're not prepared. Chat calmly and softly to your puppy. A gentle voice will help to soothe his insecurity.

REMEMBER

If you have to travel a long way, you'll need to make a puppy potty stop. That means you'll need his collar and leash or a long line to keep him safe and under control when he relieves himself. (See Chapter 5 for more on collars and leashes.) Find a safe out-of-the-way place where no other dogs have been to prevent exposure to fecal droppings or other contaminants. His immune system is not yet fully protected and is very fragile at this tender age.

Keeping His First Days Calm and Quiet

Even though your puppy was (or he should have been) socialized with humans at his breeder's, remember he's never been away from home. He will be apprehensive in a new environment, and he'll need your full attention for reassurance. Keep the first day or two low-key, and don't invite the neighbors over to see the new arrival. Ditto for your children's friends. Explain to the kids that your new puppy needs to feel comfortable and confident in his new surroundings before he meets too many people. Friends and other family members can visit in a day or two, after he feels at home.

REMEMBER

This first day is *puppy* day! Let him sniff and investigate your yard and whatever rooms of the house you designate as his territory. Show him his water bowl, crate, and toy box. Take it slow and let him investigate all the new sights and smells. Make sure the kids don't smother him to death with too much hands-on attention. Calm, quiet, and relaxing — that's the cardinal rule for his first day at home.

Teaching the Kids to Be Dog-Smart

Although most people lump kids and puppies into one big happy family, they don't always co-exist peacefully. Child psychologists say that young children are not born with natural feelings of compassion or empathy toward animals, so they're often unintentionally cruel in their behavior with a pet. They don't mean to be unkind; they just don't know any better.

Consequently, it's your job to teach your children and their friends that your new Golden puppy is a living being who will love them and play with them if they treat him gently and with respect. Show the kids how to properly pet the puppy; don't let them drag him around by the tail or carry him by the neck (or worse)!

Teach your older children the correct way to hold the puppy. Show them how to grasp him under the chest and tummy so that he won't wiggle out of their arms. Toddlers and little ones *should not be allowed to carry him under any circumstances.* Rather, they should always sit on the floor when playing with the puppy. (With toddlers and youngsters, this play session should be brief and supervised.)

WARNING

This is important! You should never leave any child and your puppy unsupervised together. If you do, you're begging for a problem. Puppy teeth are sharp, and even a playful puppy nip can easily break the skin, leaving the child or children frightened and resentful. The opposite is also true. Children can accidentally hurt the pup. They'll get along eventually, but you have to be the ringmaster for a while.

The kids should not pester the puppy when he sleeps or eats. A puppy or adult dog who is eating may be possessive of his food and think that the child is going to take his food away.

Another important kid rule: Instruct your children not to wave their hands or holler when they approach the puppy. If they surprise him from behind or wave and jiggle, they could scare him. He might also think they're playing, and he'll jump on them and chase them, which is a normal response. This is also one of the toughest lessons to teach children because silly antics are natural adolescent behavior.

Children also should never take a toy or bone from the puppy's mouth. As the adult and puppy master, that's your job to teach the puppy to drop the object and give it willingly to you.

REMEMBER

Dog-smart kids are less apt to become dog bite statistics, and as a bonus, they'll grow up to be best friends with their new Golden playmate.

Pulling Rank

If you have another dog at home, you should know how your current pet responds to other dogs before you bring your puppy home. (If your current pet is a cat, see the following sidebar for tips on introducing her to your new puppy.) If your current dog has had little or no social experience with other canines, you can (and should!) visit a local park or dog walk area to check out his response to other animals. That way, you're not caught off guard if he's less than happy with his new playmate.

When you introduce your new puppy to your adult dog, keep both dogs on leashes so that you can maintain control. It is most important that you also keep their leashes loose so that the two can sniff and feel comfortable with each other. In dog language, a tight leash may signal to the older dog that the puppy is a threat. Look for happy doggie signs like play bows and tail wags, and allow them to play together while they're still on-leash. Your adult dog may growl and protest, even bare his teeth, if he feels it's necessary to pull rank, but for the most part, dogs work out their own pecking order.

If your two dogs don't reach an agreement you feel comfortable with or if you think your puppy's in harm's way, do not discipline your older dog. He's just being a doggie. And playful puppies can be a real pain in the hindquarters for an adult dog! Just keep them separated and continue this socialization process for the next few days. If your older guy continues to protest, consult your veterinarian or other behavior specialist.

Even if harmony reigns immediately, supervise their time together to prevent squabbles and make sure that some minor incident doesn't erupt into a major confrontation. The older dog may snarl or bark loudly to put your puppy in his place, and that's okay. That's how puppies learn who's the boss dog and when to back off. Down the road, when your puppy approaches sexual maturity, there may be changes in their relationship.

After the two dogs are well acquainted, limit the amount of time they spend together. Puppies will quite naturally relate best to and bond with their own species. You want your puppy to consider you his leader and become a people dog. I'm sure I have convinced my own Goldens they're just canine versions of my children!

WARNING

Big-dog roughhousing can easily injure a puppy's tender growing bones and joints, so it's best to keep wrestling and rowdy play to a minimum during the first year of rapid growth.

REMEMBER

Your older dog has squatter's rights. Do not make him jealous by making a fuss over your new puppy when your older dog is present. He has first dibs on his own toys and treats unless or until such time as he relinquishes that privilege. To minimize his stress over a new dog in his territory, give him extra individual attention with special things he likes to do, such as Frisbee games, walks in the woods, or obedience routines.

Soup's On! Your Puppy's Dinner Plan

Most puppies come equipped with tummy timers that prompt them to eat on schedule. Give him three meals a day for the first month or two, then feed him twice a day for the rest of his life. Sure, lots of dogs eat only once a day. However, twice-daily feeding is preferred by most breeders and professional trainers. Smaller meals are more satisfying, promote better weight control, and may prevent bloating, which is a good reason all by itself. Plus, your dog will think it's a big deal getting that food bowl twice a day.

Some dog owners prefer *free feeding*, also called *free choice*, because they feel it's more convenient, and it surely is. But it's also a lot harder to housebreak a free-choice puppy — what goes in at odd times will come out when you least expect it. It's also harder to monitor the amount your puppy eats, which is important in fast-growing breeds like Goldens. And down the road, your dog may have some health problem that requires a stringent feeding protocol.

REMEMBER

Food is a primary reinforcer. A puppy who is dependent on you for basic needs like food will be less independent and more likely to consider you his leader. If he has food available at all times, he will not think he needs you for this basic need.

Feed your puppy at 6 to 7 a.m., again about noon, and dinner no later than 5 or 6 p.m. For easier house training, don't feed him after 6 p.m. and don't give him water after 7 p.m. If he needs a drink in the evening, give him an ice cube to chew on. A 10 p.m. trip outside should carry him through the night. (See Chapter 7 for more on housebreaking.)

He will need three meals a day for a few weeks. Start feeding twice a day when he's about 11 or 12 weeks old. Meal size will vary with each pup, but the average Golden puppy at 7 weeks is polishing off about ⅓ to ½ cup of dry food at each meal. Feed it dry, with a bowl of fresh water available on the side. Feeding dry will help prevent plaque and tartar build-up on his teeth, which is most important after his adult teeth have come in.

TIP

Some puppies almost inhale their food as if it were their last meal on earth. To slow the eating process to a healthier pace, you can place a clean, large round rock in the center of his food pan. That will force him to eat around it and slow down. There are also food pans available online and at pet stores with little mounds built into them that slow the eating process.

WARNING

You should not give your puppy any supplements. A quality food provides the correct proportion of nutrients that a growing puppy needs. Adding vitamins, especially calcium and phosphorus or other minerals, will upset that delicate balance and can create structural and growth problems. Veterinary nutritionists are emphatic about no additives. If your vet recommends vitamins, either ignore that advice or find another vet.

Feed your puppy in the same place every day so that he can concentrate on the business of eating. Allow about 20 to 30 minutes for each meal. If he doesn't finish during that time, pick up his food and offer the same amount of food at the next meal; don't add the leftover food from the prior meal to the next.

Feed the adult dog at the same time as the puppy's morning and evening meals, but in separate spaces in the same room, so there's no sharing (or stealing) from food pans. Offer the puppy's midday meal without the adult dog present.

When should you increase his food portion? When he's finishing every bite of food at two out of three meals, bump up his portion just a tad. I suggest going from a level ⅓ cup to a heaping ⅓ cup at first, then increase to a scant ½ cup, then a level ½ cup, a heaping cup, and up the food ladder according to your puppy's appetite.

Some pups are voracious eaters and gobble up their food like it's their last meal, and others are more finicky and just seem to nibble at their food. Some puppies also go through eating spurts and will eat with more or less vigor at certain times. Not to worry. Your only real concern should be an overweight puppy. Keep him lean. (See Chapter 10 for more on feeding your puppy and maintaining a healthy weight.)

Making the Most of Meal Time

Use your puppy's meal time to lay the groundwork for other good behaviors. Once he's learned the "Sit" command (see Chapter 9), make him sit before he gets his food dish. At first make it a quickie sit, and then hold it a bit longer as he gets more proficient. He'll learn that all good things come from this new human leader who also gives food and hugs and kisses along with his commands and dinner bowl.

TIP

Once a day, wiggle your fingers in his food pan while he eats. Occasionally remove his food mid-meal, praise him, and quickly return his food. Occasionally, stroke and pet your puppy for a moment as he eats, and then leave him alone to eat in peace. Your puppy must learn to accept your presence at his dinner table, and tolerate the removal of food and other objects from his mouth. Food guarding is a common habit in dominant or fearful dogs and can lead to biting (see Chapter 16). Proper conditioning at this tender age will prevent that.

Use this take-it-and-give-it-back routine with his toys as well, saying "Thank you" sweetly when you take them, and then return them with "Good boy" praise. Practice this frequently before he develops possessive habits. It can be rather intimidating if your adorable puppy suddenly decides to keep his toy and bares his little teeth at you. Whoops! This exercise is for his benefit as well as yours, because someday you may have to remove a fish hook or chicken or fish bones from his gullet. As with all training at this age, it's easier to teach a 15-pound pup who has no bad habits (yet!) than to deal with possessive or aggressive behavior in a 60-plus-pound adult Golden.

THE NOISE FACTOR

Equate your puppy to an infant. He should hear all the normal household noises. You don't want any sudden or unexpected moves to frighten him, but you can still clatter the pans and vacuum at a distance to condition him to the sounds of daily life and as insurance against noise sensitivity.

To accustom your puppy to loud noises gradually, once a day drop a heavy book on the floor in the next room while he's eating. Gradually move closer each time until you're across the room. If he shows fear or anxiety, move farther away until he gets used to the sound, and then move closer more slowly. He should show normal curiosity, maybe stop eating and look about. You can also substitute other similar loud noises. This is especially important if you plan to hunt with your Golden. It will condition him to sharp sounds, so he'll be ready for the training pistol or a shotgun.

Continue these mini-lessons frequently throughout your Golden's lifetime. (Put a permanent flag on this chapter!) Dogs develop dominance tendencies at various stages in their life (see Chapter 8). These measures are simple reminders of your leadership, and will ward off guarding tendencies and also warn you of impending problems you might overlook.

REMEMBER

Why is this dominance thing so important? If your dog is to grow up well behaved, he must respect you as his pack leader. The ideal time to establish yourself in this lofty position is when he's young and manageable. If you wait too long, he may start thinking of himself as *your* leader ("Me boss-dog, you under-dog") and will consider your attempts to train him as a challenge.

Discovering Puppy Antics

Playing with your puppy is important. Before your puppy left his mom, he spent most of his day frolicking with his littermates, chasing and wrestling until they all fell asleep from pure exhaustion. (The pups shown in Figure 6-1 are engaging in typical puppy play.) But what happens to all that excess energy now that he's home with you?

WARNING

Exercise is as essential to his well-being as his food and water. If he doesn't get enough, he may act hyper, refuse to calm down, and redirect his excess energy into destructive activities like chewing on your furniture.

Close Encounters of the Furry Kind.

Adopt a reasonable puppy schedule and modify it as your puppy matures. Use the activities in Chapter 17, and invent your own to keep him properly exercised. This is a busy time for both of you. Goldens are smart pups, but they won't play *safely* without your help.

Conducting a Body Search

Your puppy must learn to submit to handling his body parts. He'll need it for grooming, nail trimming, ear cleaning, vet exams, and doggie times like wiping muddy paws. Start as soon as possible. If you wait until he's 3 or 4 months old and approaching adolescence, he'll be bigger, stronger willed, and less accustomed to hands-on body games.

Hold brief daily body exams. You can make a game of them, but insist that he cooperate. Lay him down and grasp and rub his paws and touch between his toes. "Ooooohh, what pretty feet!"

When he's on his back, rub his tummy and softly whisper pretty-puppy talk. He won't care what you say. It's your voice and touch that matter. I've never met a puppy who didn't love to have his tummy rubbed. My last puppy was so conditioned to our tummy sessions that she instantly rolled over onto her back if I as much as whispered to her or reached down to touch her thigh!

Look in his ears and raise his lips to touch his teeth and rub his gums and tongue. Put your hand over his muzzle and gently hold it there for just a few seconds. Slowly run your hands along his body. Use a soft brush for a few strokes to create pleasant associations. Using a brush during these exercises also will prepare him for longer and more detailed grooming sessions later (see Chapter 13). If you begin these exercises early and continue them, your puppy will learn to enjoy the process and cooperate. Occasionally do your body exams on your lap, and offer a few tasty tidbits to make them even more enticing.

Nipping Puppy's Nails

The puppy stage is the ideal age to introduce the nail clippers. He'll need those pedicures all his life, so get him used to it now before he gains another 20 or 30 pounds.

TIP

Using a standard canine nail clipper (ask your vet which one to use), remove just the tip or the curved end of the nail. (Figure 6-2 illustrates how to hold your puppy during a pedicure.) At first, you might succeed in doing only one or two nails before you throw your hands up in despair. (A sleeping or very tired puppy is easiest to work on!)

FIGURE 6-2:
Nail clipping won't be difficult if you start at an early age.

Keep at it several times a day (or all week), and you'll get all four paws done sooner than later. Dog nails grow quickly and become difficult to trim if they're neglected, because the *quick* (the pink vein inside the nail) will grow too long inside the nail. If you accidentally nip the quick and the nail bleeds, don't panic. Check out remedies in Chapter 13 on grooming.

Puppy treats are excellent lures for pedicures. One friend of mine has done such a good job of this with his three Goldens that whenever they see the nail clippers in his hands, they automatically roll over onto their backs and hold their four paws in the air to get their nails done because they know they'll get a Milk-Bone when he's done. Now that's positive reinforcement at its finest!

Socializing Your Puppy

Socialization is a puppy's introduction to the human world. From birth to 7 weeks, he's been learning proper canine behavior from his mom and littermates. Now at 7 weeks, he's old enough to make the switch from dogs to humans. Years of research have shown that 7 weeks is the best age for a puppy to begin forming social bonds with people. (We already know that some breeders don't release their pups until 8 weeks of age.) He's now emotionally mature enough to adjust to life-style changes and begin learning new behaviors.

REMEMBER

That same research also has proven that your puppy's brain is like a sponge, and that everything that happens during his first 20 weeks of life will permanently imprint on that little brain. Both positive and negative experiences will have a lasting effect on the adult dog he becomes and everything he learns later in life.

Heed this message! The time and quality of the time you invest in your Golden puppy now will directly affect the quality of the adult Golden you will live with for the next 12 or 13 years! Make the most of this critical growth phase. Never again will you have this supreme opportunity to mold his personality and behavior. Your puppy could become a 14-karat wonder dog, a common gold-plated canine, or a tarnished, garden-variety scamp.

WARNING

An unsocialized dog will grow up to be spooky, shy, and fearful of people, other dogs, and strange places, and possibly aggressive toward humans and other animals. He'll be one unhappy fellow. Rehabilitation is rarely possible; you can't turn back the clock.

Overcoming social butterflies

A quiet, placid household without noise and people, especially children, is developmentally dangerous for your puppy. Make your house an active, puppy-friendly place. If you don't have children, invite relatives or the neighbor kids for puppy parties to play with him (supervised, of course). He has to interact regularly and often with children of all ages, or he will be uncomfortable with them later on. That's how dog bites happen.

TIP

Your puppy also has to interact with other dogs so that he learns to respect and enjoy their company. Without other canine experiences, he may grow up to be shy, fearful, or aggressive around other animals. After he's safely immunized, arrange brief, supervised play with friendly dogs once or twice a week. A puppy class also offers great puppy party times.

Building confidence

WARNING

Your puppy is especially impressionable during what is known as the 8- to 10-week fear period. This is a fragile time when object associations can leave indelible imprints. It's vital that he have only positive experiences with people, other animals, and places during this critical period.

Some situations can't be avoided, like going to the vet. In fact, it's a good idea to visit your vet just to introduce your pup and say hello. That will help make future visits more enjoyable. Your pup gets praised and petted, and later on he won't even notice those shots. If your pup shows fear or apprehension, do not offer sympathy or soothing reassurance; you'll just convince your puppy that things must be pretty awful and that it's okay to cower and act scared. Load him up with puppy treats and keep your reactions upbeat and positive. See Chapter 11 for more details on vet visitation.

REMEMBER

Puppies frequently spook at some object they perceive as strange — a lawn mower, a vacuum cleaner, a large box. Don't sympathize or force him to confront the "bad guy." Instead, go to the object, pet it, laugh a bit, and talk happily to encourage him. Let him sniff and investigate it on his own. I'm sure passersby thought it was more than strange when they saw me petting a fire hydrant.

Making the world his oyster

Once your puppy is past the fear period and your vet tells you he's safely immunized, commit to two or three away-from-home trips every week to expose him to new people, sounds, and smells. Car rides are always great fun, and the more he sees of his new human world, the more confident he'll grow up to be. Start slowly with a neighbor's yard (with his or her okay, of course), a local grocery store parking lot, or other friendly place where you can both feel safe and comfortable. Carry him if you think strange dogs have soiled the area.

Gradually add other busy outdoor places to your pup's agenda. Puppies should be exposed to all sorts of new and different situations such as stairs, elevators, different types of vehicles, people in uniform, delivery trucks — the list is endless. Hang out in front of grocery stores where he'll encounter shoppers with noisy shopping carts. On city streets, walk over the sewer grates. If, however, your puppy is worried or shows signs of fear or apprehension, be enthusiastic but don't force him. Back off and try again later. Avoid extremes, and condition him gradually to the unusual. Follow his cues and plan accordingly.

Experienced puppy-raisers often set goals to socialize their puppies, declaring that every pup should meet 100 people in a variety of settings before he reaches 4 months of age. That type of social whirl is the key to a confident puppy and adult.

Creating that golden bond

Bonding is the process of becoming your puppy's number one priority and takes a lot of one-on-one time between just the two of you. Like children, puppies need someone to love and respect, to learn from and depend on. Until now, that someone was his birth mother. Now it's you. And you begin the day you bring your puppy home.

Turn these first weeks at home into a special bonding time. Take walks together around the yard or some other quiet place, such as a field or park that is safe from road hazards, crowds, and other animals. Take advantage of his dependence on you. Chat with him to keep him close and call him to you for a treat or a hug. He's learning how much he needs you for security.

Tethering is an excellent way to enhance this one-on-one relationship. Put him on his 4- or 6-foot leash and tie or clip the other end to your belt loop. It must be long enough for him to sit or lie down comfortably, but not long enough to allow him to wander several feet away from you. Make sure that he's had an outside trip before you start so that you won't be interrupted by an accident. (If it happens, no scolding, just learn from it and forget it.) Before you start, make sure he's been introduced to his leash.

For about 15 or 20 minutes every day, tether yourself to your puppy while you go about the normal, everyday business of your house. Chat with your puppy a bit to keep him happy to be with you, but don't give any commands. Do not confuse bonding time with training. If he jumps up or bites, give a swift tug downward on the leash and tell him "No!"

The plain truth is, everything you do with or for your puppy, from cuddling right into training, will enhance the bonding process. What better reason to devote these next few months exclusively to him?

Golden Designations

Your puppy's name is more than just a cute or clever moniker. It's the word that should snap him to attention, change his focus, and make him look at you.

TIP

Make a point of using your dog's name only when you praise him or give him a command. If he gets praise or goodies when he hears his name, it will become a thing of value, and he'll respond quick as a wink. However, if you use his name too casually or frequently in normal conversation, it will lose its impact, and he'll soon ignore it.

If you talk to and about your dog often, substitute a handful of nicknames rather than his "call" name so that he doesn't become so used to his name that he tunes it out. If you use the nicknames often enough, it will become a habit. Our 10-year-old male Golden, Apache, was known around here as the Patchman, our Patchpie, the Big Man, and a few other names that are too silly to repeat here. When I said "Apache," he knew I either wanted to tell him to do something or treat him. Either way, he had an "Okay, what's up, boss?" attitude when he heard his name.

Minimizing the "No" Word

Another no-no involves using the correction word "No." Because you want your dog to love his name and respond to it like magic, don't connect it to negative words like "No." "No" does not mean pay attention or do something, as in a command word. "No" means stop doing something now. Puppies learn by doing, so "No" is a tough word for puppies and young dogs because it doesn't tell them *what* to do.

WARNING

The word "No" is often overused or used improperly (with kids, too!). Just as overusing a dog's name will teach him to tune it out, so, too, will he ignore "No" if he hears it all the time. Too many dogs think "No" is the first or second half of their name!

Save "No!" for the big-time errors, like snacking in your cat's litter box or stealing food from countertops. (You can bet your boots he'll try those things.) In early puppy training, it's more positive — and comprehensive for the dog — to redirect his behavior by giving an alternate behavior you can praise. He picks up a shoe to chew. Tell him "Drop" and give a chew toy instead. He puts his paws up on the sofa, and you know what he's thinking now. Tell him "Off!" and do the chew toy bit again.

Chapter **7**

Crate Training and Housetraining

M ost Golden puppies adjust quickly to their new human families. They are happy souls by nature and will bond with anyone who dispenses love and gentle handling and explains the rules of the new household in terms that are caninelogical.

This chapter gives you three golden *P* rules you will use for life. If necessary, tattoo them on your hand, or at least post them on your refrigerator door so that you won't forget them. In this chapter you will also read about the joys of crate training and why your Golden can't live without one. And you find out how to teach your puppy elimination skills, more commonly called *housetraining*. This is one chapter you don't want to skip!

Puppy Training and the Three Golden Ps

Praise, Patience, and Practice are the three *Ps* of puppy training. You'll need a generous supply of all three starting the moment you and your puppy leave his mom and littermates.

>> **Praise:** Goldens thrive on praise. Like candy to a baby, your puppy will respond to praise as if it were a can of yummy dog food. Praise is one tool you'll use for his entire life.

>> **Patience:** Stock up now before you run into puppy disasters that will test your mettle. You will need to save a bunch of it to use periodically during your golden life.

>> **Practice:** Hang in there and keep doing the good things you're learning from this book. You may feel like 10 thumbs now, but all things get easier with time. The more you practice handling your dog, training, and communicating properly, the better you'll both be down that golden road. When things get a little sloppy at times in your adult Golden's life, practicing will come in handy.

The Message in Your Voice

When you're teaching or otherwise interacting with your dog, you need to use your best dog voice. How you say something means as much as what you say. Give commands in a firm, commanding (but not harsh) voice.

REMEMBER

A lower voice is more compelling, which may explain why some dogs respond more to men. What dog in his right mind would give credence to a weak and pleading voice that's whining like a littermate? Now you also know why puppies don't respect a child's high-pitched, squeaky voice. It sounds just like another animal.

That low, stern voice can also have the opposite effect. A heavy-sounding voice (especially male) can be so intimidating it prevents a happy working attitude. "Good dog!" in a ferocious baritone will not make your dog feel happy or successful. You'll need a positive, upbeat tone to get positive, upbeat results. The right inflection in your voice can literally set the tone for success or failure.

TIP

Always use normal volume when you give commands. Don't shout or raise your voice. If you start out with maximum volume, you'll have nowhere to go when you want to add a little oomph to your message.

Whispering is a very effective way to hold your pup's attention if you start it early. Use a soft, whispery voice when you rub his tummy or pet his ears. Whisper lots of sweet talk nose to nose, and he'll make sweet associations with your whisper voice. Think of the advantages of whispered dog talk.

Introducing the Crate

For the first 2 or 3 months, you should confine your puppy to just one or two rooms; ideally, the kitchen and/or a room with access to an outside door. Use a baby gate so that he's contained but won't feel isolated. This gate will limit his space and play areas until he learns which exit to use for potty trips. It will also limit puppy accidents all over the house and your frustration over damaged furniture and carpets. Keep his crate in the area of confinement.

In your pup's opinion, his crate is his little hideout, his own little house within your house. If you're lucky, your puppy learned about crate life at the breeder's (although that's not very likely). Regardless, you need to start the crating process right away. Show your puppy his crate by tossing in a treat to make the den inviting and praise him when he enters on his own. You can also offer his first one or two meals in the crate (with the door open) so that he'll think it's a pretty fine place (holy cow, a restaurant *and* a hotel!).

WARNING

Never use the crate for punishment or crate your puppy immediately after a scolding. It's okay to use the crate as a disciplinary tool — just make sure that *he* doesn't realize it. You want to create only pleasant and positive associations with his room.

Pick a crate command like "Kennel" (or "House," both make sense) and use it consistently as an entry word. Toss in his treat and when he enters, use the K word. Then tell him "Good boy, Kennel!" Use that phrase consistently each time you crate him, and he'll quickly learn it through word association.

REMEMBER

You can choose any word you like to teach a specific behavior as long as you use the same word consistently. If you said "Howdy" every time you crated your Golden, he would learn to recognize that word. The words mean more to you than to the dog.

TIME OUT!

Crates are also good for puppy time-outs when he has to cool it for a while, like when your prissy aunt comes to visit and you know how she hates dog breath. Just place him in his crate so that his feelings won't be hurt. The crate also serves as a dual-purpose security system, providing confinement for your pup and protection for your house and furniture (think antique chair legs). With puppy safely crated in his little castle, he can't get into mischief when you leave the house, work in the yard, or clean the basement. A cruel prison? No. Peace of mind? You bet!

CRATING ON THE ROAD

Crates add a dimension of safety when traveling with your Golden. If he's safely crated, he can't leap into the front seat while you're speeding down the interstate. (You've heard the one about the motorist who told the officer he was speeding because his dog was licking his ear?) Many motels also welcome crated pets, and your dog will have his own room within your room wherever you stay.

For more on choosing a crate, see Chapter 5.

Dealing with crate accidents

Accidents happen. Your puppy will wet his crate a time or two, which will be your fault and not his. His puppy mat (I use old, clean towels for comfort and accidents) will absorb the urine and keep him dry and clean. It's easier to wash the towels than clean a wet crate or pup. If you put newspaper in his crate, it will leave newsprint on his fur, and you'll have a gray-looking, smelly pup. And because newspaper is associated with traditional housebreaking, keep it out of the picture entirely. You don't want him to piddle on the morning paper that lies next to your easy chair.

Crating adult dogs

I'm almost as crazy about crates as I am about Goldens. I use mine forever. But that probably won't be your bent. Still, 6 months' minimum use is a must, and for the first year is even better. Fussy housekeepers and decorator moms can't wait to run out and buy one of those cute doggie beds at the pet store and ditch their crate furniture. But if you travel or vacation with your Golden, remember those crate advantages and motel restrictions. And should any problem behavior crop up in the future, you can always return to the crate routine, and your dog won't object. So it's best to keep your adult dog conditioned to his crate.

Home, sweet home

Your dog's crate should be large enough for an adult Golden to lie down and turn around, but he doesn't need to stretch to his full body height or lie down stretched out like a rubber band. I suggest putting the crate in a people area of the house so that he doesn't feel isolated. (Also, make sure that it's not too far from the door where he goes out for potty stops — of course, you know why.) Don't leave food or water in the crate, but do provide a few safe chew toys to keep him occupied and happy. Leave the crate door open when he's not in it so that he can enter and leave it at will.

BED SHARING IS RISKY BUSINESS

To a dog and lesser pack member, sleeping on the bed means equal. Bed sharing is a luxury he gains only with permission, and he earns it only by recognizing you as leader. That goes for your kids' beds also.

I don't mean to dash your dreams of someday curling up in bed with your Golden, especially when I sleep with several of them myself. A few miles down the training road you might let your adult Golden into bed with you. But that choice is best made later in the dog's life when you know whether he can handle bed sharing without becoming possessive or territorial over it. You risk a dog bite if that happens.

Don't crate him during his first day at home. Just do the treat-toss and the first meal or two as a crate incentive. Bedtime will be soon enough. It's a good idea to move the crate into your bedroom at night (actually — it's a great idea!) and next to your bed for the first few weeks so that he won't feel left alone. Knowing you're close by will also help the bonding process. If you're lucky and own two crates, just leave one in the bedroom all the time. Another plus to having the crate in your room — you'll hear him if he whimpers during the night to relieve himself.

Cover the top and sides of your puppy's crate loosely with a large towel or blanket so that he can still observe the activity around him. Drop the covering at night for sleeping (and for naps if he takes to howling during his midday crate times). It will enhance the den-like environment and signal to him that it's time to rest.

Remember that puppy towel his littermates dragged around? Put it in the crate with him, or use an old bath rug or other towel. You'll have to use good judgment here. If your puppy chews these things up, thus rendering them useless, remove them and don't replace them.

Lights out!

When it's bedtime, drop your puppy's crate curtain (carefully away from the crate sides) so that he knows it's time for sleeping. (It's that cozy den thing again.) If he whines and you know he just pottied and doesn't have to go again, you can just wiggle your fingers in the crate to comfort him a bit. (No chewing on those fingers! I'm assuming here that the crate is next to your bed.) If the noise continues, just be patient that first night and ignore it. He's not resisting the crate itself. It's his first night away from Mom and family, and he's adjusting to a new and unfamiliar environment.

Sometimes a softly ticking alarm clock, soft music, or a humming fan will soothe a restless pup. It may work for you, too, if his whimpering keeps you awake!

TIP

If the whining persists past that first night, proceed to Crate Plan B . . . with the crate still covered, when he complains, slap the kennel lightly with your hand and tell him "Quiet." Repeat as necessary. The noise should intimidate him to be quiet.

Crate Plan C is more extreme and only if his whining gets really nutso for a few days. Again, with the crate covered, jiggle a shaker can and repeat "Quiet." Repeat if necessary.

Most properly raised Golden puppies settle quickly into their new sleeping quarters. If your pup is the exception and continues fussing night after night, just move the crate to a nearby area so that you can get some sleep. Do not, as a last resort, invite him into your bed for consolation. Like a child, he'll quickly make the natural connection that if he whines or cries, he gets released and hugged. He'll also figure out that it's okay to be on your bed, which is not a good idea this early in your relationship. Bed privileges must be earned, and you have not yet taught him you're the privilege-maker (see the earlier sidebar, "Bed sharing is risky business").

Here are some other important crate rules to remember:

>> **Never call your puppy to come to you and then promptly send him to his crate.** Puppies learn by association, and if he thinks his reward for coming to you is confinement, he may decide not to come at all. It's far better to simply carry him or walk him to the crate.

>> **Establish a daily crate routine right away.** Crate your puppy for 1- to 2-hour intervals during the day according to his personal nap and potty schedule. If he falls asleep under the table or curled up at your feet, just put him in his crate and close the door. (If you leave him under the table, the obvious will happen. He'll wake up, toddle out to piddle, and then hop on over to say, "Hi!") Be sure to close the crate door once he is inside. A closed door will force him to let you know when he has to go. At this tender age, puppies have tiny bladders, which they have to empty often. So don't ignore his message, or he'll adjust his housekeeping habits accordingly.

>> **Keep the crate door open whenever he's not in it.** In short order, he should be curling up in there on his own for naps and quiet time. (Again, don't forget to close that door gently after he goes in there!) Make sure that the kids don't disturb his down time or reach in and pull him out. Instruct them to call him gently to come out on his own.

Don't overuse your crate

Crate use can be overdone. For the first 10 weeks, never leave a pup unattended in a crate for more than 2 hours at a time (unless he's sleeping). Pups 3 months old can be in a crate for 3 hours. You can go 4 hours for the 4- and 5-month olds, and no more than 6 hours for dogs 6 months and older. If you can't be home to tend the pup, have a relative or neighbor come in to let him out or hire a trustworthy dog sitter.

If a crate won't work for you at all (I can't imagine why not, but just in case), you can use an indoor exercise pen at least 4 feet by 4 feet square. Make sure that it's sturdy enough to stand alone or secure it so that it won't fall if the puppy jumps up on the sides. Make it large enough to allow a corner for elimination and another one for play and sleeping. Cover the floor area with newspapers. When you determine which part of the pen area he has chosen to relieve himself, you can limit the papers to that corner or area. You will still need a companion to visit him at least once during the day.

WARNING

Some owners use a backyard chain link kennel or dog run to give their Golden a change of scenery and give themselves a doggie break. These work well for short periods, but their convenience makes them easy to abuse. You can't just put your puppy or dog outside in a pen and forget about him. He will be bored and lonely, and untrained and wild when he's released. If you have an outdoor kennel, be sure to use it only as an outdoor break for brief periods of time. Quality house time is essential to your Golden puppy's mental and emotional well-being. Goldens do not thrive if they are raised separated from their human families. And really, why have a dog in the first place if you plan to raise him separated from the rest of the family?

Don't rely on baby gates to contain your pup if he's unsupervised for lengthy periods. Most Golden puppies master them within a week and will scale them like a mountain goat.

Decide how you're going to handle your puppy's maximum confinement periods before you bring him home. Remember that raising a puppy without people is like raising a child in a closet. If he's merely confined without proper supervision and training, he will not learn people rules, good manners, or correct canine behavior. He won't grow up to be a Golden companion; he'll just be a dog.

TIP

If you are unable or unwilling to make appropriate arrangements for a puppy, don't despair. You can still live the Golden life. Consider adopting an adult or older Golden, a rescue Golden, or a retiree from a breeder. See Chapter 3 for details. Cats and ferrets also make good pets who do well without a lot of human interaction or attention.

Housetraining Routines

Like wolves in the wild, dogs don't like to soil their sleeping space, which is your biggest asset in teaching him to eliminate outdoors. It's the main ingredient in housebreaking. This doesn't mean he will never soil his crate. He probably will. If that happens, just clean it up, be patient, and be more vigilant. It's a rare Golden who doesn't give you a clue that he has to go.

TIP

Canines of all ages learn best and thrive on a routine that meets their daily needs. Puppies especially need a schedule to keep their body clocks in tip-top working order. Routines and consistency are your best tools for teaching your new Golden puppy the rules of the world outside the whelping box. His little brain sponge is just waiting to soak up information. Housetraining (which is a better term than "housebreaking") is his first important lesson.

Research has shown that puppies under 8½ weeks of age do not have the neurological development necessary to control their bladder or hold their urine. Your puppy may piddle as often as every half-hour that first week or two. Set your watch, phone, or oven timer to remind yourself — a half-hour whizzes by so fast. Pups between 7 and 12 weeks of age will need eight to ten trips outside each day. From 13 to 20 weeks, he'll need seven or eight trips a day for walks and elimination stops. (Trip numbers and times are average, every pup is different.) Adult Goldens should always go outside at least four times a day.

REMEMBER

Always take your puppy outside the first thing in the morning, immediately every time he wakes up or leaves the crate, within 5 to 20 minutes after eating, before you bed him for the night, and many times in between!

WARNING

If your puppy does have an accident, never use ammonia to clean it up. Dog urine contains ammonia, so you'll just make the spot a good reminder to "pee here." (See the sidebar "Odor neutralizers" for more cleanup tips.)

ODOR NEUTRALIZERS

Those accident spots have to be deodorized. Goldens have a "nose brain" that can identify odors that are ages old and in amazingly tiny amounts. (Didn't you ever wonder about fire hydrants?)

First, blot up the moisture with paper toweling or an absorbent sponge designed to sop up liquids. Clean with a crystallizing and sanitizing carpet cleaner. (Don't use dish or laundry detergents, which will leave soap residue that attract and hold dirt.) Then generously spray with an odor neutralizer (available through pet suppliers) to remove the smell. Some owners use a four-to-one water-vinegar solution with good results. Soak the area with the odor treatment, blot once more, cover with a clean, non-staining towel, and top with a heavy book for 24 hours. (Tell your friends you're teaching your puppy how to read.) Try both methods and see what works best for you.

Create good elimination habits:

TIP

» **Start teaching him "Outside" right away.** When he leaves his crate, just tell him "Outside" and take him to the door. Use it every time, and he'll soon learn that "Outside" means the door, the one he'll use to do his job. Smart owner, smart puppy, right?

» **Use the same area in your yard or other appointed spot for his outside trips.** He'll learn to associate the area for that purpose, and the odor from previous outings will help stimulate him to go. (The fire hydrant principle again.)

» **These potty trips are business trips, not time for play.** If he wants to romp or visit, just ignore him until he does his job. Once he's finished, praise him and go back inside. Reward him with his walk or other playing after he has gone.

» **Teach an elimination word.** Teach your puppy an elimination command and use it every time he goes. My personal favorites are "Hurry Up" and "Get Busy" (although I confess to also using "Go Potty," "Peeps," and "Poopers" in the past). As soon as your puppy squats to urinate or move his bowels, use your chosen command (softly, or he'll become too excited to finish the job) and offer praise: "Good boy, hurry up."

Give brief praise while he's actually going. You don't want a lot of conversation, and you don't want to praise him if he's merely squatting. (I've seen puppies simply squat and not go when they heard the magic word just to get the praise!) He'll soon recognize his key word and understand the purpose of those little trips outside. You can praise more heartily when he's done and even give a tidbit treat once in a while.

» **Don't talk or praise your puppy before he does his business.** Puppies get distracted easily — by your voice, a blowing leaf, or a daffodil. Start praising softly while he's going.

» **Be sure to use the same door or exit for his business trips.** Within a few days, you should see him go to the door on his own.

» **Teach elimination skills one room at a time.** Goldens are pretty smart pups, but even a genius Golden won't know how to find his bathroom exit if he's upstairs or several rooms away. That's the beauty of baby gates (see Chapter 5). When a puppy owner tells me her little one always has an accident in their upstairs bedroom while she's making the kids' beds, guess what my answer is? Why is he there, for heaven's sake?

After a week or two, you'll find that he may not always "go" as soon as he goes outside. There'll be irresistible sights and sounds that will distract him from the job at hand. That's okay! He's just discovering the world you take for granted. Be patient and enjoy the moment with him. Like children, puppies grow up all too soon!

In addition, resign yourself that you just can't just pop your puppy out the door to go. You must go with him on each trip to teach the potty place and give the praise. You also need to check his stools for signs of diarrhea, blood, or parasites. Rain, shine, or 2 a.m., you have to make sure that he does his job and gets his praise.

REMEMBER

Every dog develops his own signal system. Some whine at the door, a few may paw at it, others simply stare at the door, while some just sniff the floor in circles. At this age, one pass at the door is all you'll probably get before he lets it fly, so be alert! Eventually he'll be more persistent. My own Goldens never bark to go outside. They simply come and stare at me, leave the room, and then come back again and stare.

When you see your puppy squat indoors — or start to squat — quickly clap your hands and use a firm "No!" or sharp "Aahh, aahh, aahh!" (no shrieking, please), and then scoop him up and carry him outside. The sharp sounds may even startle him to stop going. Take him out even if he doesn't go again and offer praise for completing his job if and when he does.

WARNING

If your puppy makes a mistake indoors when you're not looking or if you find it later, just forget it and try harder next time. You have to catch him *in the act* to show him that indoors is not acceptable; even seconds later is too late. Puppies — in fact, dogs of any age — cannot connect a correction with something they did a heartbeat earlier. (Burn that in your brain. That truism applies to everything a canine does throughout his lifetime.)

WARNING

Never use a newspaper (or your hand or foot) to hit your dog and never rub his nose in his "mistakes." These are cruel and pointless punishments that he will not understand at all. Rather, he will only learn to fear the newspaper or your hand. If you miss his duty call, it's your mistake, not his. Punish yourself instead for not being vigilant when your puppy had to go!

One survey by the National Council on Pet Population Study and Policy found that 34 percent of people who surrendered their dogs to shelters thought rubbing the animals' noses in their feces would help housetrain them. It is, in fact, disgusting and counterproductive. The reality is that only praise and reinforcing positive behavior are effective.

RAIN, RAIN, GO AWAY

Some puppies don't like to go out in rainy weather. For starters, use a big umbrella as a weather shield. Then wait for a nice, easy shower to gently introduce puppy to the joys of playing and eliminating in the rain. It will make future trips outdoors much easier. The opposite is true of snow. He won't want to come back in!

IN THIS CHAPTER

» **Seeing through the eyes of your dog**

» **Understanding positive and negative reinforcements**

» **Redirecting inappropriate behavior**

» **Surviving adolescent agonies**

» **Controlling chewing and biting**

Chapter **8**

Canine Communication and Growing Pains

ry to think like your dog! Tough, huh? Humans do not think naturally in canine terms. What's clear to you is seldom clear to the dog. (I will say this often, so bear with me!) Given that axiom, it's also obvious that a dog will rarely understand what seems so logical to his human master. Animals enter this world as creatures of instincts and heredity, and you always need to remember that and start thinking like your dog in order to successfully teach him the rules of his new world.

Puppies are little learning machines. Everything a puppy does or encounters teaches him something, either positive or negative. That's why early intervention and positive structured learning situations are so important in raising a well-adjusted dog. Goldens are bright students with a strong propensity to please, which is a plus in their education process.

This chapter gets you inside your puppy's head and explains how and why he reacts to situations and what he learns from them. Then it explains the correct way to handle those responses and turn your little guy into a model citizen.

Welcome to Puppy Preschool

Your puppy started canine grammar (dog talk) school the day you brought him home. Just like children, puppies learn best through repetition (remember those multiplication tables?) and "Good dog!" rewards.

Everything your puppy does is motivated by his instincts until you teach him otherwise. Your Golden puppy spent the past 7 or 8 weeks learning from his mother how to be a proper dog. He knows nothing about human standards of behavior. During these next important learning stages, it's best to keep his life as simple as possible and his space uncluttered with temptation.

TIP

The most successful obedience methods today rely on positive reinforcement instead of older negative and cruel corrections such as jerking, hitting, and other forms of punishment. Your Golden must learn what's right before you can correct him for being wrong. With positive reinforcements such as praise and food rewards, correct behavior is rewarded. That makes the dog feel good, so naturally he wants to repeat the behavior.

This is true of any canine behavior, even if you are not involved in the reward process. If your dog gets away with *anything* that makes him feel good, like sleeping on the sofa or snatching food from the kitchen counter, when you are not watching, you can bet he will repeat that misdeed. He doesn't know he did something wrong; it's only incorrect behavior in people terms.

Dogs also learn behaviors only in the present tense. Take the best (and worst!) example — piddling in the house. You have to catch your puppy in the act. Timing is so critical that even seconds later is too late. A correction after the puddle, or any other undesirable behavior, even when he's been told before, will not be understandable to the dog. (See Chapter 7 for more on housetraining.)

The better your timing, the clearer message you send the dog. In some cases, you don't even have to wait for him to actually get into mischief. Say that he lingers near the table peeking at the meat that you've set out for dinner, and you recognize that "Should I?" look. Use a sharp "Aaahh, aaahh!" to stop him in his tracks. You've just redirected his behavior without his suffering the consequences of a correction. This kind of mind-reading technique avoids the use of harsher negatives and creates a more confident attitude in your pup.

WARNING

Never punish your Golden for something he did hours or even minutes earlier. Punishment must be dispensed within 3 to 5 seconds after the behavior, or your dog won't understand it. The same is true of praise.

Consistency Counts

When working with your puppy, use the same word for the same behavior every time. Add food lures and lots of "Good boy!" praise to make the action pleasant. Puppies, being greedy creatures, will be enticed to perform the action when they hear the word.

Memorize these important guidelines to successful puppy training:

» **Be clear and consistent.** It's not okay to allow your Golden on the couch with you and then scold him when he jumps up beside your visiting Aunt Agnes. Rules apply all the time.

» **Use simple one- or two-word commands such as "Buster, sit" or "Buster, quiet."** Don't nag with a long lecture he won't understand. ("Buster, why don't you ever sit down when I tell you to, for goodness sake!")

» **Dispense a correction only if your dog doesn't do what he was told to do.** Use appropriate discipline or corrections that are not excessive and do so immediately.

» **Always praise as soon as he complies.** For two important reasons. You want to praise the act of stopping the undesirable behavior. And you want him to know that you are pleased that he performed a particular behavior. You're capitalizing on his desire to please you.

WARNING

» **Never strike your dog with your hand, foot, newspaper, or other object.** I cannot emphasize this enough. It's hard to believe that in this enlightened era, some people still think they should use newspapers to swat their dog and believe that a good cuff across his nose is an okay thing to do. Cuffing any dog could not only hurt the dog, but it will also provoke fear and cringing, and sets the dog up for possible violent responses at some later time. Corrections are not random acts of violence.

» **Never call the dog to you for a correction.** That's the quickest way to turn "Come" into "Go away fast!" The dog will associate coming to you with the discipline and not the behavior that warranted the correction. (Present tense, remember?) Go and get the dog instead. And remember, by the time you reach him, he will not remember what he did moments earlier (not coming), so a correction is not appropriate.

» **Use common dog sense.** The best way to keep your Golden out of the trash is to put the trash away.

REMEMBER

» **Never discipline your Golden for something he did hours or even minutes earlier.** I can't say this often enough. The punishment (or praise) must occur within 3to 5 seconds of the behavior, or he won't associate the discipline with the act.

Your Voice Says It All

How you talk to your puppy or dog is as important as what you say. Your tone of voice relays your message as much as the words you use. In "doggese," a low-pitched, heavy sound tells him he's pushing things too far. A high-pitched voice means all is well, and it's time to play. When issuing warnings or corrections, use a lower voice and keep it short, sharp, and simple. No dragged out sounds like Nooooooo, and never plead or whine. Use your high-pitched, happy voice for praise and during training sessions to tell your puppy what a smart guy he is.

TIP

Voice pitch and inflection can be difficult for some to master. Practice using your best doggie voices to hear how you sound to your dog. Would you think obedience was fun if your boss thundered "Ruffy, heel!" in a deep intimidating voice? Would you hop right to it if she said "Drop it" in a high-pitched tone that dripped with sugar?

Correcting Your Puppy's Behavior

Of course, in all puppies' lives there comes a time for discipline. *Discipline* simply means dispensing appropriate corrections to teach the dog correct behavior.

WARNING

Do not confuse discipline with punishment. Punishment (as a physical tool of force or worse) is not appropriate and will, in fact, cause behavioral problems like aggression rather than correct them. Corrections, on the other hand, are humane disciplinary tools that help your puppy understand what he did wrong and what he should do instead.

Discipline should be mild and minimal. Goldens are smart, sensitive little guys, and you can encourage correct behavior by distracting him as soon as you see him "think about" getting into mischief (which in a puppy's mind is merely play). A sharp "Aaah, aaah, aaah" or a sharp hand clap can startle him and shift his attention from his mischief (pawing at the trash bin, chewing on the rug). Immediately offer a toy or other object as a distraction. Always praise him profusely when he stops and give him the toy or treat for a reward.

TIP

Timing is always critical. All discipline must occur while he's actually performing the misdeed, and the discipline should fit the act or misbehavior.

When your pup displeased his mother weeks ago, it took but a single snarl or snap from Mom to make him sit up and take notice. As his new pack leader, you can use the same type of tactic as a means of correcting misbehavior.

Enroll in a Puppy Kindergarten Class

In times past, it was believed that puppies were not prepared to learn or handle a classroom atmosphere until they were at least 6 months old. Not so today. The 21st-century puppy's education starts the day you bring him home and is enhanced by early group training. These programs are casual and fun and designed to allow the pups to interact with other pups and people as well as learn.

JUST FOR
FUN

Puppy kindergarten classes, such as Super Puppy, can help speed up the social learning process. The age of enrollment varies with each class. Wait until he's 11 or 12 weeks old and has completed his first two or three shots (or whatever your vet recommends). These are fun classes that will get you started on a good canine communication system. They're not structured lessons or rigid obedience. They are designed to teach your puppy how to learn, and show you, the owner, how to teach. It's the beginning of an attitude. For more about puppy classes, check with a veterinarian or a dog or kennel club in your area.

All dogs, even super-dogs like Goldens, go through predictable rebellious stages on their journey from puppyhood into grownup dog. Research on a dog's maturation process reads almost like a canine Dr. Spock. These are trying times that will add an extra dimension of challenge to your first Golden year, but forewarned is forearmed, which can make these periods less difficult and even fun.

Even though most people think of their Goldens as little kids dressed in furry coats, the fact is that dogs are not little people (but you already knew that), and they sure don't think in childlike terms, so their behavior has to be examined differently. So, if you want a well-behaved dog, you have to think like one, and make sure that you're always one dog thought ahead of him.

CALCULATING YOUR GOLDEN'S AGE

Think of your puppy as a not-quite-2-year-old. Even though some experts maintain that an adult dog can achieve the comprehension of a 5-year-old child, living with a fully grown canine is more like living with a 3-year-old who never grows up. No matter how well trained, he will always chase a squirrel into the street. He will never resist the chicken bones in your trash. You wouldn't allow your toddler outside to play unsupervised. The message here is clear.

In the past, a dog's age was multiplied by seven to calculate canine development in comparison to human age. Today, more sophisticated methods are used to evaluate age, incorporating factors such as size, breed, and temperament.

Small dogs mature more quickly than large-breed dogs, which may take as long as 2 to 3 years to fully mature. Once they have reached maturity, large dogs age more rapidly than small ones, which is why smaller dogs tend to live longer than the big guys. After age 2, each year of a Golden's life is equal to only 4 years of human life.

Golden Puppy Age	Human Age
2 months	2 to 3 years
4 months	5 to 7 years
6 months	10 to 12 years
1 year	15 years
2 years	24 years
3 years	28 years
6 years	40 years
12 years	64 years

Ages 3 to 6 months

Your puppy's 3- to 6-month pre-adolescent period is complicated (or enhanced, depending on how well you handle it!) by his gradual increase of independence and confidence. Your little guy will venture farther and farther from your side, following his nose and curiosity with grand new feelings of confidence about his human world. Through his first 12 weeks, it was instinctive for your puppy to stick close to his leader (you) and his den (your house). But suddenly the big, scary world isn't so scary anymore, and off he goes. About this time, obedience instructors often hear puppy owners complain, "My puppy was so good until this week. He never left the yard, and now I have to chase him down the street."

Your pup is entering the terrible twos of puppyhood. It's time for greater supervision, your 20- or 30-foot long line, and a basic puppy obedience class. Basic obedience is a step up from puppy kindergarten class. Those first classes offered social exposure and taught your puppy how to pay attention, which was a huge step forward for a little fellow. These next basic classes will teach specific exercises to help you mold and control his behavior — very important with a spunky Golden pup!

A smart owner will continue obedience training during these difficult growing-up periods when the puppy most needs that training. The value is in the class itself as well as the lessons learned: the multiple-dog atmosphere, assistance from an experienced instructor who will tackle your puppy's unique problems, and the incentive to teach your puppy every day so that you won't look like a jerk when you go to class. And there's nothing like a little group therapy to give you moral support when your puppy's antics move from normal and reasonable to you-won't-believe-what-he-did-last-night!

Puppy FRAPS

At about 4 or 5 months of age, puppies enter a period some experts call the "puppy crazies," the "zooms," or puppy "FRAPS." Fortunately, it's not contagious! *FRAP* stands for Frenetic Random Activity Period, a wild time in his young life when for no apparent reason he'll run like a demon possessed through the house and over the furniture, spin around in circles, and zoom back and forth across the yard for 5 or 10 minutes once or twice a day. He may even growl at imaginary beasts that exist only in his fuzzy mad-pup head.

This nutty behavior happens out of the blue, often just when your puppy starts showing small encouraging signs of maturity. I often got calls from puppy families who think their adorable puppy just popped a screw loose, and that they did something to cause his absurd behavior.

Don't worry or try to discourage that behavior, as long as he isn't being destructive. It may last 2 or 3 months, and he'll outgrow it along with his puppy teeth, although some dogs never seem to totally outgrow it. My old Golden did huge zooms around our property until he was 9 years old!

During this pain-in-the-ankle stage, it's often tempting to keep your puppy outdoors in the yard or in his kennel run. Don't! This is a vital developmental stage, and your puppy must spend quality time with you indoors, learning proper house manners and how to settle down when you insist on it. Golden puppies are such eager students at this age. Prime that learning pump while it's at its peak.

The terrible teens

Did you know puppies go through a teenage puppy adolescence period during their first 2 years just like kids do? This stage begins anywhere from 6 to 9 months of age, often after that cute puppy stage, and unfortunately, just when you think his silly puppy behavior should be over. He's entering sexual maturity, and as those big-boy hormones start pumping through his young veins, he will discover independence, confidence, and even arrogance, all of which will probably be directed at you, the loving owner he's supposed to please.

The symptoms of adolescence can be sudden and inexplicable. Suddenly your once-adoring Golden challenges your authority (I don't want to do that today, thank you!), jumps on furniture, and forgets commands he once responded to. He digs, barks, jumps, nips, becomes possessive and demanding, mounts your leg, and marks his territory. (Females just stare at you and then squat and wet the rug.) The teen period can last for several months and beyond, sometimes until the dog is 2 years old. (Dig out that P for Patient!) But if you can tough it out, you'll have a wonderful companion for the next 10 or 15 years. Sound like a teenager you used to know and love?

Your Golden's needs for stimulation, companionship, and activity during his adolescence are very high, and his tolerance for boredom and inactivity are low. Now *there's* a golden opportunity for you! Your challenge is to channel his energies in positive directions. Use exercise and games that appeal to and tax both his mind and body, and don't forget those daily walks (or jogs if you're up to it).

TIP

Provide plenty of safe opportunities for vigorous play and exercise, and safe toys to occupy his teeth and mind. Use jogging, Frisbee- and ball-chasing, swimming, and other energetic ways to entertain him and wear him out. (See Chapter 10 on exercise.) Avoid situations in which his occasional lapses in obedience could lead to disaster, such as off-leash work or play in open or unsecured areas.

The best safeguard against these adolescent problems is, of course, a good foundation in obedience to fall back on during such difficult times (see Chapter 9). Think of it as stockpiling supplies in your behavior bomb shelter. Although most teen-dog challenges can't be avoided, with lots of patience and persistence, they can be managed if the dog knows you're the boss *before* his hormones slide into overdrive. A daily Sit-Stay or Down-Stay can go a long way toward controlling adolescent antics (the youngster shown in Figure 8-1 is doing his "good dog" Sit). Use those obedience tools to insist that he obey, even if it he does it in slow motion. Never encourage aggressive play or behavior, and don't give him free run of the house when you're not home. And remember, as in all canine life stages, this, too, will pass.

FIGURE 8-1:
A daily Sit-Stay or Down-Stay can help keep your dog in line.

REMEMBER

Your year-old Golden is still a puppy even though he looks grown up. Large breeds like Golden Retrievers are not fully mature until about 2 years of age. Make appropriate allowances, and adjust your behavior expectations accordingly.

Twelve to 18 months

At some point during this period, your Golden will reach emotional maturity. Dogs with tendencies toward dominance will begin to assert themselves at this time, hoping to raise their status in the "pack" (your household!). This behavior usually occurs within a structure of familiar relationships, and surfaces when the dog is approaching emotional maturity.

WARNING

Living with a dominant dog does not mean you must "conquer" the dog, but obedience challenges must be recognized immediately and taken seriously. He must, in no uncertain terms, accept you as his leader. Punishment or discipline is not the appropriate method of dealing with early dominance and is likely to provoke a negative response. You should instead demand *rigid* obedience compliance — that means "always," with no ifs or buts. If serious signs appear, like growling or baring teeth, consult your vet, an experienced obedience trainer, or a qualified behaviorist.

The problem with most problem behaviors is that most of it is normal canine behavior; it's *your* problem, not the dog's! Nevertheless, it's your job to reshape that behavior to acceptable human standards. That's most easily accomplished when a dog is very (as in *very*) young. Otherwise, you have a secondary problem — you're working with bad habits while you try to teach the dog.

To Chew or Not to Chew

Golden puppies love to chew. So do adult Goldens. It's in their job description. It's a natural and healthy canine habit that goes way back to their wolf ancestors who gnawed their way around the den. Chewing on bones will satisfy your dog's emotional needs as well as certain physical needs that are important to his health. From a human perspective, it's *what* they chew on that presents a problem (see Figure 8-2).

Mouthing and chewing are the most normal of Golden puppy behaviors. It's how curious puppies learn about their environment. It's a stress reliever. It feels good. And it's one of the hardest habits to correct.

FIGURE 8-2:
Chewing is only natural; it's *what* your Golden chews on that's a problem. Garden hoses are an obvious no-no.

Close Encounters of the Furry Kind.

THE DOG GRUDGE MYTH

"He's just plain spiteful. He knew what he did wrong."

You've heard that one before. Maybe you've even said it yourself. The dog knew he was naughty because he had this guilty look on his muzzle every time his owner found a pile of feces or shredded Kleenex on the floor. Naturally the owner snarled at the dog, maybe even dragged him over to the crime scene to remind him just how bad he was. And naturally, the dog cringed and tucked his tail. His owner is enraged, but intelligent people like yourself understand that the dog is reacting to the anger, not the mess in the living room.

Your dog does not do destructive things to "get even" with you. He is incapable of those human emotions. Dogs are naughty because they get lonely, tired, or bored and simply act out of canine instinct. It's up to you to teach him manners and make his environment canine-friendly.

Dogs learn by association and repetition. Hereafter, whenever the dog sees the shredded tissue in the same room with his owner, he knows the boss is going to go bonkers. He will never understand it's because he tore up those tissues a few hours earlier. It's just another case of what's obvious to humans is not clear to the dog.

What should also be perfectly clear is that if you remove the tissue source, you will remove the problem. If they were thrown into the wastebasket, move the wastebasket, for goodness' sake! These are grin-and-bear-it times. If you're not at home to supervise your dog, you can't discipline him for his mischief in your absence, but you can prevent future accidents from happening. Remove temptation, take him for an extra walk, and crate him when you're gone.

Illustrating the unfortunate conflict between the human and canine minds, one survey of 3,772 pet owners by the National Council on Pet Population found that 53 percent of people who surrendered their dogs to animal shelters incorrectly believed animals behave out of spite. Dogs are incapable of that kind of rationalization. Hopefully, those same folks understand their kids better than they do their dogs!

The pros of chewing

Believe it or not, chewing does have a positive side. In puppies, chewing on hard objects stimulates the growth of their adult teeth. Chewing hard bones helps scrape away plaque, which causes bad breath and serious dental problems. Just as in people, plaque can damage the gums and ultimately allow bacteria to enter the bloodstream. People use dental floss. Dogs chew bones. Simple analogy. (Forget the fact that a puppy who is chewing on a bone is not chewing on your shoe or table leg!)

My veterinarian is always amazed at the healthy condition of my Goldens' teeth and gums. The credit belongs to the vast numbers of hard bones (the safe, sterilized, "real" bones found in pet supply stores) and Nylabones that litter their crates, kennel runs, and my living room floor.

WARNING

Never offer your dog cooked bones (they splinter!); chicken, turkey, pork, or steak bones; or any other "people" bones.

Chewing is also good therapy for loneliness. Dogs who are left alone during the day can get lonely, depressed, or anxious, and maybe all of those. Your Golden most likely waits all day to hear your key turn in the door, and a good bone or two helps a lonesome fellow pass the time. (See Chapter 5 for more tips on safe chewies and bones.) If he has no bones to chew, he may start in on the sofa pillows or the kitchen table legs. Chewing also releases pent-up energy, so dogs who don't get enough exercise will do — you guessed it — chew! Does your chewer get three or four brisk walks each day? Chase the Frisbee in the yard? Those activities will keep him mentally stimulated and physically too tired to chew.

Prevention power

To best prevent destructive chewing, you have to understand why it happens in the first place. Dogs don't chew because it's good for their teeth. They chew because it *feels* good to chew. Chewing relieves boredom and a host of other stressors. Just like kids (and even some adults), dogs who have nothing to do get bored and eventually get into mischief. Chewing is quite simply something to do with idle time.

Because Golden puppies are famous for their chewing exploits, you'll have to dig deep into your bag of Puppy Patience. It will take time to teach him what he may and may not chew or carry in his mouth.

Chew solutions are three-dimensional, involving the usual ounce of prevention, a dash of distraction and direction, and a dose of correction when all else fails.

> » **Keep your people stuff out of your puppy's reach.** That means no shoes or slippers on the floor, no open wastebaskets to tip over, or dish towels hanging within puppy range (think jumping puppy!). A good rule is to keep anything you value in high places — above puppy level. That will prevent him from chewing on forbidden objects and keep him focused on his puppy toys. He can't destroy what he can't sink his teeth into.

>> **Give him a variety of chewies to satisfy his urge to chew.** Not too many, though, or he'll be overwhelmed and bored with all of them. Keep two or three in his toy bucket and rotate them every couple of days to keep them stimulating. Add new toys occasionally to keep them interesting. Dozens of newfangled canine toys will captivate your pup — and you! So go ahead and indulge yourself!

>> **Notice what forbidden objects he takes a liking to and spritz them with Bitter Apple or Tabasco sauce.** If he chews a no-no anyway, it's too late. Do not scold or holler at the pup. You've already lost this round. Go to the puppy, say "Drop" or "Leave it" (your choice, but stick with one), praise him for releasing it, and offer him a substitute toy. (See Chapter 9 for more on commands.)

>> **Distract and redirect.** When he decides to nibble on a no-no, remember this: He does not know better. Just remove the object from his mouth with your command word "Drop," give him an enticing, safe substitute to chew on, and praise him when he takes that toy.

TIP

If he refuses to release his prize, grab his collar or collar tab, give him a gentle shake and a verbal "No," and take the object. If this refusal happens frequently, examine your relationship with the dog or pup. He's on his way to mutiny, and you need to re-establish your position as his leader with less cuddling and more obedience.

>> **Crate him when you can't watch him.** Despite Nylabones, hard bones, carrot bones, woolly toys, and squeaky toys, a puppy will still dismantle your woodwork or cabinet corners if he's left alone too long. Crating is your guaranteed ounce of prevention, as discussed in Chapter 7.

REMEMBER

You won't cure the chewing habit overnight. Your puppy will need many, many lessons and reminders before he's fully chew-conditioned. After all, the Golden Retriever was bred to retrieve and carry something in his mouth. It's hard to battle Mother Nature; the wiser course is to work with her instead.

Biting the Hand That Feeds

Biting and mouthing are different war games from chewing, although like chewing, both are natural behaviors that started in the whelping box. When your puppy wrestled and chewed on his littermates in play-fighting, he learned valuable lessons in canine communication and etiquette. When another puppy yelped in pain, it meant "Time out, I won't play with you anymore." He learned to bite more gently or his playmate would say "Adios!"

His mother also taught those lessons when she snarled or nipped him when he got too rough. Now that you're walking in his mother's pawprints, you have to round out his education to include his human family.

Biting involves anything from playful mouthing and nipping to curling back the lips to taking a chunk out of your arm. When your puppy tugs your pants leg or nips your fingertips, he's just being playful. When he shows those tiny canines, he has other thoughts.

With mouthing and play biting, you need to teach him "bite inhibition" in the same way his mother did. Your puppy has to learn that human flesh is just as tender as his siblings' ears, and he's not allowed to hurt it.

TIP

Whenever your puppy nips or attempts to bite your hand, do not pull it away. It's a natural canine instinct to view your hand or foot as a toy or prey and start nipping even more enthusiastically. The key is to hold your hand perfectly still (grit your teeth), bend toward your puppy, and issue a loud "Ouch!" This should startle him to stop biting or to release the pressure on your hand. Immediately tell him "Good boy," reward him with soft praise, and offer him a chew toy or a treat.

Ignoring your puppy also can be effective because it deprives him of your attention, which he dearly wants and needs. When your puppy nips your fingertips, say "Oouuuch!" in a loud voice, and when he stops, immediately turn away and fold your arms. Wait just a minute and then return to normal, but do not praise or pet the pup. Speak to him quietly but firmly. More nips, more isolation. Goldens are social butterflies, and this method can work wonders. You probably will have to do this repeatedly for a while. Goldens are notoriously oral creatures.

TIP

While I am not fond of the following method, I mention it here as some owners have used it with success. They use a glove to teach a puppy gentle mouthing and not to bite. With a glove you can protect your hand and keep it in his mouth while telling him "Easy" or "Gentle," which is a secondary No-Bite command that will allow you to put your hand in his mouth without his biting down.

Praise softly as soon as he stops biting, pet him gently, and offer him an alternate chew object: a woolly toy or other favorite chewie. Be consistent and make sure that the entire family does the same. Your puppy will discover who and what he may and may not chew on. If the kids don't follow these same rules, they will remain fair chomping game.

If your puppy bares his teeth during any of these maneuvers, hold his collar or collar tab and give him a gentle shake or tug with an obedience command like "Sit." That will defuse his attitude and remind him you're in charge. If such incidents continue, take a good long look at your relationship. You need to follow a more rigid training program. This is one problem that *will* escalate from minor to major unless you nip it in the bud (pun intended) in the early stages.

Do not get physical with your pup; tough tactics only stimulate and encourage aggressive behavior. Instead, use obedience reinforcements that will remind your puppy that you're the alpha dog who gives the orders.

By the time your puppy is 3 or 4 months old, he should have his play biting under control with perhaps just an occasional nip here and there. If the habit goes beyond that age, even a submissive dog may be tempted to take over as top dog. Now you're entering the danger zone. Reassert your authority with consistent leadership exercises.

REMEMBER

Obedience is the best nonconfrontational way to remind him you're his boss and master. Make him earn his meals and treats and play activities by utilizing your obedience commands. He'll be less apt to sink his teeth into his leader's arm!

If he bites or tries to bite when you correct him or take his food away, his behavior is dominant-aggressive, and he's challenging your leadership. That behavior is more threatening and hints at future problems, so it must be dealt with more firmly and immediately. Consult a professional trainer or behaviorist for advice on how to deal with it. Search the Internet for some good books on canine aggression that will help you understand your dog's behavior and how to correct it.

IN THIS CHAPTER

» Enrolling in the "good dog" school of obedience

» Offering rewards and praise

» Introducing your puppy to the leash

» Mastering basic commands

» Using training collars safely

Chapter **9**

Homeschooling Your Golden Puppy

I f there's one principle that applies to all dogs regardless of breed, size, or color, it's this: The quality of your adult dog is in direct proportion to the quality and amount of time you invest in *training him as a pup.* You'll both be glad you did.

In this chapter, I focus on how to teach your puppy basic obedience commands, like walking on a leash, coming when called, and sitting and lying down when told. You don't need much to start: a happy voice, a pocketful of goodies, a 6-foot leash, and a 20-foot long line. Proper training collars will come later.

To Treat or Not to Treat?

Proponents walk on both sides of the food fence, but both pro and con trainers suggest using treats for first-time puppy lessons because they produce an immediate and positive response, and then gradually weaning off the food rewards. Of course, you can't use food forever. Imagine offering a tidbit to a 90-pound Rottweiler who's charging you with his pearlies bared!

Food is just one of several positive motivators for *behavior enhancement*, which is just a fancy term for obedient behavior or plain old-fashioned good manners. Eventually the trainer phases out the food in favor of other rewards like verbal praise, hands-on petting and hugs, squeaky toys, and balls to chase and find. You can use all these delightful tools to teach and stimulate your puppy as well as your adult dog.

REMEMBER

Research shows that any behavior that is rewarded will increase in frequency. So, before you begin any training exercise, stockpile an arsenal of the preceding reward systems.

Begin by stuffing your pockets with tiny pieces of soft puppy treats or dried liver treats (find them at your pet store). Small slices of inexpensive hot dogs also work (cooked in the microwave until they're dehydrated), but they won't store well in your pockets.

You'll want to keep treats in *all* your pockets *all* the time. Every day, lots of training opportunities seem to fall from the sky, and you should be prepared to meet them with a goodie. Get used to soggy dog biscuits in your laundry tub.

Keep your treats small enough so that he won't have to stop to chew them up, yet big enough to make them tantalizing. A crunchy puppy-size Milk-Bone easily breaks up into three small pieces. Cheerios also work well and are the perfect size. You don't want to offer so much food that it affects his appetite or dramatically increases his food intake.

TIP

The entire family should understand the basics of your puppy's education, but only one person should do the actual training exercises. Your puppy needs the consistency of one message from one messenger. Just make sure that everyone in the household does nothing to conflict with what he's learning. You need consistency, consistency, and then more consistency.

Choosing a Release Word

Before you begin training your dog, you need to choose a release command like Free or Okay. Many professional trainers prefer Free because Okay is too commonly used in conversation. I use Okay because it's easier to remember, and I've never had a problem with it. I go with Okay for this book, but the choice is yours.

Use your release word to free your puppy from the Sit position (or whatever stationary position you have put him in). Say it in a happy tone but not so cheery as to send your pup into a frenzy. You want to keep him in a trainable frame of mind.

Mastering the Don'ts

Just as important as those things you do to teach your dog to come, are the things you should *not* do. These are training absolutes, when never means *absolutely never:*

>> **Never discipline your puppy or adult dog after he comes to you.** That's the fastest way to turn "Come" into "Stay away" or "Catch me."

>> **Never call your dog to you for something unpleasant like bathing, giving pills, crating, or kenneling.** (This does not infer that crating is negative, but it can become so if he ends up crated every time you call him.) Go and get the dog instead. If you're too busy or too lazy to go get him, give him lots of hugs and kisses when he comes on his own, and then, after a minute or two, do your dirty work.

>> **Never call your puppy when he's distracted or preoccupied.** Call him only when you're sure that he will respond. Start indoors because there are too many fun distractions outdoors. An older trained dog should respond to "Come" regardless of distractions.

>> **Never train your puppy or adult dog when you're in a sour mood.** Your Golden will sense your irritation and feel like he's displeasing you, which creates a negative attitude toward training. Keep your training sessions positive . . . for *both* of you.

>> **Never repeat any command.** Say it only once. These are not three or four-word commands. He has to learn just like any smart toddler or adolescent that he must Come or Sit or Down the first time you say the word (unlike your teenager!). There are, however, some exceptions to this rule.

>> **Never scold your puppy when he breaks his Sit to come to you.** Just use a firm "No" and return him to the Sit position, using another Sit command. Scolding will only confuse him and create a negative attitude toward training.

Introducing Puppy to His Leash

Introduce the leash within a few days of coming home. Just attach it to his buckle collar and let him drag it around the room or play area to get used to it. If he tries to chew the leash, as he surely will, spray his end with Bitter Apple. Toss a few toys to distract him from the trailing leash and use your best praise voice. After he knows how to sit when told, have him sit before you attach his leash. You're laying the foundation for your leadership.

Taking your first walk

Once he accepts the leash, put yourself on the other end and take your first walk together in the yard. Your goal during these outings is to have your puppy simply accept control and not resist walking when leashed. (Think 10 pounds compared to 30 or 40 pounds straining at the other end!) As with all other puppy exercises, fill your pockets with puppy treats before you start. Use your happy voice for encouragement and just talk to him along the way.

REMEMBER

Restraint is a new experience for your puppy, and he may resist walking with you with every inch of his tiny puppy frame. He may freeze in his tracks, spin and whirl like a roped young calf, or tug and pull with all his might. Give him a moment to settle down, but don't go to him to offer reassurance because that would reward his resistance. (It's that connection thing again.) Instead, bend down to coax him to come to you, and when he does, of course, reward him with a treat.

Now try taking a few steps with a treat lure held at your left side at nose height where he can see and smell it. Pat your knee and use a lot of happy talk to entice him to walk near your left knee.

REMEMBER

Leash walking is not heeling; that comes much later in basic obedience class. Leash walking is incremental puppy training . . . a few steps, a treat, a few more steps, another goodie. This shouldn't be a difficult process. If it becomes a daily battle, seek the help of a professional obedience instructor now or as soon as you can find a class.

After your puppy has accepted the leash, your goal is to teach him to simply walk near you like a little gentleman without tugging on his leash or yanking your arm out of its socket. Fill your pockets with puppy treats and start walking.

1. **Design your walking area.**

   Draw a mental circle around yourself about 3 feet in diameter. This is your puppy's walking space. Now memorize the walking words "This way" and "Easy." The usual "Good boy" is a given.

2. **Move forward with "Let's go" and start walking briskly around your yard or driveway.**

   Show him the treat to get him looking at you and moving next to you. All you're looking for is a few good steps. Walk briskly for just 10 or 20 successful paces, then stop with an Okay, and praise him big-time.

3. **As he follows and looks up, praise him and give him the treat.**

4. **Keep him within that 3-foot circle with "Easy" and "Let's go."**

If he wanders ahead of you outside that invisible circle, tell him "Easy" and gently tug him back, saying "Good boy" whenever he's at your side. If he lags behind, repeat "Let's go" and gently pop him forward (no dragging please, just a quick and gentle tug and quick release of the leash). If he looks away, chat sweetly to regain his attention and give a treat when he's at your side and looking at you. Be sure to praise each time he's at your side (and *only* at your side) and praise him every time he looks at you.

Your second goal is to teach your pup to look at you when you walk. Most Goldens are natural "watchers" and easily tune in on this walking business.

» **Praise only when he's near your side or when he's looking at you.** Your happy praise should make him look up at you. Don't give praise if he's lagging or pulling ahead on his leash. (Association, remember?)

» **Never scold or nag.** After all, he doesn't have a clue about what you want him to do. As with all his other exercises, you're trying to create an attitude that says, "Let's do this some more!"

» **Walk straight ahead.** Walk in a straight line at first, turning in very wide arcs or circles with no sharp or 90-degree turns.

» **Make 90-degree turns.** After a few days of walking in wide circles, add some challenge and occasionally make a corner turn and go in another direction. Give a tug if you must to get him to turn as well, saying, "This way" when you turn and tug. As soon as he joins you (don't go too abruptly or too fast), give a treat and big-time praise.

» **Once he gets the hang of it, increase your walking time to no more than half a minute in one stretch, but you can do several stretches in one session with brief play in between.** That doesn't sound like much, but count to 30 slowly. That's a long time for a puppy. Your objective is to keep his interest piqued and prevent boredom.

» **Progress slowly.** Don't move ahead to formal heeling until you start obedience class. Your goal for now is a pleasant (for both of you) walk together.

During all this puppy training, you're going to run into roadblocks — the leash will tangle around your feet, your puppy may jump and jump some more, and he may sabotage your best efforts. This is where a good puppy class comes in handy. A good instructor can work wonders!

Your Golden's leash on life

The last thing you want is a Golden who runs off to visit your neighbors or other dogs or who refuses to come when he's outdoors. How to accomplish that? Simple! Don't let your dog run free. A loose dog is in danger from automobiles, other animals, and unsavory people. Your neighbors also deserve your consideration. A loose dog may be (and probably is) digging in their compost heap or flower bed, leaving doggie deposits on their lawn, and impregnating their female dogs. These considerations far outweigh the pleasure any dog gets from running free.

WARNING

Most states prohibit dogs of any age from running loose, so be sure to consult your local leash laws. Always have your dog or puppy tethered in some fashion when training or playing outdoors.

A loose dog may react defensively if he is teased or threatened. A random bite can send him to dog jail for 10 days, raise your homeowner insurance rates, and even risk your right to own a dog.

On-leash walks are the obvious solution. It also strengthens the human–animal bond and offers you and your puppy or dog improved cardiovascular fitness. Give your dog his own leash on life and don't let him run free. He won't know what he's missing, and you won't end up missing him.

The All-Important Come Command

Coming *reliably* when called is the most difficult command to teach, yet it is the most important. This is one exercise you'll need to work on all his life to keep him dependable. As your dog grows older and more confident, and you detect a slower response to coming when called, give him a short reminder course for several days. It could someday save your dog's life. Get real — do you *honestly* believe your dog would never chase a rabbit or a squirrel across the street?

REMEMBER

Some trainers teach the Come command after they teach Stay, since that skill makes the Come process easier. I believe that you lose valuable learning time if you wait to teach Come.

Teaching "Come" starts the first day you bring your puppy home. Every time you see your puppy start to come to you, tell him "Puppy, Come!" in your happy voice. Vary your body posture at times to keep it interesting and unpredictable, squat down on one knee, open your arms wide, clap your hands, pat the front of your legs, pat the floor, and act just like a silly fool every time he comes to you. Remember to praise him while he's in the process of coming, not just when he gets to you. Use the same word and happy tone of voice every time you call your dog.

Here are a few Come reinforcements:

» **Use his meal times as reinforcement sessions by calling your pup to Come every time you feed him.** Rattle his food pan and tell him "Come" in a happy, lively tone of voice. That tasty kibble is a great reward for coming when he's called.

» **Try different places.** Practice Come in different areas of the house and vary the rewards between hands-on praise, tidbits, or a squeaky toy.

» **Add distractions.** Once your puppy is responding well, continue to work indoors, but add distractions. Wait until he's preoccupied to call him to you. If he doesn't come immediately, it's no big deal. Simply go to the pup, clap your hands to get his attention, and call him once again. Time then for a treat reward. Spend several days indoors before you move outside into the yard (see the next section).

The Come command outdoors

Your primary rule outdoors is to never allow your puppy to run free without a long line anywhere outside, in your yard or elsewhere, until he's completely trained and has proven himself reliable under very distracting circumstances. In most cases, that will take about a year. (If you think you've accomplished it in 6 months or less, you're either deluding yourself or you don't need this book!) My young Goldens usually wear a long line outdoors for their first year of life. That way I always have my "weapons" handy, and I never position myself for failure.

Outdoors, with your puppy on his 20-foot long line and you on the other end, walk away and call him. Once. Lay on the praise as soon as he starts coming to you and kneel down to encourage him. Give him a food reward when he reaches you. If he hesitates when you first call him, give a firm tug on the line and run backward, saying, "Come" with each tug. No pulling or dragging him toward you. Act like a nut and use lots of happy talk while running backward and shower him with the usual praise and treat when he arrives. Follow this yard routine for about a week.

Now mix it up with some complications. Add the leash with the long line. Walk with your puppy and drop the leash but not the line. When he starts moving away from you, give the Come command and if he doesn't come running right away, give a sharp tug on the line and say "Come." Do this for another week and then add distractions in the yard. Put a favorite toy in your walking path, a food dish or a ball, and call him when he starts toward the distraction object. Don't forget the praise and treats. This may take a while, probably more than a week. And if it sounds too complicated, remember: You're the one who wanted this puppy. And if you want to live a long, happy, and *safe* life together, you have to put in the time.

TIP

Never progress to the next phase of training until your puppy is reasonably reliable on the exercise you're working on. This principle applies to all aspects of dog training.

As he improves, switch to your 50-foot long line and repeat the process. As you progress, gradually eliminate the food rewards (first every other time, then every third, and so on) while continuing the praise and hands-on petting each and every time he comes.

Continue this process beyond when you feel your puppy is responding without hesitation. History shows that puppies will do the unexpected, especially at certain stages in their lives. The more conditioned your puppy is to Come, the better he'll react when faced with irresistible temptations.

Hit the road!

Take your puppy on the road. Practice in different locations . . . a park, a neighbor's yard (with their permission, of course), a quiet area of a retail parking lot (always using a leash and/or long line). Expect a setback each time you move. In truth, you should back up your training whenever you switch to a new place. Backing up means using the long line only, but no distractions, or whatever the process was in your next-to-last lesson. Then add each new element individually just as you do in your own yard.

The Sit Command

The Sit command is a breeze. Stand in front of your puppy and hold a bit of treat in front of and just above his nose. Slowly move it backward (not too high) over his head. As he tips backward for the treat, his rear end should slide down toward the floor into a sit position. (If he tips up off his front feet, the treat is probably too high.) As soon as his behind hits the floor, tell him "Sit, good dog, sit," and dispense his treat. When you give the treat, be sure to praise profusely, and pet or rub his ear with your other hand as preparation for that later time when you will wean him off the treat and onto strictly praise rewards. Now give a release word such as Okay to let him know this Sit is done.

TIP

If he resists setting his rump down or jumps up and paws your hand, just be patient and enjoy his puppy antics. He's merely problem solving. Your pup is one smart fella. He wants that treat, and he'll soon figure out how to get it. Just take a few steps and move about and then repeat the exercise. Your puppy should master this one by the second or third bite! Repeat about 10 times once or twice a day. As he becomes more proficient, wait just a moment longer before you give the treat.

Once he's sitting reliably, give the Sit command from a few feet away. (You also can occasionally drop your leash once he sits on command.) Make Sit a happy and fun command, almost like a trick (see Figure 9-1).

FIGURE 9-1:
This puppy is asking for approval for obeying the Sit command!

© Shutterstock.

You have countless opportunities to master Sit. Make him sit at meal times for his food dish. Make him sit at the door when he comes in from the yard and then give him a treat. Soon he'll be sitting every time he comes inside. You'll appreciate this habit when he comes in with wet or muddy paws to wipe.

The Wait Command

The Wait command is a close relative of Sit. Use it for going in and out of doors or cars or other openings. He doesn't have to sit; he just stands patiently, waits for you to proceed first, and then follows with permission. This exercise also reinforces your alpha persona, reminding him that leaders always go first.

With your dog on-leash, approach any doorway in your house, first from the inside of the room going out, and then do the reverse. Tell him "Wait," put the palm of one hand in front of his nose, and with your other hand hold him back with the leash while you go through first. Give your release command and allow him to pass through. And, of course, praise him for his expertise. Do a few run-throughs on this every day. If he already knows Sit, he'll understand the difference, and this one will be a snap.

The Down Command

Down is a great multipurpose command. This command is a normal extension of Sit, but it's a bit handier because it places your dog in a position where he can just relax, maybe even take a little snooze. It's also a submissive position that reinforces your top-dog position every time you use it, which should be at least once a day. It controls your dog at home when you eat, when you're at work at your computer, when you're watching TV, or when you have guests and you want him to behave. It also controls him in public places like your vet's office and takes him out of harm's way. There are dozens more reasons why Down is another big gun in your dog-talk arsenal. It's one command you'll want to work on and perfect.

To teach the Down command:

1. **Begin by placing your puppy in the sit position without using the Sit command.**

   You don't want to confuse him with two commands in the same exercise.

2. **Now hold your treat lure in front of his nose and slowly lower it to the floor, pushing it away from you and toward his front feet and body.**

   He should slide down in a backward motion to follow the treat.

3. **The moment his elbows completely touch the floor, say "Down. Good boy. Down," and give him the reward.**

   Be sure to follow up with praise and petting.

4. **After the praise, give him your release word to break position and another hug; then take a few steps and begin again.**

REMEMBER

As with Sit, you may have to experiment a bit and try this once or twice to master the correct maneuver. A bit of wiggling at first won't mess him up. Just be patient and keep trying. Once he's doing the Down exercise without hesitation, wait a bit longer before offering the food reward, and a bit longer before releasing him. You're conditioning him to Stay. Do at least 10 repetitions once or twice a day. Do them in various locations around the house and add distractions once he's solid and reliable. Gradually phase out the food treats (see the section "The Cookie Principle" earlier in this chapter).

Advancing to Sit-Stay and Down-Stay

Your puppy must be proficient on the commands described earlier in this chapter before you progress to Stay. You'll need your 6-foot leash. The procedure is basically the same for both the Sit-Stay and the Down-Stay:

1. **With the dog on-leash and in front of you, give the command for the desired position, Sit or Down.**

2. **With the dog in correct position, place the palm of your hand in front of his nose and then give the Stay command.**

If he attempts to move, use a quick leash pop (upward for sitting or downward for the down) to keep him in position and say a sharp "Aah!" or "No!"

3. **Wait just 5 or 10 seconds and then release him with a soft Okay (or your chosen release word) and a big hug.**

Dance a few steps together and then settle him down for a rerun.

4. **Do five or six repetitions.**

Gradually increase the Stay time in short 5- to 10-second increments. Always vary the length of time for each command, 5 or 6 seconds one time, 10 seconds, or a few more on the next, to keep his attention piqued and to make sure that he doesn't start anticipating his release. Even puppies are smart enough to figure out what you'll do next.

And remember that he's just a puppy with a limited attention span and lots of energy. Long stays beyond a minute or two are not reasonable for a very young pup.

TIP

Practice Sit-Stays and Down-Stays after your puppy has worked off most of his energy and he's ready to settle down. A fully rested, wide-awake puppy plus a Stay exercise equals a recipe for failure.

WARNING

It's hard to keep a dog happy and willing during static exercises (ones in which he doesn't move) because it places the dog in a submissive posture or position. So don't do more than 10 in a row and be sure to do fun "happy-ups" in between. It's worth the effort. A dog who stays in one place is a joy to live with!

Establish gold medal goals on your puppy's obedience exercises. By the time he's 6 months old, he should do a 15-minute Down-Stay without a fuss, and double that length of time by 9 months of age.

The Drop it, Leave it, or Give Command

You'll have lots of opportunities to work on the Drop it or Give command, considering how often your Golden will have something in his mouth! Your early fetching games should have laid the foundation for this command.

REMEMBER

It's important for him to believe in his heart of hearts that he *must* give you anything you ask him for. That means his toys, his food, and any object you don't want him to have, which includes things that could injure him or make him ill.

If your dog won't release the item willingly when you say your chosen command word, try this technique:

1. **Press his flews (lips) against his teeth and gums while saying the command.**

2. **Remove the object from his mouth.**

3. **Give him a substitute object or a treat.**

Be sure to praise. If he resists, you can add a little emphasis: Grasp his collar or collar tab, firmly tell him "Aah, aah," and repeat the command.

WARNING

Drop is one lesson that requires an A+. A dog who won't give up his toys or bones or food is a potential biter and will challenge you in other sinister ways as he grows into those 65 pounds of muscle. Think Hulk Hogan with sharp teeth. (See Chapter 16 for more on problem behavior.)

There's one more way to make your dog drop something in his mouth. Place your fingers inside either hind leg and press hard upward into his abdominal area. For reasons known only to the dog and possibly the professional retriever trainer who taught me this method, it works. I don't know if it enhances your alpha position, but it surely convinces the dog you mean it. You may have to practice this one a few times to find the exact spot and the right amount of pressure.

Teaching the Off Command

Jumping up is natural puppy behavior that started in the whelping box. Once your puppy lives with humans, jumping up becomes a problem behavior. You don't want him to jump on you, the kids, your elderly aunt, or your new sofa. Teaching Off begins soon after you bring your puppy home.

TIP

Do not use the Down command because that will only confuse him.

There are several methods that successfully teach Off, but not without a lot of practice. For starters, you can follow these steps:

1. **Put your puppy on a leash or a short cord, a line that you can tug to make your point.**

   This allows you to demonstrate what you want without physically touching the dog.

2. **When he begins to jump, command "Off" and tug downward with the lead.**

3. **When he's got all four feet planted once again, tell him to Sit and then praise your brilliant dog.**

If he thinks about trying it again, step on the lead just as he starts and force him to abort the jump. Praise him when he settles down. You also can grab his paws and hold them briefly; he will struggle to get free. After a few moments, release him, give a Sit command, and praise him when he sits. You also can release, then simply turn your back to ignore him and deprive him of your attention.

If you have a predictable jumper, you can also use a rattle can (a small empty jar or can filled with a few pennies) as reinforcement (see Chapter 5). When he begins to jump, shake the can loudly behind your back and tell him "Off!" If that doesn't work, on his next attempt, toss the can to land on the floor *near* him (never on him) and command "Off!" When he gets down, be sure to praise and have him Sit. He has to understand getting off makes him a good boy.

If neither method works, refer to Chapter 16 for more jumping corrections.

When the Message Is "Enough"!

"Enough" is a handy word to let your dog know that the game is over, or that he has to stop doing whatever it is he's doing at that moment. It's especially useful when your dog's play becomes a bit rowdy or escalates into more than you feel up to at the moment.

You teach Enough simply by using the word every time you stop playing or when you end a game. Of course, also use it when he gets a little out of hand. Say it in a low firm voice. If he doesn't stop his roughhousing or nonsense, just turn your back, which in effect deprives him of your presence and attention. Or you can grab his collar or collar tab and give a little shake while saying, "Enough," as a gentle reminder that you mean business. Always praise when he stops, but do so quietly so that he doesn't get all revved up again.

Going Beyond Puppy Class

Your puppy does not have to be "obedient" to attend a puppy class. Super Puppy classes or other puppy kindergarten classes, discussed in Chapter 8, begin as early as 11 or 12 weeks of age after your puppy has been safely immunized. These are not formal obedience classes where all the dogs walk around in circles. Rather they are structured playtimes to jump-start puppy's learning process. Puppies learn to play together and to pay attention. This early group environment helps speed up the social learning process, and will complement any obedience training you already do at home. *Do not wait* until you have mastered basic home obedience to attend a class.

But hear this! Don't stop at puppy class. Continue your Golden's obedience training at least through the novice level. It's bonding as well as training, so you'll become a better team in body and in spirit. (Your neighbors will be so envious of your dog's devotion and behavior!) You both need the practice this early in your relationship.

When you advance to the next level of obedience, novice or beyond, you'll need to change from puppy's clip or buckle collar to the chain or prong-type collar, which are designed *for training use only* after 4 or 5 months of age. They can be used separately or together, depending on how well you and your dog are mastering your techniques. Your class instructor can advise you on the proper collar to use.

The chain or "choke" training collar

A chain collar must be the right type and size. and put on the dog the correct way in order to be effective. Select a wide-link collar because the larger links are gentler on the neck, and will make a clinking noise that helps communicate your commands to the dog. Remember the pop and release you use when working on his leash walking skills? The click of the chain link collar adds one more dimension to the message in the leash.

Determine the right size by measuring the widest part of your dog's head just in front of his ears and add 2 inches to that dimension. Collars come only in even sizes, so if you measure an odd number, move up an inch to round it out.

The collar must be put on correctly to work properly. That can be tricky for the novice dog owner, so don't feel bad if you goof this up at first. My 4-H dog obedience class members learned how to put the collar on their dogs by using the letter *P* as their guideline:

1. **Begin by dropping the chain through one of the end rings — either one will do.**

2. **Hold the collar so that it forms the letter *P* around your hand or fist.**

3. **Using that position, face your dog and slip the collar over your dog's head.**

4. **Now clip your lead to the active ring.**

   The active ring is the one that allows the collar to tighten or go slack.

The secret behind the collar's use is a slack leash and the timing (ah, timing, as in all things canine) of the collar correction. Your leash must be loose or slack to create the snap-and-release effect that sends signals to the dog.

When using the collar during walking or beginning heeling, follow the same principles: Always use a slack lead (which seems to be tough to master for most novices), a snappy pop and release, and praise. The leash does the correcting, and your voice says you're the good guy.

The prong collar

With all those nasty hooks that could dig into your poor dog's flesh, the prong collar looks like something from a medieval torture rack. The happy truth is that the prong collar is actually more humane than the chain collar, which can choke your dog to death or damage his trachea if used improperly or used with a heavy hand. The prong collar is self-limiting and cannot tighten to the point of harming the dog. The prongs (which are not sharp or pointed, by the way, some even have plastic shields on the ends) pinch the neck when you tug lightly on the leash, creating immediate discomfort, which the dog will try hard to avoid. These collars are quite effective on strong and strong-willed dogs. Face it: A 90-pound woman would have one heck of a time leash-popping a 100-pound Rottweiler. Most prong collars come in three sizes, with the smallest at 17 inches, and therefore are not intended for puppy use.

I have used both collars on a dog at once, switching from one to the other as I need them. I include the choke collar as a precaution because I've had prong collars pop loose — not safe if you're walking on a busy street or if your Golden is the type who might run off.

The head collar

If you're appalled at the idea of a collar pinching your dog's neck, or if you are physically unable, undisciplined, or too discombobulated to use a choke collar effectively, consider using a head collar. Head collars look like horse halters, and lead the dog in the same fashion that halters lead the horse (which would not respond at all to a single collar around his neck). The Halti collar is available through pet suppliers. The Gentle Leader and the Promise collar — used in guide and assistance dog training — can be purchased through veterinarians. Both control the dog by controlling his head and require little physical strength from the handler, which is a blessing for youngsters and small adults. The collars come with instructions on how to introduce it to the dog, how to put it on, and how to use it — all are very simple for the human at the other end.

A chest harness, like those worn by therapy dogs, has become popular for training, and are available at pet supply stores and through "dog harness" websites.

3
Keeping Your Pal Healthy and Happy

Your Golden needs a well-rounded health-care plan, one that includes proper diet, exercise, and veterinary care to keep him looking and feeling his best.

This part shows you how to become a canine fitness and nutrition expert and keep him healthy, fit, and happy.

Find out how to prevent problems like parasites and other pests. Learn how to groom your Golden to keep him looking handsome. Look for signs of aging to keep him comfortable and healthy during his senior years.

Understand the common hereditary diseases that affect Goldens. Learn how to head off problem behaviors and aggression before they happen.

IN THIS CHAPTER

» **Dishing the real scoop on dog food**

» **Analyzing the ingredients**

» **Handling the burden of obesity**

» **Exercising for health and happiness**

» **Spaying or neutering for good health**

Chapter **10**

Healthy Habits: Nutrition and Exercise

F eeding your Golden is like putting gas in your car. You can't use watered down fuel and expect good maintenance or peak performance. Likewise, you can't feed your dog substandard dog food and expect to have a healthy, active animal who will live to a ripe old age. So what's a captive consumer to do? Get smart. Know the proper way to fill your Golden's nutritional gas tank.

But good health means more than just good nutrition. Without proper exercise, even a well-fed dog will not be healthy or content. This chapter provides information on quality dog food and explains why diet and daily exercise are essential to your dog's longevity and quality of life, as well as the health benefits of spaying or neutering.

Cheaper Is Not Better

Pet food means big bucks in the United States. According to the American Pet Products Association, in 2017 Americans spent about $3 *billion* on dog and cat food. Individual families spent between $20 and $100 monthly on dog food. And get this: Studies show that there is greater profit in pet food than in human food.

When you're planning a recipe for your Golden's happy meals, remember this: If you want to save money on dog food, don't spend less. Cheaper is not economical in the long run. It costs less to use a premium dog food than an economy brand because of the nutritional power packed in the better food. Additionally, in feeding a cheaper food, your dog can end up with a variety of health and skin problems from a lack of the vitamins and minerals he needs to support healthy skeletal structure, skin, and coat.

Dogs do not need a change in diet to keep them interested in food. Your dog actually looks forward to the same food each day. (The fellow shown in Figure 10-1 is enjoying his regular diet.) Unless some health condition requires it, frequent changes in his diet are not good for him. So, once you find a quality dog food he enjoys and thrives on, stick with it.

FIGURE 10-1: Your dog needs a quality dog food to maintain good health.

Checking Out Food Labels

When you read the information on your dog's food bags (of course you do!) the first thing you should check out are the *labels,* the panels on the side or back of the bag that contain the nutrition information. Look for these important food facts:

>> **Ingredients:** Labels list the ingredients in descending order of weight or amount in the food. You should find meat (chicken, fish, or other meat/poultry products) among the first three ingredients. (See the following section on dog food ingredients to find out why.)

>> **Guaranteed analysis:** This list breaks down the minimum percentage of protein and fat, and the maximum percentage of fiber and moisture in the food in its present form.

>> **Byproducts:** Now here's a term to watch. What's a byproduct anyway? Byproducts are things other than meaty muscle tissue, including, but not limited to, lungs, spleen, brains, blood, bone, hair, hooves, beaks, feathers, and other "hmmmm" ingredients. Although organ meat is high in protein and it provides essential nutrients to animals in the wild, much of the nutrition is removed when exposed to the high heat in the rendering process that produces commercial dried dog kibble, and should thus be avoided. And needless to say, hooves, beaks, and feathers are nasty items that add zero benefit to dog food.

>> **Manufacturer information:** These lines should include a toll-free number to call for more information. A reliable company should have professional members on staff, including a veterinary nutritionist, who you can call for information and help in selecting a formula that meets the nutritional needs of your dog's life stage. Check out the company to make sure that it conducts ongoing pet-feeding nutrition studies.

>> **Nutritional guarantee:** This will include the AAFCO (Association of American Feed Control Officials) statement. Its members are local, state, and federal officials who merely advise and provide guidelines for canine dietary needs. *They do not regulate, inspect, or run feeding tests.* The nutritional adequacy statement specifies which life stage the food is formulated for (growth, all life stages, maintenance, and so on).

Digging into the Dog Food Bag

The guaranteed analysis section of the label on the dog food bag tells you what's in the food you're feeding your dog, as well as the percentages of each ingredient. The following sections dissect the basic and most common food ingredients.

Protein

Protein is the big gun in your dog's food bowl, because about 50 percent of the muscle tissue in a dog's body is made up of protein, which is an essential component of his cell structure.

Protein contains amino acids (another word you often hear in canine nutrition), which are critical to his bodily functions like digesting food, fighting off infections, and carrying oxygen in his blood. The absence of quality protein can result in poor growth, weight loss, poor hair coat, impaired immune function, depressed appetite, energy loss, irregular *estrus* (female heat cycles), and poor reproductive performance — just to name a few! We serve our dogs "higher protein" and "all-meat protein" and hope we're dishing out a better meal.

Meat, poultry (and their byproducts), and grains like corn and soy are the most common protein sources in most dog foods. The difference lies in the balance of protein in each product. For example, beef is a higher-quality protein source than corn because it contains a better balance of amino acids.

Beef, chicken, and lamb are the most frequently utilized meat protein sources. If the label states "chicken meal," it is a lower-quality protein than real, unprocessed chicken.

TIP

Protein requirements change throughout a dog's life just as they do in humans. The animal's size and age, his individual energy demands, and daily stressors vary from dog to dog. Optimum protein intake is more crucial at certain times in most dogs' lives. For example, hunting and hard-working dogs' energy requirements increase during hunting season and they should eat more nutrient-dense food (higher protein and fat). Conversely, they should eat less nutrient-dense food during the off-season when their energy needs decline.

Growth foods

While we're on the subject of protein, foods designated as "growth foods" were at one time thought to contribute to structural problems in dogs like hip dysplasia and other skeletal disorders like OCD (osteochondritis dissecans), a painful disorder affecting elbows and shoulders. Current research holds that calories primarily from fat, not protein intake, are the likely culprit.

Large breeds like Golden Retrievers just naturally grow fast, which puts a big strain on young and fragile joints. A high-fat puppy diet promotes even more rapid growth, thus increasing the risk of hip and elbow dysplasia and other skeletal problems. While the average puppy owner may think you need to feed, feed, and feed to keep that young body growing, research has shown that over-feeding and being overweight actually contributes to poor joint development.

TIP

At least two major dog food manufacturers have developed growth foods for the various breed sizes with a lower fat and protein content to meet a large-breed puppy's restricted caloric needs. The object is to control the puppy's weight during his major growth phase of 8 weeks to 10 months. Your vet can advise you if and when to change to a different formula.

Here's another protein myth: High-protein diets cause kidney disease in older dogs. Not so. Although an already damaged kidney cannot properly metabolize protein, the protein itself will not cause the problem.

That said, most dog food manufacturers do offer a somewhat lower protein food for senior canines — in large breeds, defined as dogs over 7 years old. Because the amount of protein is restricted, the quality of the protein becomes vitally important. Healthy older dogs still require adequate quality protein to maintain lean body mass and help support their immune system.

The two faces of high fat

Fat calories *do* have their place. Dogs need fat for healthy skin and coats and to prevent constipation. An adult dog food should contain about 15 percent fat to maintain good health. Although animal fats are more palatable, fats derived from vegetable oils and fish oils are better sources of the fatty acids they need to lubricate their outsides (see the sidebar "Good and bad fats").

GOOD AND BAD FATS

Properly balanced healthy fats are vital to maintaining a healthy skin, coat, and digestive system, as well as supporting better eye and heart health. But giving your dog those extra fats isn't as simple as a bit of bacon fat or a spoonful of corn oil.

Omega-3 fatty acids are found mainly in fish like salmon, herring, and sardines. Omega-6 fats are found in meats, poultry, and eggs, have anti-inflammatory properties, and are important for a healthy skin and coat.

Veterinarians and breeders will recommend adding quality fish oil supplements to your Golden's diet. Some breeders add a weekly portion of sardines to their dog's food. (I do.) Portions depend on the dog's size.

Fat also contains more than twice the metabolizable energy of protein, so a Golden who hunts or works at other strenuous activities will need extra fat as well as extra protein to maintain his energy and stamina. Watch for terms like "calorie-dense" or "high-caloric density" in performance food; these refer to the fat content of the food.

Preservatives

Dog foods require preservatives because they contain fats, which will spoil when exposed to heat and air (a process called *oxidation*).

WARNING

Manufacturers use antioxidant materials to prevent oxidation. The antioxidants used may extend the fat life, but some add dangers worse than rancidity to the food. One preservative sometimes used is called *ethoxyquin*, which is a reputed to be a cancer-causing agent, as are two others known as BHA and BHT. All three are considered safe in very small amounts, but why risk it at all? They are used primarily in lower-quality foods, often those containing "meal," which should be avoided anyway. Yes, you'll pay more for better food, but you'll save even more because your Golden will be a healthier animal.

The preservative used will be listed on the label, and may be shown on the front of the bag as well. Most quality dog foods today are preserved safely with vitamin E, or you can purchase natural foods with no preservatives from specialized dealers. Ask your vet about those products if they interest you. You can also find information on natural dog foods on the Internet.

Artificial coloring

Because dogs don't see most colors, any color added to their food is for the owner's benefit. Today, the Food and Drug Administration (FDA) regulates the use of all color additives in human and animal food. However, canine nutritionists and wise dog owners avoid food that is artificially colored. It should not be included on the food ingredient list.

Vitamins and minerals

If you had one dog food rule to follow, it should be no vitamin supplements, ever. A quality dog food (the key word being *quality*) should be complete, with no supplements necessary to meet the life stages of the pet. In fact, supplementation can create toxicity problems, which can cause poor growth, abnormal eye conditions, and impaired reproductive performance.

Supplementation is especially dangerous for puppies. Normal tooth and bone development require

>> Adequate and balanced levels of calcium, phosphorous, and vitamin D.

>> A proper ratio of calcium and phosphorous of 1.2 to 1.

A quality growth food contains a correct balance of easily metabolized sources of these nutrients.

If extra calcium, phosphorous, or vitamin D is added to a puppy's diet, it can cause serious skeletal disorders. No extra vitamins, please. Ignore all those ads that promote XYZ for bright eyes and shiny coats.

For more information on selecting a healthy dog food, consult the World Small Animal Veterinary Association (WSAVA; https://www.wsava.org/).

Feeding Wet or Dry

Adding water to dry food is optional. Feeding dry is recommended as a dental plus, because it helps prevent plaque and tartar buildup. For that reason, most large-dog owners feed their dogs dry food. Canned dog food (*quality* canned food!) is just as nutritious, but a large-breed dog would need 3 to 4 cans a day, which many consider impractical. A few breeders, as well as some dog owners, add a can of wet food to a portion of the kibble, adjusting portions according to the weight requirements of the dog.

Dogs who gulp their dry food like it's their last meal may inhale the dry particles or choke on them, and may do better with a generous splash of water in the food. It's also thought that adding water helps reduce the risk of bloat. I add a healthy splash of water to each dog food pan immediately before offering it. The food is still crunchy enough to preserve dental benefits, and, in my opinion, the water releases flavor and adds to palatability (although eating slowly has never been my dogs' problem). Some foods *require* the addition of water to release the digestive enzymes in the food.

Always have clean, fresh water available for your dog, in addition to any water you add to his food (see Figure 10-2).

FIGURE 10-2:
Your dog should always have access to fresh water — but it should always be from a bowl and not an outdoor faucet!

The Real Skinny on Obesity

Studies indicate that obesity is the number one nutritional disorder in dogs and that a large percentage of pet dogs seen by veterinarians in this country are overweight. An extra 10 pounds on your should-be-65-pound Golden would be comparable to an extra 20 pounds on a woman who should weigh 120.

Just like people, every Golden is an individual with different metabolic needs. The same food/exercise ratio that keeps one dog lean and physically fit may lead to obesity in another. You have to know your Golden.

Your dog should have an hourglass figure when viewed from above, with a *defined* waistline behind his rib cage and in front of his hind legs. Put your hands on his back with your fingers curled around his rib cage. You should be able to feel his ribs beneath a layer of muscle with very slight pressure.

Obesity is simply excess consumption — too many calories in and too few calories used — and is no healthier in dogs than it is in humans. It can lead to diabetes and skin problems and will aggravate orthopedic problems, heart conditions, and nervous disorders. It *will* shorten your Golden's life. Either cut back on food portions and/or the type of food, or increase his exercise. Doing both is better.

USING DIET TO DEAL WITH ALLERGIES

Because allergies top the list of Golden health problems, diet can have a major impact on your dog's overall well-being — and your mental health as well! Natural foods and hypoallergenic diets use protein sources such as lamb or fish, and even duck or bison.

Some highly allergic dogs do well on homemade diets. Homemade may help your dog, but it requires a full understanding of nutritional requirements and a firm commitment from the owner to follow a strict dietary regimen.

If your dog has food allergies, work with your vet or a canine nutrition specialist (find one through your veterinarian, kennel club, or a veterinary teaching institution) to develop a diet he can tolerate.

Here are some tips for keeping your Golden slim and trim:

» See your veterinarian before you put him on a diet.

» If he's overweight, switch to a quality food with less fat and higher fiber. Fat delivers twice the calories per gram as carbohydrates and protein. More fiber provides more bulk with fewer calories, making the dog feel full.

» Eliminate all table scraps and check the contents of his biscuit treats. (See the following section, "Scrap those table scraps!") Many are very high in fat and sugars.

» Always feed him twice a day. He'll have more to look forward to and will feel more satisfied.

» Step up his exercise. Every day walk farther, throw more Frisbees, take him swimming, and expend more energy. (You'll probably look better, too, even without a diet!)

Scrap those table scraps!

Dog owners love to gooey up their dog's food. It's another way of lavishing attention. Bad idea. It usually makes the dog fat and unhealthy. Table scraps are no big deal if given in moderation (as in not much and not often!). A bit of fruit or vegetable won't hurt most dogs occasionally. (Raw carrots are great for his teeth.) Although it adds a few extra calories, a taste or two shouldn't upset the nutritional balance of a good-quality diet.

Feeding table scraps carries another subtle danger: the finicky eater. If a dog gets used to goodies in his food bowl, he might refuse to eat his normal diet. Offer him a veggie treat separate from his dinner time.

WARNING

Never feed your dog old or moldy leftovers, especially aging cheeses, nuts, or other similar food. He could become ill and later recycle the food on your bed or pillow. Not a healthy idea.

WARNING

Pure chocolate is toxic in doses that are proportionate to the dog's weight. About 2½ ounces of unsweetened chocolate can be fatal for a small dog, and a 2-pound bag of chocolate chips can kill a 50-pound dog.

Onions are also highly toxic to dogs. They contain an alkaloid that ruptures the red blood cells, causing fever, darkened urine, and death. Cooking does not eliminate the danger.

Exotic diets and the raw food debate

The big news in the dog food world today focuses on feeding strategies that use raw and natural ingredients. Claims abound about such diets that have conquered lifelong allergies and other chronic ailments in Goldens as well as other breeds. Just as common are the health issues arising from feeding diets that do not contain the vitamins and amino acids essential to a dog's well-being. Currently, there are studies underway at several university veterinary schools and hospitals researching recent illnesses, and even deaths, with diet as the primary cause.

This is a highly volatile subject among breeders and trainers as well as pet owners. Before you embark on a "new food" journey for your Golden, have a serious conversation with your vet and other dog owners who have been down that road. And of course, *read.* You can find several good books on alternative feeding methods on the Internet.

Exercising Your Dog

Exercise is more than a good health habit. It's as essential to your Golden's overall well-being as food and water. It's also important to your own mental health, because a Golden who is not exercised will redirect his energy into creative mischief and destruction. You'll swear he's suddenly become possessed.

If you think dogs will exercise by themselves, you'd better think again. Most dogs, including Goldens, are just like you and me. They only move about if they have a reason to do so. A fenced backyard will not provide physical stimulation for your Golden. *You* are your dog's motivation to run, play, and get physical.

WARNING

Whatever your exercise pleasure, when he is out and about, always keep your Golden on a leash! There are dozens of doggie temptations that could turn your morning mile into a nightmare chase scene. Even the most reliable dog can defy his owner and zip off after a squirrel, often across a busy street. A leashed dog is seldom a statistic.

Golden energizers

Your Golden needs high-energy retrieving games like Frisbee toss and fetch-the-tennis-ball. Capitalize on your Golden's natural instincts and throw canvas or plastic bumpers for him to retrieve. If he doesn't bring them back, run in the opposite direction to entice him to chase you. This retrieving business is in his genes; he'll catch on fast. A 15-minute (minimum) backyard retrieving session every day will help keep the average dog in shape.

Your dog also needs his daily walk. How far and how long depends on the individual dog, so just make sure that he can keep up with you (and vice versa) without undue stress (on you, too!) and don't push beyond his endurance level. Many dogs don't know what's best for them and will extend themselves beyond their limits. Goldens are notorious for that.

Is your Golden still a growing pup? Young bones should not be unduly stressed because the growth plates are still forming. Puppies need more frequent, shorter walks. Your vet can tell you how much walking a young dog can handle without injury. A healthy adult will enjoy, indeed thrive on, a longer, faster pace. If he's a senior citizen, slow down and watch for signs of weakness or aching muscles the next day. (See Chapter 14 for more on caring for your older dog.)

JUST FOR FUN

Try to find a park, field, forest preserve, or beach where there are no traffic hazards and plan a hike or bicycle outing once or twice a week. You don't have to be creative. Just get him outdoors for exercise.

STREET SALT IS BAD FOR THE PAWS

The street salt used on roads and sidewalks during the winter can burn your dog's paws. Be sure to clean his paws after a walk outdoors. It's best to wash, not just wipe, because wiping may actually rub the salt into cracks on and between the toes and do more damage.

Check the forecast

On warm days, walk during cooler mornings and evenings and rest if you notice that your Golden is panting excessively. He can become overheated very easily. Hang a water canteen on your belt and stop occasionally for a drink. In extremely cold weather, walk at midday when it's warmer.

Examine his footpads frequently, and if cracks or bleeding occur, clean them and apply petroleum jelly to soften and soothe. In winter, check his toes for ice buildup after a run in the snow and wipe his paws to remove any salt and chemicals he may have stepped in.

WARNING

On summer walks, avoid walking on hot cement or tarred and blacktop surfaces, which could burn your Golden's footpads. If you can't walk barefoot on the pavement, neither should your dog. Blacktop is especially dangerous because he can also get the hot gooey tar on his feet. If he accidentally steps on hot tar and it sticks, don't put his paws in cold water and then peel it off because that will also remove healthy tissue and make the damage worse. Instead, rub his paws generously with vegetable oil and apply a bandage. The tar should wash off the next morning.

If your dog is exposed to extended periods of summer sun during exercise or on long summer walks, protect his nose with a sunscreen formulated especially for dogs. Check your pet supply house or catalog for approved products.

Hit the jogging trail

If you're a jogger, your athletic adult Golden Retriever is a perfect running partner. He not only loves to run, he'll inspire you to stay the course, and you'll both benefit from the emotional bond that will grow from running together.

Before you decide to do the 3-minute-mile with your Golden, a quick health check with your vet is a good precaution. Then start out slowly. Out-of-shape dogs will gladly run themselves into exhaustion and then collapse. Make sure that he can hang in there before you up your speed.

TIP

If your dog licks his feet after running through a field, he may have picked up tiny pointed grass and weed seeds, which wedge themselves into the foot tissue. If not removed at once, the seeds can become painfully embedded and infected, which means another trip to your friend, the veterinarian. Always check his feet after an outdoor jaunt.

Spaying or Neutering Your Dog

Everyone knows (or should know) that spay/neuter helps prevent pet overpopulation. Statistics vary with different organizations; according to the ASPCA (American Society for the Prevention of Cruelty to Animals), more than 3 million dogs end up in shelters every year. And sadly, many of those dogs will be euthanized because there aren't enough adoptive homes for all of them.

It doesn't take a genius to figure out that spay/neuter is the obvious solution.

Most animal shelters require that all pets adopted out be spayed or neutered before going to their new homes. Most breeders also require puppies sold as pets be spayed or neutered at some point in time. However, conformation rules require that all competitors must be shown intact. So, if a client plans a show career for her puppy, the breeder may waive the spay/neuter requirement, at least until she knows the client is serious about her puppy goals.

The kicker here is that the owner must be extremely vigilant to prevent her Golden from having accidental "contact" with another dog. Stuff happens!

When to spay/neuter

In past years, early spay/neuter was recommended as a preventive measure for a host of reasons: no "surprise" puppies because your male Golden (or your neighbor's mixed breed) impregnated your female in an instant; no ill-informed owner-breeders raising unwanted litters; no intact females dripping estrus fluid for 3 weeks; no amorous Romeos lurking about in search of romance.

In recent years, however, research has determined that early spay/neuter can actually do more harm than good. Sex hormones are necessary for a dog to achieve optimum bone density. Interfering with that growth process increases the risk of developing hip dysplasia and torn cruciate ligaments. Studies also show early spay/neuter increases the risk of certain cancers, and even the occurrence of incontinence in females as well as males.

On the plus side, females spayed after their first heat cycle, as recommended by many breeders, have a 4 percent risk of mammary cancers. Waiting until after the second cycle ups that risk to 13 percent. If spayed before the first heat cycle, the risk decreases to less than 0.5 percent.

Risks aside, many breeders recommend spaying females after their first heat cycle, and to neuter males between 12 and 24 months of age. Such decisions, of course, depend on the individual dog and owner. My advice is to always do your own research and have a serious discussion with your veterinarian and your breeder.

TIP

The decision to delay spay/neuter for health or other reasons will conflict with animal welfare organizations, who always advise altering your pet as soon as possible. That advice is important and well-intended. If you're not sure, have a conversation with your vet or breeder. The importance of spay/neuter cannot be understated.

The benefits of spay/neuter

Spaying or neutering has many health benefits to your dog (and to you!). Keep the following points in mind:

>> Spayed females at any age have a reduced risk of breast cancer, cystic endometrial pyometra, false pregnancies, mastitis, venereal sarcoma, ovarian and uterine tumors, cystic ovaries, chronic endometriosis, vaginal prolapse, and uterine torsion or uterine prolapse.

>> Neutered males have a reduced risk of testicular cancer, benign prostatic hyperplasia, acute prostatic abscess, tumors around the anus, infection of the testicles, anal hernias, and venereal tumors. A neutered male will also hang closer to home and not become macho with other male visitors.

    You, on the other hand, will also benefit, thanks to absolute birth control for life and relief from hormone-induced aggression toward other dogs, especially males, territorialism at home, wanderlust in search of romance, urine marking at home and in new places, dominant and overt sexual behavior such as riding or mounting your leg or your mother's, licking and arousal, and your own frustration when intact male dogs feel their hormones and resist doing what they're told.

>> Most importantly, spayed/neutered animals are less likely to bite or exhibit temperament problems that would affect your family and neighbors.

It's a myth that surgical alteration will affect your dog's true personality. He or she will still be the silly, fun-loving Golden critter you know and love!

TIP

Spay/neuter can cost between $150 to $400, depending on your neighborhood and veterinarian. However, some animal shelters offer low-cost spay/neuter clinics to the general pet-owning public. Check with your local shelter to compare costs.

IN THIS CHAPTER

» **Choosing a veterinarian**

» **Understanding vaccines and diseases**

» **Reading your dog's body signs**

» **Giving medications**

» **Handling ailments and emergency situations**

» **Winning the war against allergies**

Chapter **11**

Golden Health Care 101

Choosing a veterinarian is a major decision. In essence, you're selecting your Golden's HMO. The vet will be there for you through sickness and health, hopefully more of the latter than the former. This chapter helps you understand all his or her ministrations, poking, prodding, and advice.

Choosing a Veterinarian

Finding a veterinarian in most U.S. cities is easy. Finding a *good* veterinarian will take a little more time and research. It's worth the extra effort.

Today's veterinarians wear a dozen hats. Many specialize in specific areas of canine health — orthopedics, ophthalmology, oncology, cardiology, nutrition, dermatology, reproduction, internal medicine, acupuncture, or holistic and integrative medicine (healing-oriented medicine that considers the whole dog, including all aspects of lifestyle, is informed by evidence, and makes use of ALL appropriate therapies, both holistic and conventional). Even the general practitioner vet often has some special area of expertise.

Ask your dog friends where they go for veterinary care. Ask your breeder, or call the secretary of the local kennel club or area Golden Retriever club. If you can, find a veterinary clinic with at least two doctors, more if possible. In an emergency or the onset of some mysterious ailment, several vets are better than one.

Your puppy's first visit

Select your veterinarian well before your pup's arrival and make his first appointment within his first 2 or 3 days of coming home. He may not be due for a shot, but you'll want a health check anyway, especially if his breeder gave a health guarantee. (Most breeders guarantee a puppy's health for 3 days to a week.) Bring his health record from the breeder of all shots and wormings to date, a fresh stool sample in a small clean container, and a pocketful of puppy treats. This veterinary visit is your one exception to "no outings during your puppy's early fear period," so make it a pleasant one.

Hold your puppy in your lap until the vet can see your pup; his little paws should not touch the clinic floor. There are too many things lurking there that could infect your puppy. Carry him into the office, place him directly onto the table in the exam room, and pet him lavishly so that he's not scared.

If you've chosen wisely, your vet will gush over your puppy to make this visit a positive experience. If your pup is apprehensive, use lots of sweet talk and stay happy and relaxed. He'll think it's pretty neat to get all this extra hands-on attention.

With gentle hands, the vet should examine all your puppy's body parts — eyes, ears, throat and glands, genitalia (especially to make sure the testicles have dropped), skin and coat for fleas or flakiness, heart sounds for irregularities, and temperature. He should also palpate for swollen glands and hernias.

Use your dog radar during this first visit. Does the vet's hands-on manner put your pup (and you) at ease? Does she come across as a caring and capable professional? Does she encourage you to ask questions or call her any time? If not, keep looking until you find a vet you're comfortable with.

Annual checkups are important

Your Golden should have, at the very least, an annual check-up, annual heartworm test and fecal exam, and a hands-on physical exam. That hands-on exam can detect small lumps and bumps that could be overlooked by the owner. Regular visits also help your vet become familiar with your Golden, which is vital to establishing a solid doctor-canine client relationship. If you ask questions and keep notes, you can transform these visits from simple routine health care into a Golden learning experience.

When you make your dog's appointment, tell the receptionist why you're scheduling this visit — illness or routine visit — so that she can allow enough time for the exam.

Avoid appointments in the early morning and late afternoon during the week because these are prime drop-off and pick-up hours for pets who are boarded or hospitalized. Both you and the vet will be less hurried during the hours in between those times.

If you have questions, write them down before your visit so that you won't forget to ask. Get all pet care instructions in writing, and don't leave until you read and understand them. Your vet will appreciate the extra time you take to be careful and follow through. It makes her job easier, and your dog healthier in the long run.

Holistic veterinary medicine

Acupuncture, acupressure, chiropractic, homeopathic remedies, natural foods — all are today available to pets as well as people. Many breeders and pet owners who struggle with a constant plague of health and fertility problems have found relief by using natural foods, herbal remedies, and holistic medicine. They use herbal products to treat everything from allergies, insect bites, bruises, digestive upset, and whelping problems to fleas and internal parasites, and they claim to do so successfully. Natural is always better, but it's very important to research thoroughly before introducing any new product or protocol.

Acupuncture and acupressure are often used on dogs (by licensed practitioners) to treat arthritis and arthritic symptoms, seizures and other ailments, and even immune problems. I've seen acupuncture benefit a couple of my own gimpy Goldens who showed dramatic improvement after just one treatment.

Massage therapy, a relative of acupressure, will strengthen the circulation and flow of energy in your dog, and it's something you can do yourself. Geriatric dogs especially benefit from a good massage. If you're really into hands-on treatments for your Golden, you can find good books and tapes to help you learn the process. Some veterinarians have massage therapists on staff. They can demonstrate the process for you.

Proponents of holistic veterinary medicine stress that natural remedies should not replace traditional medical care for serious illnesses, but they definitely have one foot in each medical camp. This is an area of canine care that's worth exploring. Start with a good book on holistic medicine and decide for yourself.

Your Puppy's Health Agenda

Your puppy's initial health-care program should include a series of shots. These early shots are critical to your puppy's long-term resistance to canine infection and disease. Puppies are born with an umbrella of antibodies (gifts from their mother) and receive more natural antibodies from the colostrum in her milk. These immunities last through very early puppyhood and gradually wear off. Because no accurate test can confirm when those immunities are completely gone, puppy shots are scheduled at 3-week intervals after the initial shot to provide maximum protection. This is a vulnerable period, because those maternal antibodies may be strong enough to override the vaccine, putting a pup at great risk during his first 12 to 16 weeks of life.

Most vaccination schedules consist of shots given at 3-week intervals, starting with that first shot given at the breeder, through 16 to 20 weeks. Your pup will need a booster shot 1 year later, and every 3 years thereafter, according to the current suggested guidelines from the American Veterinary Medical Association (AVMA) and your dog's individual needs. (If you decide to do titer tests as described in "The case for titer testing," below, he may not need those booster shots.)

REMEMBER

Always ask your vet exactly what vaccine your puppy is getting, and what is in it. A "5-way" shot contains the core vaccines recommended by the AVMA, which protect against the core diseases. A 6-, 7-, or 8-way shot contains additional vaccines for non-life threatening, non-core diseases. These are not essential vaccines, and they unnecessarily impact a puppy's immature and fragile immune system. Always request — in fact, insist on — the 5-way shot.

Some breeders give only a first and second distemper/parvo vaccination, then do titer testing to determine if the puppy needs a third vaccine. That eliminates vaccinating against non-fatal diseases. If that protocol is not available at your veterinarian, insist on the 5-way shot. (See the following section for more on core and non-core vaccines.)

Your puppy should receive his rabies vaccination at least 3 weeks after the final puppy shot, a rabies booster 1 year later, then a booster every 3 years instead of annually, unless otherwise mandated by local public health laws. Unfortunately, there is no titer test allowed for rabies.

Most vets offer to give a rabies shot at the same time as the final puppy shot. My personal protocol, and the one I strongly recommend for you as well, is to never give more than one vaccine at a time. Wait at least 3 more weeks to give the rabies shot. Yes, it means an extra visit to the vet. And yes, you *can* request the separation of vaccines: It's your dog and your call. Consider this: Just as a segment of today's medical world believes humans have overdosed on antibiotics and vaccines and thus weakened their own immunities, a large segment of the canine medical camp subscribes to that same theory, especially given the increase in cancers and other autoimmune diseases that were rare in dogs of yore. Over-vaccination is believed to cause weakened immune systems, auto-immune problems, thyroid issues, and is suspect in the rise of cancer in the breed. Why take that risk?

Your vet may also prescribe a *heartworm preventive* to protect your little guy against heartworm disease. Heartworm is found today in all 50 states, although they are most prevalent in in warm regions where mosquitoes are common. In such cases, dogs may need to take the preventive all year long. In colder climates, the medication can be given only during mosquito season. If you reside in a tick-prone area, your dog also should be protected against tick-transmitted diseases, which can be life threatening. If your vet doesn't discuss these options, be sure to ask about them. (See Chapter 12 for more on heartworm and tick-borne diseases.)

Core and non-core vaccines

The following section breaks down your puppy's disease prevention program into core vaccines (recommended by the AVMA) for all dogs due to severity of disease and ease of transmission, regardless of circumstance. These protect against diseases that are too dangerous to risk any absence of immunity. Non-core are recommended only for dogs where exposure to an outbreak of a particular disease puts them at risk.

Core vaccines include

>> **Canine distemper virus (CDV):** Viral. Attacks the lining of the intestines. Highly contagious. Symptoms include cough, fever, vomiting, and diarrhea. Method of exposure: Airborne. Risk: High; usually fatal in puppies. Usually included in the initial 5-way puppy shot.

>> **Canine parvovirus (CPV):** Viral. Attacks the lining of the intestines. Highly contagious. Symptoms include bloody or watery diarrhea, fever, vomiting, dehydration, and intestinal pain. Method of exposure: Infected feces. Risk: High; usually fatal in puppies. Included in the initial 5-way puppy shot.

>> **Canine adenovirus (CAV2):** Viral, respiratory, part of the kennel cough complex. Highly contagious. Method of exposure: Airborne. Symptoms include harsh, spastic cough. Risk: High, although less than CDV and CPV; puppies are at greatest risk. Immunization usually included in initial 5-way puppy shot.

» **Infectious canine hepatitis (CA1):** Viral. Affects the liver (not related to human hepatitis). Highly contagious. Symptoms include fever, appetite loss, and vomiting. Method of exposure: Infected urine, saliva, respiratory discharge, or contaminated clothing. Risk: High for puppies. Immunization included in initial 5-way puppy shot.

» **Rabies:** Viral. Affects central nervous system. Symptoms include lack of coordination, seizures, and aggression. Method of exposure: Saliva, found in some species of wild animals, including raccoons, skunks, foxes, and bats. Risk: Very high; usually fatal. Immunization is usually at 16 to 20 weeks or at least 3 weeks after final puppy shots. Boosters thereafter as required by law.

Non-core vaccines include

» **Canine parainfluenza:** May be included in the core vaccine. Viral. Respiratory, part of kennel cough complex. Symptoms include harsh, spastic cough. Method of exposure: Airborne. Risk: High.

» **Canine coronavirus:** Viral. Intestinal. Symptoms include diarrhea, vomiting, and persistent fever. Method of exposure: Infected feces. Risk: Moderate. Vaccine is no longer widely recommended unless there has been an exposure to the disease or an outbreak in the area.

» **Leptospirosis:** Bacterial. Affects kidneys and liver. Method of exposure: Urine of infected animals such as cattle, sheep, and wild animals. Risk: High in rural and remote areas where the named animals may be present. One vaccine can produce severe side effects. Immunity less than 4 to 6 months. Immunize only after 12 weeks of age and where there is risk of exposure. Many vets do not recommend this vaccine.

TIP

My personal experience with the lepto vaccine: Upon recommendation of three veterinarians, I agreed to the lepto vaccine for my 10-year-old Golden. He had a severe reaction and developed immune-mediated-thrombocytopenia, a condition that destroys blood platelets. After 7 months of intensive treatment and several hospitalizations, he went to the Rainbow Bridge. For obvious reasons, I do NOT recommend this vaccine.

» **Bordatella bronchiseptica:** Viral. Canine/kennel cough. Method of exposure: Airborne. Symptoms include harsh, spastic cough; wheezing; and fever. Most common in a boarding situation. Can lead to weakened immunity, bacterial infections. Immunization is one injection or intranasal dosage. Immunity is short-lived. Not necessary unless required in boarding situations or where there is risk of exposure.

>> **Lyme (borreliosis):** Bacterial disease from tick bite. Affects joints. Symptoms include lameness, fever, appetite loss, and swelling at joints. Risk: High in tick-prone areas. Immunization is controversial at this time; the efficacy of the vaccine is debatable. Can produce severe side effects. Some flea/tick products protect against tick bites (see Chapter 12). The best prevention is a thorough body exam after any time spent in woods, grassy areas, or other tick-prone areas.

The case for titer testing

Titers are antibodies in the dog's (or human's) blood that detect immunity from a certain disease. Many dog owners today are having titer tests performed for CDV (canine distemper virus) and CPV (canine parvovirus), the most dangerous canine diseases, rather than unnecessarily revaccinate their dog.

Dr. Ronald D. Schultz, professor of immunology and founding chair of the Department of Pathobiological Sciences at the University of Wisconsin–Madison School of Veterinary Medicine and an author of the WSAVA and AAHA guidelines, has conducted controlled studies on the duration of immunity in vaccinated dogs. He has found that dogs maintain immunity to CDV, CPV-2, and CAV 7 to 9 years after vaccination.

Dr. Schultz further suggests using titers to know whether or not the animal does need to be revaccinated rather than automatically revaccinating on a set schedule. (Arbitrarily revaccinating if the immunity is still present is not the best choice for the dog.) While few practitioners would have thought of doing titers 10 years ago, Dr. Schultz sees more and more titer testing today and acknowledges that owners are increasingly choosing titer tests in order to avoid unnecessary booster shots.

Dr. Schultz is emphatic that dog owners be aware of the importance of core vaccines for every puppy and kitten. Beyond those initial shots, antibody (titer) testing will ascertain whether the pet has developed an adequate immune response to a particular core vaccine.

Unfortunately, not all vets believe in titer testing or offer it to their clients. If you opt for titer testing (and I hope you do), seek out a veterinarian who offers such testing and understands how to use it.

Keeping a Golden Health Calendar

If your pet is ill, even for a day or two, keep written notes on your Golden calendar about whatever problems you observe, including changes in eating or elimination habits, appearance, or behavior. Also keep notes of even minor changes like the following:

>> Has he been picking at his food pan lately instead of gobbling it up in his usual slobbery manner?

>> Does he occasionally stumble during your walks or limp once in a while after exercise?

>> Does he take more time than usual to catch his breath after a romp in the park?

>> Is he sleeping more, chewing his rear at night, or scooting across the floor on his behind?

>> Has he been urinating more frequently than usual?

>> Does he frequently strain when moving his bowels?

>> Do you notice anything unusual or different in his habits or his attitude?

These observations will help your vet diagnose a condition that may not be apparent during a brief examination. (They are also symptoms that warrant a phone call to your vet when they occur.)

REMEMBER

With older dogs, it's especially important to note any changes in their habits or behavior. Even the slightest differences should be noted on your canine calendar. They may signal the start of a problem your vet might not discover for weeks or months ahead, and early intervention could literally save, or at least extend, your dog's life. Also, if your vet asks you any questions, you can refer to your calendar notes about when certain symptoms began to occur or when you noticed a specific change.

Always call your vet if

>> You find a lump anywhere on your Golden's skin.

>> Your Golden seems unusually short of breath.

>> Your Golden has an abrupt change in appetite, up or down.

>> Your Golden starts losing weight for no apparent reason.

>> Your Golden drinks more water than usual and urinates more frequently.

>> Your Golden becomes uncharacteristically fearful or aggressive.

>> Your Golden has been coughing for more than 24 hours.

Healthy Body Signs

Your Golden should be the picture of perfect health, but what does that look like? From nose to toes, here are your dog's body signs:

>> **Body temperature:** A dog's normal body temperature is 100.5 to 101.5 degrees. Take his temperature with a rectal thermometer or "instant" digital thermometer that "dings" when done. Dip the bulb into petroleum jelly, lift his tail, and gently insert the bulb into the anus. Be meticulous about your hygiene.

>> **Heart:** At rest, canines register 90 to 100 beats per minute, with puppies and senior dogs a little faster. You can feel your dog's heartbeat on the inner side of the hind leg or just behind the flex of the front leg. The pulsing action should be easy to locate. A normal pulse can range from 70 to 120 beats per minute.

>> **Nose:** His nose should be black and smooth, never crusted or cracked. *Note:* A dry, warm, wet, or cold nose is not a dog's health barometer. His nose may turn dark pink in cold weather, a normal reaction to the lower temperature.

>> **Ears:** Inside the flap and canal should be pink and free of wax and debris. A smelly or waxy substance or discharge indicates ear mites or an infection. (See Chapter 13 for ear care and cleaning instructions.)

>> **Teeth:** Your dog's teeth should be white and free of plaque. Offer hard, sterile bones and Nylabones to chew his way to dental health. (See Chapter 13 for more on dental care.)

>> **Gums:** The gums should be firm and pink with the edges adhered closely to the teeth. Some pigmentation or dark spots are normal. A black spot on the tongue is also common. Very pale gums can reflect a lowered body temperature and may mean hypothermia. This can also be an indication of blood loss somewhere in his body and requires immediate emergency attention. Bright red gums are a sign of elevated body temperature and the onset of heatstroke, which is life threatening and also requires immediate emergency measures. (See "Heatstroke," later in this chapter.)

>> **Skin and coat:** The skin should be supple without scaling or flaking. The coat should be thick and shiny, although many variations exist in length, texture, and density.

REMEMBER

A warm, dry nose does not mean your dog is sick. Whether the nose is cold and wet or warm and dry, either condition can be normal for a canine.

Incidentally, dogs who eat grass are not sick and do not have worms. Even veterinarians don't know whether dogs ingest grass for the moisture content, for a nutritional imbalance, or because of an ancestral instinct. Until research provides an answer, don't worry about it unless it's excessive. Only the dog knows the answer to this one. I always try to discourage excessive grass ingestion, as my sweet one usually returns the grass to me, during the night, on my bed.

Giving Your Dog Medications

Most dog owners dread giving medications because the dog either struggles and wins, or spits the pill on the floor an hour later. Here's how to make the job easier for both of you. Be firm yet gentle and follow these steps:

1. Stand behind the dog and grasp the top of his muzzle, placing your thumb and fingers of one hand on each side of his canines (the long tooth on each side).

2. Tilt his head back at a 45-degree angle.

3. Squeeze gently while pulling the top of his muzzle upward to open his mouth.

4. Holding the pill between the thumb and index finger of your free hand, grasp his bottom jaw from underneath with your three remaining fingers and gently lower the jaw.

5. Once the mouth is open, place the pill as far back as possible on his tongue and use your index finger to poke it down toward the side of his throat.

6. Close his mouth and hold it closed.

7. Elevate his nose slightly and gently rub his throat with downward strokes to stimulate swallowing and tell him to "Swallow."

Some dogs will swallow if you blow gently directly into their nose.

Always praise lavishly when he swallows the pill.

If he's too stubborn and refuses to allow you to handle his head or mouth (hmmm, when did *that* happen?), use the old hide-it-in-the-cheese trick or bury it in a dollop of peanut butter. (Make sure that the pill is compatible with the bribe.) You also can use Pill Pockets, available at pet supply stores, to hide the pill. Success guaranteed!

TIP

Try storing pills or capsules in a closed container filled with moist or meaty treats. The pills will absorb the flavor, and you may even fool your dog into thinking it's a treat. At the very least, he'll be more receptive to accepting it.

To give liquid medications, use a syringe base minus the needle or an eye dropper. Tilt his head upward, open his mouth, and insert the tool from the side into the back of the throat. Inject the liquid, hold his mouth shut tightly, and stroke his throat.

Always check the label on liquid medication to see whether it requires refrigeration.

Often, dogs can take over-the-counter medicine for common ailments. However, always check with your veterinarian before giving your dog any medication to make sure the medicine is appropriate for each situation. Be sure also to ask for instructions on the correct dosage for your dog and how to best administer the medication.

WARNING

NEVER giver your dog acetaminophen (Tylenol) or ibuprofen (Advil). It can be dangerous or fatal for dogs.

The following table lists some common medications, dosages, and uses.

Medication	Dosage	Use For
Baby aspirin/ Ascriptin	5 mg per lb.; given every 8 hours; 65 lbs. + one 325 mg tab. Do not use with steroids, if a bleeding disorder is present, or post-surgically. Long-term use can damage the kidneys.	Pain relief
Benadryl (antihistamine)	1–2 mg per lb.; given every 8 hours; 65 lbs. + four 25 mg tabs.	Allergies, itching
Hydrogen peroxide	1–3 tsp. every 10 minutes.	To induce vomiting
Imodium A-D	1 caplet per 25 lbs., 1–2 times daily.	Anti-diarrheal
Kaopectate	1 ml. per lb. every 3–4 hours; 65 lbs. 3–4 tbsp.	Treats diarrhea and vomiting

Applying Eye Drops and Ointments

Always wash your hands both before and after administering eye medication to your dog. Do not allow the tip of the applicator to touch the surface of the eye, eyelids, or other surface. With warm water and a soft cloth, gently clean away any debris around the eye.

To apply eye ointments, tilt your dog's head back slightly, as shown in Figure 11-1. Use your thumb to roll the lower lid gently downward, and squeeze the ointment into the exposed pocket. Close the eye, and gently hold it closed for just a second. Be careful not to allow the tip of the applicator to touch the eye, which could contaminate the medication. If you're using a dropper, roll his lower eyelid down so it can act as a pouch to receive the drops. Drip the medication into the pouch and close the lid *very* gently.

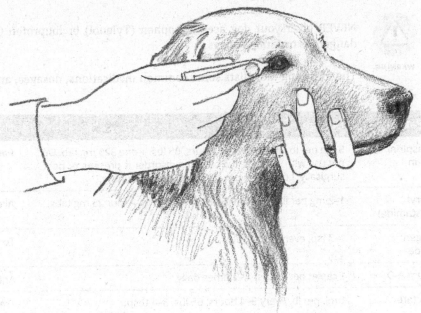

FIGURE 11-1:
Apply eye ointment very gently.

If you suspect something in the eye, inspect it by gently parting the lids under a bright light. If the eye has been irritated by dust or wind, rinse the surface with all-purpose eye drops using the bottle or an eye dropper.

PREPARING A FIRST AID KIT

Every Golden owner should have a well-planned emergency kit for the home (it can serve double duty for your family), plus a backup kit for the car if your Golden frequently tags along for the ride. Check with your veterinarian for specific items, but the following items should give you a good start. (Refer to the earlier table for dosage, or check with your vet).

- First aid instruction book. Read it cover to cover at least once!
- Gauze (2- and 3-inch pads)
- Adhesive tape
- Vet wrap (a stick-to-itself gauze bandage wrap)
- Cotton swabs
- Hydrogen peroxide and alcohol
- Syrup of ipecac to induce vomiting
- Kaopectate and Imodium A-D
- Eye wash
- Rectal thermometer
- Tweezers
- Eye dropper
- Syringe without the needle to give oral medications
- Ascriptin 325 mg
- Tourniquet (a wide rubber band and a pencil will do)
- Muzzle (use a leash, tie, or pantyhose)
- Benadryl
- Towels, one per animal in a vehicle (it can be wet with water or alcohol to cool an overheated dog)
- Blanket (one per vehicle to use as a stretcher or for treating shock)
- Large water container for traveling (an absolute necessity in summer)
- Your veterinarian's office and emergency telephone number

Your first aid kit is just a start. You have to be prepared. This is like taking your emergency SATs.

You can remove small seeds from under the eyelid using a dampened cotton swab to gently slide the seed onto the swab.

Do not attempt to remove other foreign objects. See your veterinarian. Excessive tearing could indicate a blocked tear duct. Again, check with your vet.

Ailments and Injuries from A to Z

Accidents happen. As a responsible dog owner, of course you take every precaution to keep your Golden safe and healthy. But knowledge is power, so you should be aware of what *could* happen, and what to do if it does. In most cases, a call to your veterinarian is your first course of action. The following information will help you understand and deal with each situation.

Bleeding

Bleeding can be *arterial* (spurting of bright red blood) or *venous* (oozing of dark red blood) or sometimes both. Both require immediate veterinary attention. Your pet is in danger from shock, coma, and death. Picture your dog's bleeding wound on a child to help determine your emergency situation. Common cuts and scratches are superficial and should be kept clean and dry to prevent infection. Fresh lacerations over one-half-inch deep or long should be sutured by a vet to prevent infection and scarring and to speed healing.

WARNING

When dealing with bleeding, there are two *don'ts* to remember. *Don't* pour hydrogen peroxide on a fresh wound. That will make the bleeding harder to control. *Don't* wipe a wound that has stopped bleeding because that may dislodge the blood clot that has formed.

There are three main pressure points on your dog, which, along with direct pressure on the wound, will help control bleeding on the limbs and tail while you rush him to the veterinarian:

>> **The upper inside of the front leg.** Pressure here will affect bleeding of the lower forelegs.

>> **The upper inside of the rear leg.** Pressure here will help control bleeding of the lower hind legs.

>> **The underside of the tail.** Pressure here helps control bleeding of the tail.

You may need a tourniquet to control a spurting artery. Apply it to the leg or tail between the wound and the heart.

1. Loop a strip of towel, a tie, rope, or belt around the limb. A wide rubber band and a pencil will also work.

2. Tighten the loop by hand or by inserting and twisting a stick beneath the loop.

WARNING

Your dog could lose a leg or his tail if his blood supply is cut off for too long. You must loosen the tourniquet every 15 minutes to allow blood flow to the limb. Apply direct pressure for 3 or 4 minutes and then retighten the tourniquet. Your best recourse is to see your vet as soon as possible.

Bloat

Everyone's familiar with the human version of bloat. Too much Thanksgiving dinner, too many mashed potatoes. Not quite so with dogs. *Bloat,* or GVD (gastric dilation volvulus), is a buildup of gas that can't escape from the dog's stomach. As the gas accumulates, the stomach swells and will quickly twist, blocking food passage in or out of the stomach and blood flow to other internal organs. The dog is in great pain and on the brink of shock and death within the hour.

WARNING

Large breeds, like Great Danes, Irish Setters, and retrievers, are most affected, especially dogs who eat large meals, eat once a day, or gulp their food. Symptoms of bloat are sudden discomfort paired with labored breathing, restlessness, roaching (humping) the back, drooling and unproductive vomiting, and abdominal swelling. Tapping the dog's sides will produce a hollow sound. Get veterinary attention ASAP, or your dog can die!

Preventative measures make good common dog sense. Divide your dog's food into two smaller meals and feed him twice a day. If your dog is a ravenous eater who inhales his food, you can add water to his kibble and use a food pan designed for such eaters. Some have lumps or humps built into the pan, forcing the dog to eat around them. Or put the food on a large flat pan, even a cookie sheet. Avoid strenuous exercise for 1 hour before and 2 hours after a meal (same as swimmers' rules).

Research at Purdue University shows that underweight, fearful, and nervous dogs are at higher risk for GVD. (Fear, nervousness, and excitement all increase air swallowing in humans, too.) A calm, relaxed dog is less likely to get GVD. Keep him happy as a clam!

Burns

Electrical shock and burns are most common in puppies who chew on appliance or extension cords, but don't rule out a curious adult Golden. If the burn is severe, the dog will incur tissue damage and retain fluid in his lungs. If he's unconscious and not breathing, give artificial respiration (see "Choking" below) and get immediate vet attention.

Thermal burns are caused by contact with open flames, boiling water, stoves, or any heated object or surface. First apply ice packs or ice water to the area for 20 to 30 minutes. Follow with a soothing antibiotic ointment twice daily and cover with a nonstick gauze pad or vet wrap (a stick-to-itself gauze bandage wrap) to make sure he doesn't lick it off.

For a caustic acid or chemical burn, you should flush the area immediately and liberally with cool water. Apply an antibiotic preparation and ice to reduce swelling. Apply a pad or vet wrap to prevent licking the injured area, as with thermal burns above.

REMEMBER

Always check with your vet when treating any type of burn.

Choking

Dogs can swallow anything from chicken bones to balloons. If you believe this has happened, you need to keep him still while you attempt to remove the swallowed material. First, wrap the dog in a blanket to keep him still. Wedge an object (such as a clean, tightly rolled sock, washcloth, or small towel) sideways between the back teeth on one side of his mouth to keep it open.

Pull out his tongue (cautiously to avoid a dog bite) to check for foreign bodies behind the tongue or in the back of the mouth. Use your fingers or needle-nosed pliers to remove the object. If it won't come out, lift the dog and hold him upside down by the hind legs. If this is a large, adult dog, this may require two people. Shake him vigorously to try to dislodge the object and clear his airways. If you're unsuccessful, use the *Heimlich maneuver*. Lay the dog on his side and use your fist or your knee to apply sharp quick pressure to the abdomen at the base of the breastbone. If he stops breathing, give mouth-to-nose resuscitation — artificial respiration — or CPR as described below.

WARNING

If your dog has swallowed thread, pantyhose, or something long and stringy, do not attempt to pull it out. You could make things worse. Ditto for his other end: If he is evacuating something long and stringy, let him push it out on his own. If he's unsuccessful at either end, rush him to your veterinarian.

To perform artificial respiration:

1. Place the dog on his side and extend his neck.

2. Open his mouth and check for food or vomit if necessary.

3. Hold his muzzle closed and place your mouth over his nose.

4. Slowly blow into his nose so that his chest expands.

5. Repeat every 3 seconds.

To perform CPR:

1. Place the dog on his side.

2. Place both hands, one on top of the other, over his heart (where his elbow meets his rib cage) and apply rapid, downward pressure.

Compressions should be about 100 per minute.

3. Stop every 30 seconds to see whether a heartbeat has returned.

Dehydration

Dehydration is an excessive loss of body fluids caused by fever, inadequate water intake, and prolonged vomiting and/or diarrhea.

To test your dog for dehydration, gently lift the skin around the top of his neck. It should snap quickly back into place. If the skin hangs loose or remains in a ridge, it means he's dehydrated, an emergency that requires immediate vet attention.

You can treat a mild case of dehydration with electrolyte fluids given by mouth. If he won't drink copious amounts of water or electrolyte fluids, your veterinarian will give fluids intravenously.

Diarrhea

There's diarrhea, and then there's *diarrhea!* Loose stools can be due to a dozen things: a sudden change in diet or drinking water, emotional upset or excitement, scavenging in the garbage, parasites (see Chapter 12), or other serious problem or disease.

Examine the stool for color, consistency, odor, and frequency and keep a record for your vet. If the diarrhea is bloody, persists for more than 24 hours, or is accompanied by vomiting, fever, or other signs of toxicity, take your dog directly to the vet. Always take a stool sample with the dog.

TIP

You can treat ordinary diarrhea at home. Withhold all food for 24 hours. Offer very small amounts of water or ice cubes for his thirst. Give him Kaopectate (same weight dose as humans) or Imodium A-D (one capsule per 25 pounds of dog). Resume feeding with small amounts of a no-fat diet: one part boiled hamburger to two parts cooked rice, cottage cheese, or cooked pasta. Follow for 2 or 3 days before going back to regular dog food. Small amounts of canned pumpkin can soothe the digestive tract and help with vomiting, too.

Ear hematomas

These soft lumps on the ear flap sometimes come as a surprise as you're scratching your Golden's velvety ears. This thickening is nothing more than a large pocket of blood from a ruptured blood vessel within the flap that popped when your dog was shaking his head or a dog friend punctured it during play. It sometimes indicates an ear infection as well; that's why he shook his head so hard.

Only your veterinarian can repair a hematoma, so visit him as soon as possible.

Flatulence

Flatulence, or gas, is rarely serious, although it can be annoying. It's more common in older dogs who are less active and experience slower intestinal function.

TIP

If gas is a chronic problem, you might try feeding your dog two or three times a day. Some experts think that gas is created when the dog wolfs or gulps down his food. It may also be a reaction to a certain dog food, so experiment with different (but not lesser-quality) foods. (See Chapter 10 for more on choosing a dog food.) If you feel the problem is extreme, it may be caused by digestive upsets, and you should talk to your veterinarian.

Frostbite and hypothermia

Just because your Golden has a long fur coat and loves the snow doesn't mean he's not at risk for either of these serious conditions. Dogs of all breeds can get frostbite just like people do. Dogs exposed to prolonged wet or very cold conditions are prime candidates for frozen body parts.

Frostbitten areas will be very cold and pale and may have a bluish cast, followed by redness and swelling. Ears, tails, and genitals are the most susceptible areas. Gently warm the affected areas without rubbing. (Rubbing can do more damage.) You can use a heating pad on the low setting or try warm — not hot — compresses. See your veterinarian as soon as possible.

Hypothermia is even more dangerous. Prolonged exposure to the cold, especially if the dog is wet, can cause a dangerous drop in body temperature. Your dog will shiver and may appear disoriented or lethargic, even collapse. His body temperature will fall below 97 degrees.

If he's wet, give him a quick warm bath and rub vigorously with towels to dry his fur. Slowly rewarm him using a hair dryer on the lowest setting. Offer him a warm drink and warm him under blankets, with your own body heat if possible. You also can apply warm-water packs or heating pads to the armpits, chest, and abdomen until his body temperature rises to 100 degrees. Then take him to the veterinarian as soon as possible.

REMEMBER

Indoor living does not prepare a dog or his coat for the vagaries of very cold weather. Never clip his long hair in winter. That shaggy fur will keep him warm outside, and regular grooming will keep it healthy for maximum protection.

So what about outdoor living? While most Goldens are indoor companions, those who live outdoors should have a warm, sturdy dog house to shelter them from cold or rainy weather. The entry should face away from the wind. It should be filled with clean straw or soft hay to burrow into. Never use blankets since they can freeze when wet. Of course, the better plan is to bring your dog indoors for warmth and comfort. He is part of the family, after all!

Heatstroke

Dogs overheat more easily than humans do because they aren't blessed with sweat glands. They cool off through their footpads and by panting, neither of which is very efficient. All breeds are vulnerable to heatstroke, but puppies, older dogs, and overweight dogs are more susceptible. Too many people fail to see the risks or recognize the symptoms of heatstroke until their dog is close to death.

WARNING

NEVER leave your Golden (or any pet) in a closed car during warm weather. In spring through early fall, the inside of a car, even with windows cracked several inches on a sunny, breezy 75-degree day, can heat up to more than 120 degrees in minutes. A confined animal will suffer heatstroke and die an excruciating death. That extra 5 minutes in the store may be fatal. Leave your Golden at home!

Symptoms of heatstroke include

>> Excessive panting

>> Drooling

>> Rapid pulse

- ➤ Dark red gums and tongue
- ➤ A frantic, glazed expression
- ➤ Possible vomiting

Treat the symptoms immediately and then rush your dog to the vet to continue emergency care. Immediately move him to a cooler area, either into air-conditioned indoors or in the shade. Use a rectal thermometer to check his temperature (remember that first aid kit?) Heat exhaustion typically occurs when his temperature reaches between 103 and 106. Above 106 is the danger zone and requires immediate vet attention.

If you're near a body of fresh water, even a baby pool, take or place him in it to cool him down, or hose him with a garden hose. You can also use cool, wet towels and place them on his neck, groin, armpits, and between his hind legs. Gently wet his ears and paw pads with cool water.

Give him cool, not cold, water to drink. If he won't drink, wet his tongue instead. Do not feed him ice cubes, which could cause his temperature to drop too quickly and send him into shock.

Then get him to the vet ASAP. His body temperature can rise again very quickly during the next 48 hours, so strict supervision is necessary.

REMEMBER

The best cure is prevention. Keep your canine cool.

Hot spots

If you own a Golden, you probably have or will experience *hot spots* — inflamed, infected areas on the skin that are very uncomfortable for your dog. Caused by a condition called acute moist dermatitis, they are more common during the warmer months. They can develop from repeated scratching, licking, or chewing, or appear out of the blue for no reason at all and spread rapidly, in as little as 24 hours. One day you brush your Golden, and underneath the long hair on some body part you find an oozing, hairless sore. Hot spots can be painful and horrific. If you find one, tackle it immediately before it spreads.

First, clip the hair around the affected area with clippers or scissors to eliminate the damp undersurface. (If your dog becomes anxious due to the area of pain, you may need to have your vet handle treatment of the hot spot.) Cleanse the area carefully with a product that is formulated to treat hot spots (available at pet stores) that will not sting Allow the area to dry completely, then apply a topical hot spot treatment, hydrocortisone spray, or cream from your vet, several times a day. Keep the area dry and exposed to speed healing. Some experienced Golden owners have used Wonder Dust, a horse powder found in most feed and grain stores and tack shops, as a healing agent to dry the wound area.

Most importantly, you must prevent your dog from licking or gnawing at the hot spot wound. You might have to use an Elizabethan collar or plastic cone if necessary. Hot spot healing time usually lasts anywhere from several days to a couple of weeks. You must continue to clean and check the affected area daily. If the wound does not show improvement in a couple of days, or if it worsens, contact your vet for further treatment. She may prescribe antibiotics in addition to topical healing agents.

TIP

Always check your Golden for hot spots and other coat irregularities frequently during the summer months, after a stay at a boarding kennel, or if he's been swimming a lot. Most Golden coats take forever to dry, and a constant damp coat, especially behind the ears, provides a perfect host site for a hot spot. Regular brushing and bathing, especially in warm weather, will help remove any allergens and irritants from his skin and coat and prevent hot spots from forming. Always think prevention!

Lick sores

Officially called *acral lick dermatitis* (ALD), lick sores are born through excessive licking of one spot, usually the front of one or both legs or feet. ALD sometimes starts with a minor injury, a bee sting, splinter, or irritation that the dog licks and chews and then continues licking long after the wound has healed. The resulting aggravation may be due to boredom, stress, or some environmental change known only to the dog.

If you can prevent his licking with anti-chewing sprays, or in desperation with an Elizabethan collar, the spot should heal on its own. A few dogs, however, persist and go back to licking the healed area or start working on a new one. Get creative, keep your Golden busy, and ask your vet for more advice.

Pyometra

Pyometra is generally an "old lady" disease and usually shows up in unspayed females over 5 years of age, although it can occur in younger females as well. The uterus becomes filled with pus before or after her estrus cycle. Symptoms usually appear several weeks after she has finished bleeding or she may appear to be having a prolonged season. Early-stage symptoms can include excessive licking her back end, a longer than usual season, feeling lethargic or a bit "off," lack of appetite, unquenchable thirst, excessive urination, and vomiting. Pyometra can be fatal if not caught in time, and spay surgery is usually the only medical solution.

In a few cases, a heavy round of antibiotics may help a bitch (female) survive the infection. Obviously, spayed bitches are never at risk — another good reason to have your Golden girl spayed (see recommendations in Chapter 10).

Shock

Shock is the lack of adequate blood flow to support the body's needs. It's caused by a sudden loss of blood, heatstroke, poisoning, dehydration from prolonged vomiting or diarrhea, or severe trauma such as being hit by a car. If not treated quickly, the animal will die.

Symptoms of shock are a drop in body temperature, shivering, listlessness, mental depression, and a weak, faint pulse. Keep the dog calm and comfortable, cover him lightly with a coat or blanket, and get to the nearest veterinarian immediately.

Urinary incontinence

Urinary incontinence is inappropriate passing of urine, usually unintentional, sometimes not. Owners will complain their dog leaks urine when relaxed. It typically occurs in older females, although males can be affected, too. Old age means a weak urethral sphincter muscle. Most cases respond well to drug therapy, but if the underlying cause is renal failure, diabetes, or other abnormality, your vet will have to perform tests to make an accurate diagnosis. (See Chapter 14 for more on aging.)

Don't confuse incontinence with the tendency of some male dogs to lift their leg and "sprinkle" every bush even after they've relieved themselves. This "marking" system is behavioral and not at all related to a dog's bladder.

Vomiting

Follow the same protocol as for diarrhea (see earlier section). You need to watch *how* your Golden vomits and notice *what* he vomits. (More notes for your Golden calendar!) Vomiting can be due to eating too fast or eating grass or some other tasty indigestible stuff. If you suspect your dog ingested toxic plant material or something equally hazardous, save a sample of the vomit for your vet.

Secure your outdoor garbage cans with tight lids and keep your compost pile well out of reach. Rotting garbage smells like haute cuisine to most dogs. Your dog can die from eating bacteria-ridden garbage.

If the vomiting is repeated, sporadic with no relationship to meals, is bloody, or forceful and projectile, always seek veterinary help. If the vomit contains feces or foreign matter or is accompanied by drooling, whining, or trembling, get to the vet ASAP.

If your Golden swallows something dangerous like mouse bait, follow the same guidelines as for people (should he vomit or should he not). You should keep a list of vomiting do's and don'ts on your Golden calendar, your refrigerator, or taped inside a kitchen cabinet door. Do not induce vomiting if your dog

» Swallows an acid, a solvent, or other toxic cleaner

» Swallows a petroleum product (gasoline, turpentine, and so on)

» Swallows a sharp object, which can perforate his esophagus or stomach on the way back up

» Is comatose or more than 2 hours have passed since he ingested the poison

WARNING

Regurgitating any acidic or toxic material should be avoided as it could easily enter the lungs, damage the tissue, and create breathing problems.

You can induce vomiting by giving 3 percent hydrogen peroxide every 10 minutes (1 teaspoon for every 20 pounds of dog). Use a turkey baster poked to the rear of his throat. You can also give syrup of ipecac at 1 teaspoon per 10 pounds of dog.

WARNING

Never use table salt to induce vomiting. Only 2 grams (less than half a teaspoon) per pound of body weight is considered lethal to dogs.

MUZZLING

An injured dog might easily bite the hand that's helping him. A soft muzzle will prevent you from being hurt along with your dog and make your first aid ministrations more effective.

Using a tie, belt, pantyhose, or strip of cloth, wrap the strip around the dog's nose with a half knot on top. Wind the ends under his muzzle and make another half knot under the jaw.

From under the jaw, bring the strips along each side of his neck and tie a bow behind his ears. Remove the muzzle as soon as possible because dogs perspire through their tongues.

Combating Allergies

Golden Retrievers have more than their fair share of health problems common to the breed. (See Chapter 15 for common hereditary problems.) That's in addition to the usual dog illnesses and emergencies that all canines experience. That's just a fact of Golden life. But since you can't fight Mother Nature, you have to be smart enough to fight the problems when they do arise.

Goldens are one of several breeds that are highly predisposed to allergies. Some allergies are seasonal, some appear at various life stages, and some skin diseases become lifelong problems requiring frequent or continuous treatment by a veterinarian.

Dogs with allergies don't usually sneeze or get runny noses like people do. (A few do, however.) Instead, they itch and scratch, chew, lick, and rub their feet, ears, belly, and any part of their body they can reach. Left untreated, the irritated skin becomes traumatized and damaged and subsequently infected. Allergies are caused by the dog's reaction to various allergens. The most common types of allergens are flea saliva, inhaled substances (pollen, mold, dust), and food ingredients.

Flea allergies

The most common and most debilitating is flea allergy dermatitis, which is a hyper-sensitivity to the protein in flea saliva. It's most commonly diagnosed after age 2, is most severe from midsummer through fall, and always requires veterinary care. In warmer climates, it can be a year-round plague. (For more on fleas, see Chapter 12.)

In flea-allergic dogs, it only takes one tiny flea bite to set a major allergy machine in motion. Flea-allergic dogs will scratch and bite themselves raw, with most of the intense itching and biting occurring near the base of the tail.

Your veterinarian can prescribe anti-inflammatory medication, an oral or spot-on flea preventive medication, and also recommend stringent flea control, which includes the environment (house and yard) as well as the dog. Routine grooming, brushing, and thorough body inspections are also vital for flea allergy preventive maintenance. Some of these products can be toxic, so make sure you read the labels, know what's in the product, and understand any possible side effects. Don't be shy — ask questions!

Inhalant (also called atopic) allergies

These are the second-most common culprit, with grasses, pollen, molds, danders, and even dust making your dog completely miserable. Atopic dogs rub their faces, muzzles, and eyes, scratch their armpits and ears, bite their feet and legs, and may develop red and swollen patches. Indoor air cleaners, air conditioning, and good environmental sanitation are helpful in keeping indoor inhalants to a minimum. Veterinarians commonly treat inhalant allergies with antihistamines, steroids (see comments in the next section), and fatty acids, and recommend topical therapy with shampoos and rinses to make the dog more comfortable. Your vet also can refer you to a veterinary dermatologist for allergy skin testing to determine the offending allergen. If your dog is treated with a steroid, you need to know all about side effects and long-term effects to make the best decisions for your dog.

Occasionally, a dog will react to some everyday element in his environment, like carpet fibers, bedding, cleaning agents, plastics, or lawn products. He may scratch himself hairless, especially in his armpits, lower abdomen, groin, and bottom of his feet. Finding the culprit can be difficult, but then at least you can make him comfortable by eliminating it from his life.

WARNING

Avoid fertilizers unless they specify they are safe for animals, and NEVER use weed killers and pesticides! They contain organophosphates, which are proven to cause cancer. Don't put your dog at risk. Wash his feet after running on freshly mowed grass, and use shampoos that contain healing agents and are free of perfumes and dyes. (Ask your vet for recommendations.)

Food allergies

Although food allergies are uncommon, they also are not seasonal and do not respond to corticosteroids. As with inhalant allergies, food allergies can cause itching, which makes the dog scratch, rub, chew, bite, and lick at his skin. The most common offenders are beef, pork, chicken, milk, eggs, fish, corn, soy, and preservatives. Diagnosis takes time because your vet must remove the dog from all commercially prepared food and replace it with a two-ingredient diet with adequate supplementation of vitamins and minerals for a period of 3 to 5 weeks, then gradually introduce a food to the dog.

I know one retriever who reacts violently to all commercial and people foods and exists solely on a special fish and potato dog food.

Here's another food fact you should know: Food allergy is sometimes confused with food intolerance. *Food intolerance* is an abnormal physiologic response (like intestinal upset) to food, while *food allergy* is an immunological response to an ingested substance.

REMEMBER

Topical remedies can provide short-term allergy relief, but they don't address the problem. Shampoos and rinses, anti-itch sprays, and soaks between baths can help make an itchy dog more comfortable.

IS YOUR DOG INSURED?

Along with your home, car, life, and health, you can also now insure your dog. It's not just trendy, it's practical as well. Typical doggie maintenance health care can run well beyond $200 to $300 a year, and more if he gets sick.

Doggie health insurance offers a wide range of costs and coverage, from routine health care to ultrasounds and CAT scans. Premiums generally range from $30 to $50 a month. Benefits vary within policies and companies, so do your homework before you sign on the dotted line. Ask the carrier for specifics about its coverage:

- Does the policy cover regular checkups and tests, emergency visits and treatment, unusual care (such as ultrasounds and CAT scans), and non-life-threatening surgeries (such as hip replacements)?

- What does the policy not cover or specifically exclude — certain illnesses, surgeries, and so on?

- Does the policy allow you to use or choose your own veterinarian?

- How much is the deductible?

- Is there a policy limit on certain procedures or conditions?

- Is there an age limit on any part of the policy?

Ask your veterinarian for more information about policies, her personal experience with dog insurance, and her recommendation on a carrier.

Cortisone and other steroids will make your dog feel better, but it's a quick fix that will not make allergies go away. They also have other potentially damaging side effects, so they should never be used long-term. And they only treat the symptoms; the dog is still stuck with the allergy.

Antihistamines can offer relief from certain inhalant allergies. Additives containing omega-3 and omega-6 fatty acids often help because they address the inflammation that causes the itching.

Desensitization is a slow, expensive process, and although some dogs improve, there's no guarantee it will work. (It didn't work on one of my allergy-prone Goldens.)

TIP

Some Golden breeders and owners have had success using natural diets to conquer allergies. While such anecdotal evidence is not a substitute for long-term studies, it's worth investigating and may provide one more recourse for the frustrated owner and his poor allergic dog. See Chapter 10 for more on diet and nutrition.

Chapter **12**

The Ins and Outs of Bugs and Worms

L ike all furry beasts, your Golden is a natural magnet for an army of nasty little organisms, all determined to create a life of misery for your dog. Bugs and worms are nasty subjects, but you need to know about the more common parasitic critters that can invade or torment your Golden. This chapter will launch a major attack on parasites like fleas and ticks and a bunch of other nasty critters that plague most furry animals.

The Parade of Parasites

A *parasite* is an organism that lives in or on an organism of another species (its host) for its own survival. Some of these little devils invade the bodies of other animals; i.e., dogs, and even people.

REMEMBER

Most parasites are sneaky creatures that will appear the moment you relax your guard. To prevent a sudden infestation of the unknown, keep your dog and dog areas scrupulously clean. Examine his stools frequently for out-of-the-ordinary signs (such as loose or watery stools) and have your veterinarian perform a fecal exam twice a year. Call your vet immediately if your dog has any diarrhea, fatigue, vomiting, weight loss, chronic scratching, or bloating. Always consult your vet before using any anti-parasitic product on your dog or in his environment.

Internal parasites

Roundworms and hookworms account for about 90 percent of all internal parasitic infections.

Roundworms

Roundworms are the most common parasite found in dogs (cats, too). These little fellows migrate through the lungs, into the bronchial tubes, and then to the intestines, where they settle in for the long term. A heavy infestation will cause a pot-bellied appearance in your dog, a dull coat, and failure to gain weight. A large colony can seriously weaken and even kill a young puppy. Sometimes visible in the stool or vomit, adult roundworms (and hookworms, see next section) appear as small to large long, spaghetti-like strings that are off-white to tan in color. They compete for the dog's dinner, robbing him of valuable nutrition and leading to possible starvation even though the animal is eating large amounts of food. Infected dogs shed the microscopic roundworm eggs in their feces. Other dogs may become infected by sniffing or licking infected feces. Roundworm eggs can also be spread by other animals such as rodents, earthworms, cockroaches, and birds.

Roundworms are equal opportunity invaders and do not discriminate against humans. In poor sanitary conditions, they can be easily transmitted through fecal contact, especially when people fail to wash their hands after touching or cleaning up stools.

Primary human victims are children under 3 years old who are most apt to eat soil or other contaminated matter. (Think sandboxes.)

Most puppies are born with roundworms. Although most adult bitches (healthy ones, that is) don't have active colonies residing in their pregnant bodies, they can pass along the dormant parasites to the whelp still in the womb, or through their milk after the birth. The puppies pass the microscopic eggs in their stools, the bitch cleans it up, and the cycle repeats itself. Most breeders worm their pups routinely after 3 or 4 weeks of age. Your vet will prescribe a safe wormer depending on the types of parasites found in your puppy's stool.

WARNING

Symptoms of a minor to serious infestation include degrees of the following: dull, dry coat and skin; distended abdomen; loose, watery stools; insatiable appetite; dry cough; and abdominal discomfort with whimpering or crying.

Treatment consists of oral medication in two doses, one for the adult roundworm, and a second for the undeveloped larvae.

For prevention, schedule twice-yearly fecal exams, follow careful clean-up procedures, and maintain a consistently clean environment. You can also control roundworms with regular use of heartworm preventives. (See "Flea and tick preventives" later in this chapter.)

Hookworms

Although second on the parasitic popularity scale, hookworms are the most harmful of all canine intestinal parasites, especially in puppies. Like roundworms, they can be passed through the mother, through fecal contact, and can also enter by burrowing into the animal's exposed skin. They take up residence in the dog's intestines, but attach to the intestinal walls to suck blood rather than digesting the dog's food, resulting in severe anemia and even death in very young pups.

WARNING

Symptoms include bloody diarrhea; a dull, dry coat; weight loss; weakness; distended abdomen; and insatiable appetite. However, in otherwise healthy adult dogs, no symptoms may appear.

Treatment consists of oral medication in two doses.

For prevention, schedule twice-yearly fecal exams and keep a strict sanitary environment. As with roundworms, you can control hookworms with regular use of heartworm preventatives (see the "Heartworm" section, later in this chapter).

Tapeworms

Tapeworms come from fleas. Dogs can get one of six types of tapeworms by eating an infected flea or an intermediate host — a rodent, bird, or critter (or part of one) that carries the flea. (Goldens are notorious for gobbling up dead birds and bunny parts.) Tapeworms look like wiggly grains of rice. Many dog owners discover their dog is infected when they see the worm segments in the dog's stool, or in a worst-case scenario, crawling in the fur around his anal area. Tapeworm segments can also contaminate rugs and furniture and the dog's bedding.

WARNING

Symptoms include increased appetite and weight loss, alternating diarrhea and constipation, and chewing at the rectal area. Healthy adult dogs may show no signs other than mild diarrhea.

In my own experience with tapeworms (which is considerable because I live in the country and my Goldens are forever foraging for some dead or rotting animal part), my dogs have never developed diarrhea, but I'm sure that's because I find them *early*. Not to brag, but I'm *always* looking at their stools!

Treatment includes oral medication.

For prevention, practice rigid flea control, inspect your dog's fresh stools frequently, and maintain a sanitary dog and people environment. If possible, don't allow your Golden to eat potential host creatures. (Lots of luck!)

Whipworms

Dogs acquire whipworms by ingesting the eggs through either direct fecal contact or microscopic fecal matter on their coat or feet. Whipworms are tough to diagnose and may require more than one fecal exam. They are also very resistant to many disinfectants used to destroy the larvae.

WARNING

Symptoms include watery, slimy, or bloody diarrhea, which can be intermittent; increased appetite; weight loss; a dull, dry coat; and abdominal pain.

Treatment consists of oral medication.

For prevention, keep the dog's living area clean and dry with good exposure to sunlight. You also can prevent whipworms with heartworm preventive.

Heartworm

This one will kill your dog if not diagnosed and treated. Heartworm occurs when an infected mosquito bites your dog and deposits the heartworm larvae into the animal's bloodstream. The larvae migrate to the body tissues, where they spend 3 or 4 months maturing into small adult worms. From there, they make their way into a vein, move to the heart, and set up housekeeping in the right side of the heart as sexually mature worms. They mate inside the heart; the female worm can produce up to 5,000 microfilariae in a single day. That colony will sit and wait for the next mosquito bite so that they can hop a ride and continue the same life cycle in another dog.

Adult heartworms will reach lengths of 4 to 12 inches in the heart and arteries of the lungs. The results are obvious: decreased circulation, heart failure, and ultimately, your own heartbreak.

WARNING

Symptoms of heartworm disease may not appear for up to a year after infection first occurs. The most constant sign is a soft, deep cough, which gets worse with exercise. The dog will become listless and tire easily and lose weight. His coat will become dry and dull, and he may cough up bloody sputum. Treatment is expensive and risky, but without it, the dog will die.

Heartworm medication will prevent the disease, but your dog must be tested annually for the disease before taking any preventive medication. Why? The medication will kill any heartworms present, and if the dog already has a large colony residing in his heart, they will die there and clog his heart and lungs.

Your vet will prescribe medication that is appropriate for your geographic area. Dogs who live in warm climates where mosquitoes thrive all year should be kept on year-round medication. In North America, heartworm is found in all 50 states. In areas that experience seasonal changes, use preventives only during hot, humid months when mosquitoes are present. In cold climates (that is, no mosquitoes), medication isn't necessary. Skip the maps that suggest giving a preventive during certain months and use common sense. No mosquitoes, no medication.

Your puppy was born heartworm free. Discuss preventive medication on your first visit with his veterinarian.

Giardia

Giardia is a one-celled parasite, not a worm, bacteria, or virus. It can be found in soil, food, or water that has been contaminated with feces from infected animals or humans. Dogs, being dogs, may ingest infected stools or swallow infected water in public places, including kennels, dog parks, pet supply stores, and animal shelters. These nasty parasites are capable of passing from cattle to dogs, dogs to humans, and so on down the contagion chain. The microscopic cysts attach to the dog's small intestine, and can be fatal in very young pups.

Symptoms include severe, watery, or persistent extra-smelly diarrhea that may occasionally contain blood, and dehydration.

Treatment includes long-term medication, most commonly metronidazole (Flagyl) and/or fenbendazole (Panacur). Reinfection is not uncommon. The parasite is hard to diagnose because it shrinks after shedding in the stool and may not be present or detectable in every stool sample, so further testing may be necessary.

For disinfecting surfaces such as floors or crates, you can use chlorine bleach at a rate of 1–2 cups per gallon of water. The longer the disinfectant stays on the surface, the better the chances that all cysts will be killed.

The most effective prevention is through strict sanitation of the dog's living area, and by avoiding contact with possible contamination in lakes and ponds frequented by wildlife. For obvious reasons, this is especially important with young puppies.

Coccidia

Coccidia are single-celled organisms that pack a wallop that belies their size. Coccidia is spread through the feces or through contaminated food or water. It can also be passed from a nursing dam to her whelp. It develops quickly in the dog or pup's intestines. Diagnosis requires fresh stools and special testing procedures designed to reveal this type of parasite. My introduction to coccidia was brutal when three pups in my 4-week-old litter of Goldens suddenly became listless and presented watery yellow diarrhea. After three high-speed runs to my veterinarian, several days of subcutaneous (under the skin) hydration, and round-the-clock neonatal care, we all prevailed triumphant, although I was by then considerably weaker than the pups!

WARNING

Symptoms include loose, watery stools; listlessness; vomiting; and weight loss.

Treatment consists of oral medication that contains sulfamethazine in pill or liquid form. It must be quick and aggressive, but is usually successful.

For prevention, practice conscientious hygiene in your dog's living environment, keeping it dry and clean, with good exposure to sunlight.

REMEMBER

If you haven't noticed by now, a scrupulously clean environment is critical to your puppy and adult dog's overall health.

External parasites

If it's not bad enough that you and your poor dog may have to deal with creepy crawlers on the inside, there's more. External parasites include fleas, ticks, and other mighty mites.

Fleas

Holding steady as the first and foremost canine adversary, the flea, along with the cockroach, has outmaneuvered all attempts at its extermination. Under the right conditions (warm and humid) one adult flea can produce 25,000 fleas in 30 days.

TIP

It's almost guaranteed that you and your dog will encounter fleas at least once during his lifetime. If you hope to wage a winning battle, you first must understand the enemy.

Adult fleas who have had their first blood meal must dine every 24 hours in order to survive. For that reason, and their own convenience, most adult fleas will remain on their food source, which is your dog or other warm-blooded animal.

The following describes the life cycle of a typical flea population:

1. The eggs will hatch into first-stage larvae within 21 days.
2. The first-stage larvae will mature into second-stage pupae from 9 to 200 days.
3. The second-stage pupae can become adults in just a few days or take as long as 9 months, depending on their food source, and will live in the environment rather than on the dog.

Most eggs are laid on the dog and then fall off onto your carpet, bedding, furniture, or grass, where they move along in their life cycle.

TIP

You can find out if you have fleas in your carpet or house by donning a pair of white socks and walking around the house for a couple of hours. If you end up with black specks on those socks, it's a good bet you have fleas. Double-check by scraping the specks onto white paper and wetting them with water. If the specks turn red or reddish brown, they're flea droppings filled with blood.

FLEA AND TICK PREVENTIVES

With such huge numbers and so many life stages, the flea battle is a tough war with several strategies. Fortunately, flea prevention and eradication has become easier, thanks to modern dog-science. Today, in addition to traditional flea management, several revolutionary new flea weapons put effective flea (and in some products, tick) control in every dog house. They are available from pet supply stores, pet pharmacies, and online.

WARNING

These products contain toxic chemicals that can produce mild to severe side effects and should be used with extreme caution. Although touted as safe for your dog, they remain controversial due to short-term, and possible long-term, side effects. Home remedies such as garlic, apple cider vinegar, and essential oils have been used, but have not been proven to be totally or permanently effective. Read the labels and do your research. Check with your vet for recommendations.

>> **Frontline Plus (Fipronil):** Frontline Plus is a safe *adulticide* (a product that disables the flea's nervous system). A spot-on treatment that is applied to the dog's skin between the shoulder blades, it provides 100 percent control within 24 hours. The dog, however, must be kept dry for about 48 hours after application. The best part for water dogs like Goldens is that Frontline Plus is water-friendly, so after the initial 48 hours, your dog can swim without reducing its effectiveness.

Frontline Plus does not enter the dog's bloodstream; it spreads across the body through the hair follicles and oil glands in the skin, killing fleas within 4 hours of contact and ticks within 12 hours. (Blessedly, the flea does not have to bite the dog.) One application will control fleas for up to 90 days on dogs and ticks for up to 30 days. It's safe for puppies *in appropriate doses* (be sure to check with your vet before using). It is now available over the counter. Generics are also available, but can pose the risk of side effects.

- » **K9 Advantage II (Imidacloporid):** Advantage II is a safe spot-on treatment applied between the shoulder blades, which, like Frontline, quickly spreads across the surface of the dog's skin. Also an adulticide, it kills 98 to 100 percent of adult fleas within 24 hours. It is not absorbed into the dog's bloodstream and remains effective for 30 days. (Advantage II does not offer tick prevention.)

- » **Seresto:** This relatively new preventive is a polymer matrix flea and tick collar that offers a continuous supply of two active ingredients: imadicloprid and flumethrin, and is effective for 8-month protection against fleas and ticks. Seresto protects your dog from fleas, flea eggs, flea larvae, ticks, and sarcoptic mange. It remains effective even if your Golden swims or splashes in the backyard pool.

- » **NexGard** is a bite-sized, beef-flavored chewable tablet used to kill adult fleas before they lay eggs to help prevent infestations; it also kills ticks. NexGard can be given with food or on an empty stomach. The most common adverse reactions recorded in clinical trials were vomiting, itching, diarrhea, lethargy, and lack of appetite. NexGard is said to be safe for dogs and puppies who weigh 4 pounds or more and who are at least 8 weeks of age.

  NexGard, the brand name for the insecticide afoxolaner, targets and kills adult fleas before they can lay eggs. NexGard kills Lone Star ticks, black-legged ticks (deer ticks), American dog ticks and brown dog ticks.

The following traditional remedies now take a back seat to the popular products like Frontline and Advantage. Some are less effective, and often more toxic, than the products discussed above, and you should know their names and the dangers they pose to your dog (if in doubt, consult your vet):

- » **Flea collars (other than Seresto):** Traditional flea collars contain time-released insecticides and will not control a serious flea infestation. Flea collars may also cause allergic reactions if used long term. Always remove prior to bathing and never combine with dips or sprays.

- » **Sprays and powders:** Although they're easily applied, they will not penetrate oily or heavy coats. They are ineffective in serious infestations and do not provide long-term protection. Never combine with other flea preventives. Read the product labels carefully and watch for side effects.

- » **Shampoos:** Shampoos will kill fleas if properly used, but they also contain strong chemicals, so be sure to rinse them off very thoroughly.

- » **Dips:** Dips contain organophosphates and are highly toxic. They should not be used on your Golden. If there are extreme circumstances where your vet recommends it, my recommendation is to get another opinion before dipping.

Combs: Flea combs are useful for short-term removal; however, because they have 32 tiny teeth per inch, flea combs are difficult to use on heavy- or long-coated dogs.

» **Premise sprays:** Sprays applied to the house or yard kill adult fleas or inhibit larvae growth. Use with extreme caution. Your dog can inhale the product or get it on his skin.

» **Foggers:** Forget it. They don't work and cannot be used with animals or humans present. Foggers do not penetrate carpet fibers, so they will not kill imbedded flea eggs. They do, however, release pesticides, which, while killing fleas, also leave residue on all exposed surfaces. Human and canine exposure to those pesticides remains long after the area has been fogged, making them unsafe to use.

NEVER use pesticide sprays and/or any products that contain organophosphates and carbamates. These are highly toxic and easily absorbed into the animal's system, and can be fatal. They have been proven to cause cancer.

WHAT DO ALL THOSE TERMS MEAN?

Here are some terms you should know when evaluating traditional flea remedies. Pay special attention to the key word here: *toxic.*

- **Amitraz** is a toxic chemical used in tick collars. It kills ticks, not fleas, and can be used in combination with other flea and tick products. (Many others cannot.)

- **Organophosphates** and **carbamates** are toxic chemicals that are proven to cause cancer. However, many are still used in flea-killing products. They are absorbed into the animal's system and can be fatal, especially if mixed with certain other flea products. Forget using with caution. Do not use at all! If you don't know what the ingredient is, ask your veterinarian.

- **Pyrethins** are a natural plant extract from the chrysanthemum family found in Africa. It's easily metabolized when taken orally, so it offers lower toxicity to pets.

- **Permethrins** are a synthetic pyrethin with longer residual action, commonly used with quick-killing natural pyrethins to control fleas and ticks. Permethrins and pyrethins are fast-acting adult flea-killers with low to moderate residual effects (retained in the dog's system).

As a precaution, remember the cardinal rule of fighting fleas: *Always* read labels and directions carefully and *never* combine flea preventives (such as a flea collar with a topical flea spray or oral medication) without first checking with your vet. For example, never place a flea collar on a dog who has been recently bathed, or — heaven forbid — dipped. Some of those chemical combinations can be fatal! In addition, do your homework before using flea products. The Internet and Google can provide a plethora of information, all of which will make you a more informed Golden owner.

Some dog owners are firm believers in natural remedies such as garlic, brewer's yeast, eucalyptus, citronella, or pennyroyal oil, and claim to have success with them. Although no scientific research exists that brewer's yeast and garlic actually prevent fleas, both will contribute to good health, so they can't hurt. Some oils, however, can be toxic if ingested or improperly used. Do not combine any of these products with other flea-control products. These are uncharted waters — why take chances?

TIP

Get the jump on fleas and start prevention *before* they find your dog. Use a three-pronged attack that covers your dog, your house, and your yard. For your dog, consult your veterinarian and use whatever flea preventive she recommends. Groom your dog with a flea comb (dipped in soapy water to snag and drown the fleas) after every trip outdoors, and use it weekly to check for fleas and flea dirt. If you find suspicious dark specks on his underside, between his hind legs, or on his back at the base of his tail, rub them with a moist tissue. Flea dirt will turn a reddish-brown color.

In your house, routinely vacuum and clean all floors, furniture, and beds, especially areas where your Golden sleeps, plays, or rests. This simple household chore is more effective than pesticides in controlling fleas. Drop a 2-inch section of a flea collar in the vacuum bag to kill any fleas or larvae you might pick up.

Handling fleas in the yard is harder. Ask your vet for safe and affordable remedies.

YOUR PERSONAL FLEA TRAP

If you suspect fleas in one or more rooms, plant a flea trap. At night, put a small lamp on the floor, place a shallow bowl of soapy water beneath the light wherever you think fleas are hiding, and leave the light on all night. The fleas will jump at the light and fall into the soapy water. They will be unable to climb out of the water and will drown. If you don't find fleas in the morning, move the bowl to different rooms and various areas of large rooms to continue your detective work.

You can buy similar flea traps at your local pet store if you don't want to create your own.

Ticks

Modern science has yet to discover why ticks were created in the first place. These ugly bloodsuckers are everywhere, just waiting for some warm-blooded creature to hop on to.

Ticks are major carriers of disease and must be removed as soon as possible to prevent infection. If you spend time outdoors, especially in the woods, check your dog (and yourself) afterward. Tick-borne diseases do not discriminate and affect humans as well as dogs.

Ticks love warm, moist places, so confine your walks and play to open sunny areas and use a tick preventive.

Safe tick removal is also important. You want to avoid crushing the tick so that its bloody contents don't spurt out and contaminate you or your dog. Follow these steps to safely remove a tick:

1. Spray the tick with a bit of alcohol to make it loosen its mouth parts that are attached to the skin.

2. Use tweezers (or the little gadget in the Tip below) to gently pull the tick straight out (not up) from the bite site.

3. Drop the tick in a jar of alcohol or bleach or flush it down the toilet.

TIP

A clever little gadget called Pro-Tick Remedy is the easiest and safest means of tick removal. It always (well, almost always) gets the head out, too. You can order from several sources on the Internet.

Here are some tick-borne diseases:

» **Lyme disease:** Named for the Connecticut city of Lyme where it was first discovered in 1977, Lyme disease is found today in every state. The current vaccine for this disease is still controversial, has side effects, and is not recommended, so the best protection against infection is still prevention.

Spread through at least two species of the tiny deer tick, Lyme disease attacks dogs as aggressively as it attacks humans, invading the joints and causing painful swelling, lameness, and lethargy. Prolonged exposure can cause permanent damage to the heart and kidneys, so early diagnosis and prompt treatment are important. False positives are common in the testing process, and your vet may have to run two or three titer tests to confirm a diagnosis. Several weeks of the antibiotic tetracycline is the most common treatment.

Lyme arthritis is the most treatable form of the disease, but many affected dogs have recurring symptoms even after treatment. Cardiac and neurological disorders respond to antibiotics, but kidney Lyme disease is almost always fatal.

For more information about Lyme disease, contact the Lyme Disease Foundation at 800-886-LYME, which is a 24-hour hotline, or go to www.lyme.org.

>> **Ehrlichiosis:** Similar to Lyme disease, ehrlichiosis is transmitted through the bite of the brown dog tick, with at least one other tick species under suspicion. The disease attacks the blood platelets and may produce Lyme-type symptoms of mild fever, appetite loss, swollen lymph nodes, and abnormal discharge from the eyes and/or nose. The symptoms may come and go, making an accurate diagnosis difficult. Current treatment involves aggressive use of antibiotics, and affected dogs are more prone to reinfection. Ehrlichiosis is more common in tick-prone areas, so tick prevention and prompt tick removal is still the best preventive measure.

In 1994, ehrlichiosis was also discovered in humans. It can be fatal in both dogs and people, with advanced stages causing kidney failure and respiratory problems, which makes early diagnosis critical.

>> **Rocky Mountain spotted fever (RMSF):** Its name implies its origin and whereabouts. Symptoms of RMSF include fever, bloody urine, loose or bloody stools, difficulty breathing, and unexplained nose bleeds, and usually show up within 2 weeks of a tick bite. See your veterinarian for tests to confirm infection. RMSF can be fatal if untreated.

Ear mites

Mites are less visible than ticks but are just as pesky. These microscopic eight-legged parasites love to feast on the various body parts of the dog.

Adult ear mites settle into the lining of the ear canal, causing irritation and extreme itching. Your dog will scratch and dig and try to shove his paw into his ear. He'll shake his head a lot and maybe even walk a little crookedly. Mites usually produce a smelly, brownish wax in the ear. A vet exam is necessary to diagnose these mites.

A regimen of 6 to 8 weeks of ear drops will squelch the infestation. Mites are transmitted by direct contact and are highly contagious, so they are often shared with other canine family members. If one of your Goldens has ear mites, have everyone in your dog family checked by your vet, and give each one a thorough mite-specific shampoo to whack any stray pests that might be wandering around on the dog. Ear mites are not transmissible to humans.

Mange mites

There are three cousins in the mange mite family, each one rendering its own brand of havoc on your dog:

>> **Sarcoptic mange:** Sarcoptes (also known as scabies) can be devastating. This crab-shaped mite burrows under the dog's skin to lay its eggs, causing continuous, intense itching. The infected animal will be miserable and will scratch, dig, and literally chew himself raw until much of his body is scabby and hairless. The damage is often compounded by secondary bacterial infections resulting from the open sores.

   Scabies mites are microscopic and may require several deep skin scrapings to confirm their presence. Your vet can prescribe proper medication and treatment. Scabies is highly contagious to humans as well as other dogs, so if you develop an itchy rash around your midsection, call your vet before you call your physician.

>> **Demodectic mange:** Both localized (confined to parts of the face) and generalized (invades other body parts), this type of mange is considered by some to be the scourge of the mange family. Sometimes called "red mange" or "puppy mange," it is passed to puppies during the nursing process. Demodex usually exists harmlessly in the animal's hair follicles and oil glands. Then, for some still-unknown reason, one or more pups become stressed for who knows why, and the mites multiply in the coat, causing bare patches around the eyes, face, neck, and front legs. If itching occurs, scratching can lead to secondary bacterial infections of the skin, further stressing the young victim's immature immune system.

   Early diagnosis and treatment are important to keep the demodex under control and localized. That includes superb health care and a stress-free environment to minimize the impact on the pup's immune system.

   Despite an owner's best efforts, about 10 percent of localized demodex progresses into generalized demodex (see the following sidebar).

>> **Cheyletiella mites:** These dandruff mites are often called "walking dandruff" because they travel across the surface of the skin, munching lightly as they move along, causing mild itching and flaking on the head and along the back. Your dog will, of course, bite and scratch those areas. Your vet can control the condition with prescription treatments, and follow-up shampoos or sprays to target any leftover mites who escape the treatment.

GENERALIZED DEMODEX

When localized demodex develops into generalized demodex, the hair loss will spread across the puppy's body, causing inflamed and itchy bald patches, secondary infections, and a serious condition called deep pyoderma. Generalized demodex is extremely difficult to control, requiring special bathing, skin scrapings, dips, and antibiotics, and all while the animal is in great pain due to skin damage from the infection. Generalized demodex can sometimes be controlled, but it is rarely cured. Treatment is long term requiring intense management. In some cases, veterinarians may suggest euthanasia to end the animal's suffering.

Thank goodness this condition is noninfectious.

Because it is believed that there is a strong hereditary predisposition for generalized demodex, all dogs with the disease should be sterilized. In fact, some experts recommend that parents and siblings of affected dogs also be removed from breeding programs to protect future generations from the agony of the disease.

IN THIS CHAPTER

» **Grooming from the skin out**

» **Assembling a grooming tool kit**

» **Understanding the importance of dental hygiene**

» **Giving your dog a bath**

» **Cleaning paws, ears, and other areas**

Chapter **13**

Golden Grooming Basics

Grooming your Golden Retriever is about more than keeping your dog pretty or handsome. It's also about hygiene and good health. It's all body parts, not just the furry coat. Your own hygiene means more than a shampoo. It's teeth, toes, underarms, and other appendages. Your dog has those same needs, too. In this chapter, we'll dig out the brush and comb and groom your Golden buddy.

Grooming Is a Year-Round Job

A well-groomed coat is very important all year long. The flow of air through a dog's coat helps regulate his body temperature, and that process is hampered if the coat is dirty, matted, or full of mud. During winter months, we have to pile on warm coats and heavy blankets. Not your Golden! He is blessed with a double coat of long outer hair and a downy undercoat that will protect him from those freezing temperatures. Keep it clean and well-brushed.

WARNING

Summer grooming is just as important as winter care. Professional groomers tell horror stories about double-coated dogs like Golden Retrievers and other heavy-coated breeds like Samoyeds that arrive for grooming with their heavy coats hiding inch-deep holes in their flesh from maggot eggs. Flies love to visit unclean dogs and lay their eggs in filthy or badly matted fur. When the larvae mature, they eat into the dog's skin or move up into the rectum. Severe cases can destroy huge areas of flesh and require surgery to repair the wounds. There are reported cases of dogs who died because the problem was so severe, but the owner never bothered to brush their dog or look under all that matted fur, so the problem was invisible to them.

Grooming does more than untangle and remove dead hair. It also stimulates the oil glands, which keeps the skin healthy, reduces dander, and keeps that Golden fur coat gleaming. It's also a weekly body check for lumps and bumps and critters that hide in the skin and coat (especially important during summer months). It's weekly ear checks, and cleaning those ears whenever necessary. It's weekly dental care and monthly pedicures. If all of this sounds like overkill, remember, you're the one who bought this dog!

JUST FOR FUN

Your attitude toward grooming can make it fun instead of inconvenient. Most Goldens love the hands-on attention involved in grooming, so think of this as bonding rather than a burden. It's one more aspect of living the Golden life. Your toddler eventually grew up to bathe and shower without help. Your Golden never will.

Your Grooming Tool Kit

You'll need more than that slicker brush you bought when your Golden puppy first came home. You'll also need a steel comb with wide and narrow-spaced teeth, a flea comb, a mat rake, nail clippers, and small sharp scissors. Some Golden owners use a pin brush. I also have a shedding comb, but I end up using my steel comb-slicker brush combination instead. (I also have one of those grooming gloves that collects loose hair when you pet or rub your dog, but I never use it. I like the feel of my dog's fur between my fingers!) Pick your breeder's or your groomer's brain for good tool choices.

Now get out that brush and groom! Brushing will be easier if you follow a pattern on the dog. Always brush with the grain of the coat and start at his rear, working in small sections at a time (in Figure 13-1, this owner is working on her puppy's ears). Part the coat all the way to the skin as you brush along. Use one hand to hold the hair aside, and then brush from the skin outward through the hair. Work in continuous sections, always brushing upward and forward. Pay special attention to the feathering on the legs and behind the ears, and on and under the tail, as these areas are more prone to matting.

Remove mats and tangles slowly without yanking so that you won't hurt your dog. On larger mats, rub in a few drops of a canine hair conditioner (you can also use a horse conditioner) and then work gently with a comb or mat rake. A slicker brush should handle smaller mats. If you must resort to scissors, cut upward at an angle into the mat rather than a straight-across angle cut, as that would leave an unsightly gap in the fur. (Even if he's not a show dog, you don't want him looking nerdy!) While you're brushing, check for fleas and ticks, rashes, hot spots, and other skin problems.

Close Encounters of the Furry Kind.

TIP

Your choice of scissors can be confusing and overwhelming — straight cut, curved, thinning, ear and nose, bent shank, and styling — and some cost more than a designer haircut. Most pet owners don't need elaborate shears to neaten up their Golden. I use a good-quality, medium-priced thinning shears for everything from ears to toes with good results. But then I'm not prepping show dogs. I just want my furries to look tidy.

Don't Forget the Paws

Feet and nails are the most neglected home-groomed areas. I see too many Goldens with paws that look like mops, with long hair spraying from between the toes. Can you picture those feet wet or full of mud?

Hairy feet not only look sloppy, but they collect burrs, ice balls, and mud — all uncomfortable for the dog. Trimmed and tidy feet also track less mud, snow, and ice into the house.

Clip the hair around the foot and between the toes and pads, cutting it level with the bottom of the pads. (The owner in Figure 13-2 is using a thinning shears to clip the hair beneath the foot pads.)

You can't work on the feet without tending to the nails. There's great value in 16 well-trimmed nails. They're easier on your furniture and clothing, plus think of your dog playing with your kids and grandkids. It's also healthier for the dog because nails that are too long can splinter or tear and cause sore feet. Long nails can also cause the toes to splay and spread apart. In the long term, that will damage the structure of the foot, which eventually affects the dog's legs. It's amazing what a good pedicure can prevent.

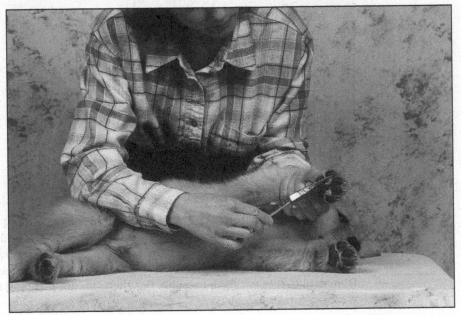

FIGURE 13-2:
It's easier to trim your puppy or dog's feet if he is lying on his side.

Close Encounters of the Furry Kind.

There's a confusing variety of nail clippers for your dog in the pet department. Ask your vet which one he recommends, and ask him to demonstrate how to use the clippers properly. It's included in your puppy's visit.

The awful truth is that most Goldens, actually most dogs of any breed, do not like to have their feet handled. (This might be an ancestral thing . . . who knows.) So, it's best to begin the process when your Golden is still a pup. At first, you may have to settle for one foot or just a few nails. Take your time, and just nip the tip of the nail to avoid cutting the *quick* (the pink vein visible down the center of the nail). If that accidentally happens, the quick will bleed, your pup or adult Golden will instantly object, and you may have to end the session. To staunch the bleeding, apply a few drops of Kwik-Stop styptic powder or liquid (or use your own shaving styptic). A bleeding nail is not a tragedy, but it is to the dog, and probably for you, too (I'm no exception!).

Some Goldens have black or very dark nails where the quick is not visible. If you can't see the quick, hold a flashlight beam directly under the nail to reveal the lighter line of the vein. If you're not sure, make small clips in the tip or curved part of the nail. Always cut at a 45-degree angle with the clipper facing the same direction as the toes.

Trimming a small amount of nail often is better than trying to cut neglected nails that have grown too long. Walking on cement sidewalks or running and playing in concrete kennel runs helps keep nails ground down. Indoor dogs will need more frequent pedicures.

Handle your Golden's paws frequently during play and petting, and give him a food reward during and after trimming so that he associates it with good times. That can help to minimize (sort of) his reaction to nail trimming. If you dread this chore, or it is or has become a problem for you, have your vet or groomer keep his nails trimmed regularly. Some major pet supply stores also offer grooming services that include nail trimming.

WARNING

Never let your dog's nails get so overgrown that they curl downward and under the toes. That can cause deformed feet and damaged foot tendons. You will need a veterinarian or very experienced groomer to fix those nasty nails.

Be a Plaque Attacker

Home dental care is vital to your Golden's long-term health. Neglected oral hygiene will lead to periodontal disease, which is severe and irreversible. Once the disease has advanced, it will cause chronic pain (which your very stoic dog will instinctively hide, so you will be unaware of it), inflamed gums, tissue destruction, and bone loss.

Plaque and tartar are perfect hosts for bacteria, which break down gum tissue and leads to all the above oral damage. Worse yet, it can also cause systemic health problems that can affect the liver, kidneys, heart, and lungs. Your pet does not deserve such a fate.

Gum disease often has no outward signs or symptoms. Noxious breath can be one indicator of tooth decay and infected gums. Symptoms of more advanced disease can include bleeding or red gums, loose teeth, bloody or ropey saliva, chewing on one side of the mouth, and blood in his water bowl or on his chew toys.

Studies show that 80 percent of dogs show early signs of oral disease by age 3. Scary, isn't it? Another survey conducted at one veterinarian congress in Vancouver, B.C., determined that dog owners can literally add 3 to 5 years to their dogs' lives simply be providing routine dental care. Isn't that reason enough to preserve that Golden grin?

Prevention is just a toothbrush away!

You don't need a lot of fancy tools to work on your dog's teeth. Cleaning teeth is more elbow grease than gadgetry. You can use a soft-bristled toothbrush and chicken-flavored toothpaste made just for dogs. (People toothpaste will make him sick.) Brush his teeth the same way you would do your own, from the gums down with gentle strokes (see Figure 13-3). If he objects, try wrapping a gauze pad around your index finger and rubbing it across his teeth instead. If your Golden has learned to accept your hand in his mouth since puppyhood, dental maintenance shouldn't be a struggle.

Obviously, daily brushing would be best. But in the real dog-people world, that's sometimes not possible. Twice weekly is probably a more reachable goal.

If your Golden isn't fond of toothbrushes or gauze pads, try a finger brush, which is a flexible toothbrush that fits over your finger. You can find it in most pet supply catalogs and pet stores.

Dry dog food will help scrub his teeth as he chews. And plaque-attacker chew products like sterilized hard bones and Nylabones, hard Kong toys, and balls where you can hide treats will help keep plaque under control. Keep his chewie bucket full. Please, no animal bones or cow or pig hooves, which are not only stinky, but can also fracture his teeth.

Always include a dental checkup in your annual visit to the vet. Some dog's teeth may need professional cleaning. Your vet should advise you when that is necessary.

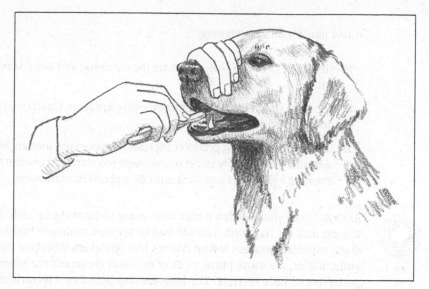

Ear Care

Ear problems are easy to prevent. Just pay strict attention to ear hygiene during your weekly grooming sessions. Clean ears are pink and odorless and require cleaning only when you notice a change. Infected ears usually emit a foul odor and may have a rancid-smelling discharge. The ear canal will be red and inflamed and/or contain debris or a dark, smelly, waxy substance.

If your dog is scratching at his ears or shaking his head more than usual, or tilting it to one side, it may be time for an ear cleaning. However, if the ear is red and inflamed, smells yeasty, or if he is in pain, these symptoms could indicate an ear infection, ear mites, or allergies. Do not attempt to clean them as it can create more problems. Take him to your veterinarian.

Ear cleaning is really pretty simple and requires few supplies. You'll need a quality ear-cleaning solution and cotton balls. No cotton swabs, ever. They can push dirt and debris deeper into the ear, and even cause damage to the ear's inner structure.

If your dog is anxious, a few tasty treats can make him more accepting of the process. First, fill his ear canal with the cleanser, then gently massage the ear for about 30 seconds. You should hear a squishing sound as the liquid dislodges the buildup of wax and dirt. Then let him shake his head and prepare yourself for a small shower from the resulting spray. When he is done shaking his head, use the cotton balls to gently wipe the ear canal. If he shows signs of discomfort or pain, discontinue the process and see your vet.

A few don't's on ear cleaning:

>> Never use peroxide — it can irritate the ear tissue and even damage the ear canal.

>> Too-frequent cleaning can cause excessive irritation. Clean only when necessary.

>> Use only ear-cleaning products approved by your veterinarian. Most are available in pet supply stores. Homemade solutions can contain harmful or irritating ingredients and most don't do a good job of cleaning.

TIP

Always check your Golden's ears after every swimming session. Dry the inside of the ear and ear flap with a cotton ball to prevent moisture buildup. Floppy-eared dogs, especially water- loving critters like retrievers who love to wallow in ponds and puddles, are more prone to dirty ears and recurrent ear infections than those perky-eared little terriers. The long ear flap acts like a terrarium cover that prevents air flow and keeps the ear canal moist and ripe for organism growth.

WARNING

Dog owners make two mistakes when fighting ear infections. They postpone going to the vet until the ear has worsened and the bacteria have multiplied into a more severe infection (what they can't see doesn't appear serious), or they stop treatment too soon, before the infection has been killed. If treatment starts as soon as possible, you will avoid secondary problems, and the cure is faster and easier on the dog and your pocketbook. Always continue treatment for the prescribed period, or the problem will surely reoccur.

Bathing Your Dog

Bathing is an area that's often overdone (in dogs, that is!). Most Goldens need a bath every few months, although some fastidious owners have their Goldens professionally groomed and bathed every month. The dogs usually don't need it, but it makes their humans happy, and it does help to minimize shedding.

Goldens may need more frequent bathing in the summer if they swim in muddy ponds or have an oily undercoat that tends to smell. Two of my Goldens (who happened to be related) sometimes had an unpleasant body odor that is unique to certain types of skin and coat. (As a result, in the summer our bedroom often smelled like you-know-what.)

TIP

Your Golden's coat must be brushed and dematted *before* you bathe him. Mats tend to set in like cement when wet, and you'll have one heck of a time getting through them after a good lathering.

The after-bath process is just as important as the bath itself. If his coat is not thoroughly dried and brushed out, the damp undercoat can attract fungal and staph infections. Wet is the first half of bathing; drying is the second part.

WARNING

Some ponds and lakes can be vulnerable to a toxin called blue-green algae during the hot summer months. These toxic "blooms" are actually a *poisonous bacteria* known as cyanobacteria. It often gives the appearance of algae when clumped together in bodies of water. Toxic algae is often found in non-flowing freshwater during hot seasons with little rainfall. Toxic algae can even grow in backyard pools or decorative ponds if they are not routinely cleaned. Swimming or playing in infected water can be toxic to canines and is most often fatal. Several fatalities were documented in 2019, with exposure to toxic algae suspected in more deaths. If you think he has come in contact with blue-green algae, rinse him off immediately with clean water and call your vet at once.

Harmful algae blooms can be blue, vibrant green, brown, or red, and can be mistaken for paint floating on the water. Be aware the toxins are not always visible. Your water-loving Golden can ingest the toxin just by licking his paws or fur. Keep him out of water that appears dirty, foamy, or has mats on the surface of the water. Never let him drink out of ponds and lakes.

Wet the entire dog with lukewarm water (a shower-type sprayer works well) and suds the entire body. If you bathe him outdoors, your garden hose works, too, although the water won't be lukewarm. Outdoor bathing is obviously not possible in cold or winter weather, so move the chore indoors or use a grooming service. Some owners bathe their dogs in their personal shower space and claim it is easier on the dog as well as themselves. Just prepare yourself for a very wet bathroom!

Make sure you plug his ears with cotton balls and keep his eyes dry. I prefer a squirt or spray bottle to apply shampoo. Follow the directions for whatever shampoo you use (see the sidebar "Choosing a shampoo") and be sure to rinse thoroughly. Shampoo residue can irritate his skin. A warm water rinse may help loosen the dead hair.

Most Goldens are eager movers and shakers, especially after a bath, so wear grubby clothes and be prepared to get a bath yourself. Towel your dog dry, and then use your hair dryer to finish the job. If he air-dries in warm weather, just make sure that he dries completely.

CHOOSING A SHAMPOO

The variety of dog shampoos is as confusing as those made for humans. Choices include oatmeal, citrus, herbal, protein, tea tree, hypoallergenic, medicated, flea and tick, antibacterial, tearless, lusterizer — the list is endless. Ask your breeder, groomer, or veterinarian for suggestions.

One cleaning product I consider worth its shipping weight is a waterless shampoo. I use it often as a spot treatment when my Goldens roll in something smelly (emphasis on the word *often*). It saves me bending over the bathtub when I'm busy.

Never use human shampoos because they have a different pH formula that can dry or damage your dog's coat and skin. Order your shampoo from a groomer or a pet supply store.

Cleaning the Anal Sacs

You have to make sure that both ends of your Golden are clean and in good working condition. That includes his *anal glands*, which are two scent glands under his skin, one on each side of the anal opening. The gland pockets fill with fecal fluid, and when a dog eliminates, the sacs empty from the pressure of the expelled solid matter. Sometimes the fluid collects in the gland, and the dog becomes uncomfortable. That's when you see him scooting his rear end across your carpet doing the proverbial choo-choo — always in front of your nondog guests who will find it absolutely gross.

Not all dogs have anal glands that tend to fill and need to be "expressed." But if your dog has "rear-end issues," you should empty these stinky compartments before each bath, or every couple of months if bathing is less frequent. If you don't want to do it, have your veterinarian or groomer do it. Anal glands can become swollen and impacted if not emptied, which can lead to infection and even surgical correction, so regular tending is important.

The glands are at 4 o'clock and 8 o'clock on either side of the anus. Using your thumb and two fingers of one hand, press inward and upward in those spots to express the fluid contents. Place a paper towel over the opening when you squeeze, or you risk a nasty shot in the eyes. Trust me — it's *not* pleasant!

Chapter **14**

Caring for Your Senior Golden

L arge breeds like Golden Retrievers mark the beginning of their geriatric period at about 8 years of age. Your Golden may still look and act like a puppy, but don't be fooled. He's entering his sunset years.

Of course, you want to make his golden years as healthy as your own, and being a smart dog owner, you know that senior dogs need special care. Besides his checkup once a year, what else can you do to prolong his life and keep him healthy longer? This chapter explains common old age problems and gives you advice on how to add quality and hopefully longevity to your aging Golden's life. For starters, rigid weight control and proper oral hygiene are the two primary canine life extenders.

Slim and Trim

Obesity strains every major system of a canine's body and *will* take years off his life (see Chapters 10 and 11). As your Golden ages, his energy needs will decrease, so you should adjust his food portions accordingly as well as the type of food he eats. Overweight dogs need a higher-fiber, lower-fat diet. Most dogs over 8 years old who are not active in competition or working in the field should eat a "senior" diet designed for aging dogs. If you're changing diets, consult your veterinarian first.

TIP Do a rib check every month. You should be able to feel your dog's ribs with *light* pressure, but you shouldn't see his ribs. Even an extra 5 pounds puts added stress on older bones and joints.

Healthy Teeth and Gums

Just as important as his weight, good dental hygiene will add healthy years to your dog's life (see Chapter 13). Too many dogs suffer from heart, kidney, liver, or respiratory infection and disease, conditions that often start at the gum line, and could have been prevented with good dental hygiene. Gums that are loaded with plaque and tartar easily become infected. Left untreated, that bacteria will enter the bloodstream and attack a dog's vital organs.

Studies show that 85 percent of dogs over 6 years of age have some form of periodontal disease, which is an infection in the deep portions of the teeth and gums. If it's not treated promptly, the infection invades the body and can become life-threatening, especially in an older dog with an equally old immune system. The infection will attack his vital organs, resulting in heart, respiratory, kidney, or liver disease.

One prominent veterinarian tells of dogs in his practice who have come in for seemingly innocent gum or mouth problems such as an abscessed tooth. The bad tooth has caused a major infection in some vital organ, the owner doesn't even know it, and the dog is in effect dying. If that doesn't make you brush your dog's teeth, nothing will!

TIP An older dog's gums are often more pigmented than when he was a youngster. His teeth should still be white, although some yellowing is normal with age. Very pale or whitish gums are warning signs that say, "Take me to the veterinarian!" They are symptoms of a circulation problem that can be due to any number of serious and life-threatening conditions.

Exercise, Arthritis, and Your Aging Dog

Exercise is important at every life stage, but it is especially important for the senior dog. A senior dog who is sedentary for long periods will grow out of shape more quickly and will take longer to handle an exercise routine. However, geriatric exercise should be tailored to fit your dog's age and physical condition.

Walking and running are still the best maintenance workouts (the dogs in Figure 14-1 are enjoying a good run on the beach). Even the change of scenery will stimulate him mentally, and he'll be extra grateful for the time you spend together. Just be careful not to overdo it. Some Goldens have more heart than stamina and will press on even when exhausted. (Sound like someone you know and love?) If he seems to tire quickly or appears to be hurting the next day, slow down and see your vet.

FIGURE 14-1: Exercise is a primary ingredient for your dog's health.

Close Encounters of the Furry Kind.

Be conscious of your dog's mobility. If your old guy is stiff getting up in the morning or after heavy exercise, he may have arthritis or degenerative joint disease. Your vet should examine him and perhaps take x-rays and prescribe medication to reduce inflammation and ease pain. If steroids are prescribed, ask about side effects and watch for them. Steroids, especially used long-term, can create a whole new set of problems.

If your dog has arthritis, make sure that he has a soft, warm place to rest and sleep. If your Golden doesn't already have one (he should!), surprise him with one of the many cushy orthopedic dog beds, and put it in his favorite place and away from drafts. I guarantee he'll sleep like a baby. (Ummm, I mean, a puppy.) My old Golden has several beds all over the house, so she can be comfy whenever she's with me. For some reason, my other Goldens never even try to sleep on one of her beds.

TIP

Arthritic conditions are significantly more prevalent in obese dogs. Watch that diet!

If your senior Golden has trouble getting on or off the couch, his bed, or other favorite spot, treat him to a pet ramp, available at pet supply stores. You'll find a variety of pet ramps suitable for every dog and situation. Indulge your aging buddy.

Changes in Vision and Hearing

If you notice a change in your senior Golden's eyes or vision, it may be due to cataracts, genetic disease, or simply old age. In many cases, a veterinary ophthalmologist can surgically remove the cataracts and dramatically improve his vision.

Many geriatric dogs develop *lenticular sclerosis*, a hardening of the lens that causes a bluish-gray haze or tint in the eyes. It does not affect vision or require treatment. However, whenever you notice any change in your dog's eyes or vision, see your veterinarian to determine if it is a problem and whether it is treatable.

Some dogs grow deaf with age, while others never do. Try to distinguish between *selective hearing*, when he just wants to ignore you, and actual hearing loss. When my 13-year-old Golden stopped hearing the treat jar open, I knew she wasn't faking it. Like most hearing-impaired dogs, she startled easily, so I avoided sudden movements and gently stomped the floor before I touched or petted her so that she didn't jump. We developed a communication system of hand signals to say, "Time to come in," "Let's go," "I mean right now!" and other conversational commands.

WARNING

Beware of hearing loss in a "city" dog. He won't hear a car approaching on the street or in his driveway. I personally know of dogs who were killed because they were deaf and didn't hear the oncoming danger.

OLD DOG, NEW TRICKS?

Yes, you *can* teach an old dog new tricks — and good behavior! It may take more time and patience, mostly because you're working around previously learned (and possibly improper) behavior. But if you use logical and practical training methods, your older dog can learn all sorts of good manners as well as fun things to do with you.

Monitoring Lumps and Bumps

Some lumps and bumps are normal, but many are not. While grooming or just petting your Golden (of *any* age), feel his entire body for lumps and bumps. Although skin masses like cysts, warts, and fatty tumors are common in older dogs, you should always have your vet inspect any new growths you find. Cancer in all breeds of dogs has become more common and can attack any organ or body part. Breast and testicular cancers are common in unspayed bitches and intact males. Spay/neuter is the best prevention (see Chapter 10).

Skin and Coat

A little gray hair here and there is normal, but overly flaky skin and hair loss can indicate a late-onset hormonal problem with the thyroid gland. (A dog's thyroid gland gets tired and wears out just like its human counterpart.) Your vet can diagnose hyperthyroidism and treat it with an oral replacement dose of supplemental hormones.

More frequent brushing will help stimulate his oil glands and decrease the extra shedding (see Chapter 13). Your vet may recommend a nutritional supplement to add lubrication to his skin. Senior foods are low in fat and can contribute to dry skin and coat.

Signs of Kidney Disease

Does your dog urinate more frequently? Does he now have accidents in the house or have to urinate in the middle of the night? Does he drink more water than he used to? All can be symptoms of kidney or bladder disease or diabetes.

Unfortunately, by the time you see any of these symptoms, there may already be significant and irreversible damage to his vital organs. His kidneys will be over 50 percent damaged before those signs show up. And if you miss the signs of increased thirst or urination, the dog will continue to get worse.

REMEMBER

The prevention key in all of these old age diseases is to know your dog and be observant!

TIP

Dogs over 7 years of age should have annual blood work and urinalysis to test for kidney and liver function before those visible signs appear. Dogs who are already in kidney failure can be managed with special diets prescribed by the veterinarian to reduce the workload on the kidneys.

Most veterinarians offer a geriatric exam that includes a thorough physical exam, blood work, urinalysis, thyroid profile, and EKG to diagnose problems in the early stages. It's not cheap, but your Golden is worth it. It may save his life.

Detecting Heart Disease

How do you know if and when heart disease occurs? Changes in sleeping habits, restlessness, coughing (especially at night or on first waking in the morning), panting, shortness of breath, and decreased exercise tolerance can indicate cardiovascular problems. If you catch the problem early, you will have greater success in treating it.

TIP

Coughing can be serious. It's the most common sign of heart disease in canines. If your Golden has been coughing more than 24 hours, see your veterinarian.

Incontinence

Urinary incontinence is a common problem in older spayed bitches. They start to unconsciously dribble urine. You may be surprised to find wet spots on her bed in the morning. This is one condition that is easily remedied with a supplemental hormone that can improve the muscle tone of the bladder.

Saying Good-Bye

Living the good life with a Golden also means the inevitable — you will probably outlive your dog. Despite your best efforts to keep him young and healthy, the time will come when you have to say good-bye. If your Golden friend suffers from cancer or other terminal disease, he will look to you, his caretaker and best friend, for relief from constant pain or inability to function. Euthanasia is the most difficult decision of dog ownership and possibly the most unselfish.

After many years of living with this magical breed, I've faced that moment many times. Each time it's a brand-new decision, never easier, and always filled with the same gut-wrenching pain. But the sad fact remains, your dog deserves your help when it's time for him to go.

You'll know when it's time. He may stop eating, no longer get up to walk, show signs of discomfort or pain, or look at you with sad, pleading eyes. So, however he is telling you, please believe me, you will know when that moment comes. I learned that again years ago when one of my older Goldens fell ill, and I knew it would soon be time. But as I heard the bad news in the emergency clinic on a Sunday morning, I didn't have that deep gut feeling that I needed to be sure. We had 3 more grand days together, he and I. He was comfortable and very loved and spoiled. He left with grace and dignity and died peacefully in his sleep, sparing me for once that dreadful final trip. Fortunately, this time, waiting was the right decision.

Your veterinarian will help you make your decision. My vet did exactly that years ago when my senior female Golden was stricken with a tumor and suffered an exceptionally bad day. She assured me it was not yet time, and pleaded with me to believe her, that my heart would tell me when. She was right, and a week later, I knew that moment had arrived. I treasure those last days we had together.

Staying with your dog

Most owners elect, as I do, to remain with their dogs to hold and comfort them during their last moments. It's best to stay as calm as possible, but I believe in my own heart that my dog understands why he's there and needs to hear me say, "I love you" one more time. The veterinarian will inject a drug, which takes but a second to make him drowsy and fall asleep; then a second shot, and within seconds, his heart will simply stop. If you are unwilling or unable to be with your dog, be sure a family member or a friend he loves stays with him. As difficult as this is, he does not deserve to die alone.

When I began this book, my 14-year-old female Golden napped on her cedar bed next to my desk, my constant companion as I wrote. Sadly, she left us the day after her 15th birthday, and I am so grateful she was here to supervise most of these chapters. Now my 11-year-old male has replaced her beside my chair, still in apparent good health. But each day I am reminded that today is one more gift.

REMEMBER

Grief is very personal and individual. Some people can't even talk about losing their dog without breaking down completely. Many will cry and grieve for weeks and months before they can move beyond their sorrow and remember the happy times without a tear. That's normal and okay. Your dog's death is a huge personal loss, and you should let your emotions show. There will be those few who claim "It's just a dog" and won't understand why you continue to grieve. Some non-pet people just don't get it. Be patient with them but don't let other people tell you how to grieve, or for how long. Share your grief with other dog lovers who have traveled this lonely road. It's going to take time. All those memories will eventually bring smiles instead of tears.

Adding a new dog to the family

Some people don't want to endure another heartbreak and vow never to get another dog. Some of those people will change their minds. Others want a new dog right away. Most of my friends own two or more dogs not only because they love living with a bunch of dogs, but because they won't be without a dog when one dies. I could not deal with losing one of my dear friends if I didn't have a Golden army here to comfort me. But that does not diminish the unique "specialness" of the dog I lose. It just represents my personal consolation zone.

Whether you get a new dog right away or wait until your heart has healed, approach your new dog as a special individual and don't compare him to your last one. None are the same, and each one is your best friend.

Burial

For many years my husband and I buried our Goldens in one of their favorite places, up on a hill on our farm under a grove of trees where I walked our dogs each day. Today cremation is available (ask your veterinarian), and we bury their ashes with their Golden brothers and sisters on that hill. Friends may question my sanity, but I always wave a big hello whenever we walk past their spot. I believe they're watching over me.

You may choose to bury your dog or his ashes in your yard or under a tree or bush in some favorite place. You can keep his ashes in a sealed vase or urn on your desk or mantle, or scatter them in your yard or over a pond where he loved to swim. Pet cemeteries offer plots and headstones. Whatever your choice, your Golden will live on in your heart forever.

CHILDREN AND PET DEATH

The death of the family dog is often a child's first experience with a serious loss. Don't try to trivialize it by saying, "You'll get over it" or "We'll get another dog." Your child doesn't want another dog; he wants the one who died. Be honest with him that your dog is gone forever. Avoid phrases like "putting him to sleep." The child may wonder when he's going to wake up. The words "death" and "died" could be replaced by "dog heaven" and will not accentuate his grief. It may, in fact, help him face the reality that his pet will not come back.

Share your own grief with your child; it's good therapy for both of you. Knowing you also grieve will help your child understand that it's okay to feel sad about the dog. It will also help a shy or quiet child who is reluctant to display his feelings. And if he's angry or feels guilty, it will help him open up to you.

For your child's sake, don't rush out to buy another dog. Depending on the individual child, doing so might minimize the departed pet's importance in the family scheme. Wait until your child feels better. Children heal differently, and some may be ready for a new dog sooner than others.

If I Die Before You Go . . .

What will happen to your dog if you die before he goes to the Rainbow Bridge? Will your children take him in? Do they even like or want him? You have to make sure that your Golden will be cared for and provided for if you leave this earth before he does. You can do that in your will. First, decide who, besides yourself, loves your dog enough to live with him and care for him until he dies. Think about family members, other Golden-owner friends, or maybe your breeder. Would they be willing and able to give him the kind of home he needs and deserves? Are you willing or able to provide a yearly stipend for his care (and can you trust them with that money)?

Some people who own an elderly Golden believe the dog would be unable to adjust to a new home and request that their dog be euthanized after their own death, and perhaps have their ashes buried with them. In my personal Golden family, I have dictated individual wishes for each of our dogs. Our old dogs and those with severe physical limitations are left with family members who will care for them until they make the decision to send them to the Rainbow Bridge. The younger, healthy ones are to be placed with various family members or friends who adore them and would provide homes we would approve of. Of course, this is adjusted as my old Goldens leave this earth or as new ones join the family.

If you don't have a will, at least draw up a formal statement of your wishes and perhaps have it witnessed and notarized. Hopefully, your family will honor your request.

TIP

The Rainbow Bridge is a place where deceased dogs and other pets wait for their owners to pass and they are then reunited. This happy thought often adds some comfort to the sadness of losing your precious friend. Search online for Rainbow Bridge and you will find words of comfort and support, including the "Rainbow Bridge Poem."

Chapter 15

Hereditary Disease

A re you ready for some serious discussion — can we talk? Unfortunately, the very popular Golden Retriever comes with a predisposition to several serious hereditary diseases that can shorten his life span or make life difficult or painful. This chapter reveals the not-so-good side of this very special breed.

Hip Dysplasia (HD)

The most common and well-known hereditary problem in Golden Retrievers and other large breeds is hip dysplasia (HD). Despite many years of x-ray screening before breeding, hip problems in the breed have prevailed.

Simply stated, *hip dysplasia* means poor development of the hip joint. It is polygenic (also called multifactorial) in nature, which means that a single characteristic (in this case, hip dysplasia) is controlled by more than two genes. This is a common problem in many breeds, and a severe case can render a working dog incapable of performance. It is also complicated by environmental factors such as over-nutrition, rapid growth, and excessive trauma during developmental growth stages. The condition covers a broad range of severity that includes mild, moderate, and severe levels of dysplasia. Even a mild case can cause painful arthritis in a sedentary companion animal, although many dysplastic dogs live normal, active lives. The condition worsens with age, and dysplastic senior dogs can experience great discomfort and very limited mobility.

The only currently accepted diagnosis is through x-ray. X-rays, taken by a qualified veterinarian, are evaluated by the Orthopedic Foundation for Animals (OFA), and dogs with "clear" or "clean" hips are issued an OFA number that includes a rating of Excellent, Good, or Fair. This rating will appear on a dog's AKC registration certificate. Dogs must be at least 2 years old before their joints are eligible for OFA consideration. OFA will, however, evaluate the hips of younger dogs and give a preliminary rating. Breeders often obtain a preliminary rating to screen hips before they embark on a training program with a dog who may not later pass OFA scrutiny.

PennHip evaluation is a second method of detecting HD that was developed at the University of Pennsylvania School of Veterinary Medicine. Known simply as PennHip, it also uses x-rays, but it requires more specific positioning of the hips. This method examines other hip qualities such as joint laxity and can be used to evaluate dogs as young as 16 weeks of age. Although relatively new, PennHip has gained greater acceptance every year, and some breeders now use both methods to screen their dogs.

REMEMBER

At this time, only OFA-approved dogs should be used for breeding. A pedigree with a minimum of one or more generations of OFA-certified ancestors is still the best insurance a Golden puppy buyer has for obtaining a Golden who hopefully won't be plagued with hip problems early or later in life. Responsible breeders always screen their breeding animals, and will proudly produce those OFA clearances on their dogs (see Chapter 3).

Elbow Dysplasia (ED) and Osteochondritis Dissecans (OCD)

Both of these diseases are developmental irregularities of the elbow and shoulder and are a major cause of front-end lameness in many large-breed dogs. Both ED and OCD affect young dogs, with typical symptoms of recurring or intermittent lameness usually appearing between 4 and 7 months of age. X-rays taken of the elbow joint will verify the condition.

In 1990, OFA created an elbow registry to provide a database for dogs who have been x-rayed and certified free of ED and OCD. Although both diseases are believed to be hereditary, nutrition is also thought to be a contributing factor in their development. Feeding diets high in calories, calcium, and protein are suspect, and at least two major dog food manufacturers now produce puppy growth foods that are lower in calories from fat and protein and recommended for fast-growing large-breed dogs (see Chapter 10).

As with hip dysplasia, Goldens with ED or OCD should not be bred.

Eye Disease

OFA also has created an eye registry (Companion Animal Eye Registry — CAER), a database for dogs who have been examined for hereditary eye disease. Breeding animals should always be examined by a board-certified veterinary ophthalmologist, who will then issue a certificate of his findings. The owner can then submit the form to OFA for entry into the OFA database. The Golden Retriever Club of America (GRCA) now recommends that Goldens be examined annually for their entire lifetime due to the increase of Golden Retriever Pigmentary Uveitis (GRPU). (See the later section "Pigmentary Uveitis" for more information.)

Cataracts

A *cataract* is defined as an opacity of the eye lens, and several types are common in the Golden breed. At least one hereditary type shows up early in life. Some cataracts don't interfere with the dog's vision, while others progress into partial or complete blindness. Cataract surgery is successful in some cases, but it's expensive. Dogs with cataracts should not be bred.

Progressive retinal atrophy (PRA)

A few Goldens are affected with PRA, which is progressive deterioration of the retina that can result in complete blindness. There is no surgical solution to correct PRA. Although the incidence of PRA is low in Golden Retrievers, afflicted dogs should never be bred.

Retinal dysplasia (RD)

RD is an inherited defect of the retinal lining and is more common in Goldens than PRA (see the preceding section). Unlike PRA, RD does not result in complete blindness, but it can render a hunting dog worthless in the field or for other working tasks. RD-affected Goldens should be eliminated as candidates for breeding.

Pigmentary uveitis

Pigmentary uveitis is a serious eye disease that affects primarily Golden Retrievers. Commonly known today as *Golden Retriever Pigmentary Uveitis (GRPU)*, the disease causes reduced or complete vision loss, and in some cases, surgical removal of one or both eyes. Affected dogs may present with redness of the conjunctiva, color changes to the iris, abnormal pupils, cloudy eyes, light sensitivity, and low intraocular pressure. Although this is not considered an "old dog" disease, affected dogs are not usually diagnosed until they are 8 or 9 years of age, making early intervention difficult. Since GRPU can only be diagnosed by a board-certified veterinary ophthalmologist, the average vet is unable to detect it in the early stage. And unless breeders recertify their dogs for CAER certification, most dogs and breeding stock will seldom see an ophthalmologist.

A recent study of Goldens in the Midwest revealed that nearly 10 percent of Goldens 8 years of age were affected with GRPU. CAER exams in one area of the Pacific Northwest revealed GRPU in 25 to 33 percent of GRPU-affected Goldens over 4 years of age.

Because of the late onset of GRPU, the GRCA now recommends annual eye certification (that means the ophthalmologist!) for the entire lifetime of the dog.

Eyelash and eyelid problems

A few hereditary eyelid and eyelash problems affect the breed. Trichiasis, distichiasis, and entropion are eyelash disorders most commonly seen in young dogs, but dogs of any age can be affected. All are painful conditions that can damage the cornea or conjunctiva of the eye.

In trichiasis, the eyelash on the upper eyelid grows inward, rubbing the eye and causing irritation. Distichiasis involves extra eyelashes that also irritate the cornea. In entropion, the eyelid rolls inward, with the eyelashes rubbing against the cornea. It can affect both upper and lower eyelids, and may appear in both eyes. All three conditions can be surgically corrected. Affected dogs should not be bred.

TIP

The bluish haze often seen in the eyes of older dogs is a normal aging process and is not hereditary or a breeding problem.

Epilepsy

Epilepsy is a seizure disorder caused by abnormal electrical patterns in the brain. It can be hereditary or caused by a variety of environmental factors, including viral and infectious diseases, trauma, and chemical or nutritional imbalance.

Inherited epilepsy usually appears between 6 months and 3 years of age. Some experts believe that epilepsy that occurs in later years may be genetically induced as well. Recurring seizures can be controlled with medication, but long-term medication sometimes causes other health problems. If your dog suffers a seizure, regardless of how slight, always consult with your veterinarian for possible causes and treatment options.

Although hereditary epilepsy is difficult to diagnose, dogs who suffer recurring seizures should not be bred, and experts familiar with the breed also recommend against breeding parents and siblings of those dogs.

Hypothyroidism

Goldens join a long list of dog breeds who suffer from the malfunction of the thyroid gland. Symptoms of hypothyroidism include obesity, lethargy, recurrent infections, and skin or coat problems such as hair loss, dryness, and thinning fur. (The opposite condition, hyperthyroidism, is rare in dogs, and when it does occur, it is usually associated with thyroid cancer.) Treatment of hypothyroidism consists of daily oral thyroid supplementation, which may continue for the dog's entire life.

Diagnosis can be tricky, and supplementation can be a problem in itself. Get a second opinion before starting thyroid treatment. Early-onset hypothyroidism may be inherited, and dogs so affected should not be bred.

Many veterinarians, both traditional and holistic, believe that the huge increase in canine thyroid problems may be due to environmental factors such as overuse of vaccines and exposure to lawn chemicals (not a good scenario for overall health!). If your Golden develops thyroid problems, check with your vet, your breeder, and other experienced Golden breeders before you get into long-term supplementation.

Testing is rather tricky and should be handled by a veterinarian familiar with thyroid problems and this breed. Dogs who are diagnosed with hypothyroidism should be retested annually to continue therapeutic levels of the hormone. Most breed experts agree that dogs with confirmed hypothyroidism should not be used for breeding.

Subvalvular Aortic Stenosis (SAS)

This disease is as bad as it sounds. A dog with SAS will simply drop dead without any symptoms or a moment's warning. The disease involves a stricture (abnormal narrowing) in the left ventricle of the heart, which restricts the blood flow out of the heart, leading to sudden and unexpected death after normal activity or exercise.

While only a small percentage of Goldens are affected by SAS, as a hereditary disease, there appears to be greater incidence of the disease in certain lines or families of Golden Retrievers. Goldens as young as 8 to 16 weeks of age can be examined for SAS, although they should be reevaluated at 12 to 24 months before they are considered as breeding candidates. Diagnosis requires examination by a board-certified veterinary cardiologist.

Von Willebrand Disease (VWD)

VWD is the most common hereditary bleeding disorder in canines, wherein puppies may inherit a lack of clotting ability (the specific protein that helps platelets form clots to seal broken blood vessels) from their parents. Many affected dogs never show any signs that they have the disease, while others may experience spontaneous or prolonged bleeding after some trauma or surgical procedure. On certain tragic occasions, it isn't diagnosed until the dog is spayed or neutered and bleeds uncontrollably during surgery. The mode of inheritance is complicated, with seemingly unaffected animals passing the gene on to some of their offspring. VWD is also sometimes linked to hypothyroidism (see earlier section), creating a double whammy for those poor affected animals. A reliable blood test exists for VWD, and while the incidence of the disease appears to be low in Goldens, some breeders still opt to test.

Neuronal Ceroid Lipofuscinosis (NCL)

First diagnosed in 2015 at the University of Missouri, NCL has rapidly become a major concern of Golden breeders. This is a neurological disease that research has determined is due to a mutation in the CLN5 gene in the brain.

Typically, early symptoms usually appear at about 15 months of age, when the dog becomes uncoordinated, anxious, and agitated; bumps into objects; and paces and circles for no apparent reason. He may snap at invisible flies, no longer recognize known commands, and even suffer mild seizures. Within a few months the seizures become more frequent, prolonged, and severe. He may become aggressive toward people and other dogs. Quality of life rapidly diminishes, and the dog will be euthanized at about 2 years of age.

Fortunately, genetic testing is now available to determine if a dog is a carrier of the CLN5 gene. The test involves a simple cheek swab, and is commercially available from the University of Missouri/Orthopedic Foundation for Animals (https://www.ofa.org). Responsible breeders today are (or should be) testing potential breeding stock before they embark on a breeding program.

Ichthyosis

It is known that most Golden Retrievers in the U.S. and 50 percent of Goldens in Europe are carriers of ichthyosis. This skin disease causes copious amounts of dandruff on the body of the dog. The first symptoms can appear as early as 4 weeks of age. Between 6 and 18 months of age, large dandruff flakes will be visible on the dog's back and belly. Skin will be dry and rough-textured, and look hyperpigmented, dirty, and scaly. In severe cases, the skin turns dark and thick and may develop painful lesions. This condition is incurable and will require lifetime maintenance to keep the dog comfortable. Special shampoos and prescription ointments are recommended to prevent infection.

DILATED CARDIOMYOPATHY (DCM)

While it's not a hereditary disease, DCM has recently been diagnosed in Golden Retrievers as well as several other breeds. This is a disease of the heart muscle that results in weakened contractions and poor pumping ability. The number of Golden deaths attributed to DCM has raised concern in the veterinary community as well as with Golden owners. It is suspected that there is a potential dietary link between DCM and dogs eating certain "BEG" (boutique, exotic, and grain-free) dog foods. Although it is thought that foods containing large amounts of peas, potatoes, and lentils may cause low taurine levels and contribute to DCM, some veterinary cardiologists suspect that other nutrients in the BEG diets may play a role.

While all this is being researched and dissected, be sure to choose a well-researched dog food that is backed by expert research and formulation. ("Balanced and complete" on the bag does not mean superior quality or safety; see Chapter 10 for more on nutrition.) You can also consult the World Small Animal Veterinary Association (WSAVA; https://www.wsava.org) for more information on selecting a healthy dog food.

In mild cases, owners may be unaware and consider it just a case of dry, flaky skin. Veterinarians may not recognize the flakiness as ichthyosis and dismiss it as simply dandruff. The vet should perform a skin scraping and submit the samples for DNA testing and analysis to diagnose the disease. Testing is offered by Antagene (https://www.antagene.com/en), a European company based in Lyon, France, that offers more than 100 DNA tests in 50 countries worldwide. Given the recent discovery of the prevalence of ichthyosis, breeders are encouraged to screen their breeding stock for carriers using the ICT-A DNA test.

Chapter **16**

Problem Behaviors and Aggression

The problem with most canine problem behaviors is the human who perceives it. If you were a dog, wouldn't you love to jump into Dad's lap or dig in Mom's pretty flower bed? These and other objectionable behaviors are fun and quite natural to the dog; humans are the ones who have decided that such conduct doesn't conform to the rules of their house or neighborhood.

This chapter deals with the good, the bad, and the ugly of your dog's behavior and offers tips on handling the more common canine social misbehaviors. It also shows you how to be the alpha person in your home, which will prevent some typical dog problem behaviors.

Jumping for Joy

Who among you hasn't had muddy paw prints on your best white pants or butted head to canine head when walking in the door? The dog was out-of-his-mind glad to see you, but you can't quite share his rowdy exuberance.

Jumping up is a perfectly natural canine behavior. Your puppy has been doing it ever since he was about 3 weeks old. He jumped up to lick his mother's muzzle and started pouncing on his littermates before he left the whelping box, and then progressed to jumping on gates or barriers or whatever else stood between him and the person on the other side. What's more, he was such a cutie he was actually rewarded for that behavior with a scratch behind the ear, or even a healthy scoop into loving arms. Talk about reinforcement!

The usual prevent-it-before-it-becomes-a-habit theory is obviously hopeless under these circumstances, considering all that early positive reinforcement. As the "jumpee," your only option is reconditioning and teaching alternative behavior. That's not an impossible task, but it will take time, patience, and the absolute cooperation of your family (especially the kids) and your friends. You may have to run interference for your children on this issue. And if your friends refuse to cooperate, don't invite them over until your dog is 2 years old and fully trained. You might also remind them about those gritty paws on their designer clothes.

REMEMBER

Consistency is a key element in correcting jumping. You cannot allow it one day and then correct it the next. Neither can anyone else. Never means never. Everyone means any human being who comes into contact with your dog.

Also understand what you should *not* do when your dog or puppy jumps. Never make *his* jumping *your* joy! Your worst response is to pet or hug him. That will only encourage him to jump some more! He's already revved his motor because you came home from the movies or someone came to visit.

The following sections describe jumping corrections. The most successful usually involve a leash or a spritzer bottle.

Use the leash

Start with your 4-foot leash on your puppy. When he starts to jump up on you or someone else, grasp the leash about 2 feet from the collar, give a quick snap downward and sideways (so that you won't injure his young neck and throat), and command him "Off" in a firm voice. Don't use the word "Down" because he'll confuse that word with the obedience exercise. As soon as he has all four feet back on the ground, quietly (*quiet* is a key word here — he's already too excited!), and tell him what a good boy he is. If he knows the Sit command, you can then immediately tell him to "Sit." *Now* he has done something you can praise him for. Use soft, easy praise so that he doesn't get excited again and jump up some more!

Turn the other cheek

Isolation often works well without using the leash. When your puppy jumps or starts to jump on you, say "Off!" and quickly turn away with your arms folded in front of you. Keep turned from the dog and refuse to look at him for a minute or two. Do not give any praise afterward; just resume your normal behavior. The puppy should discover that every time he jumps, he is deprived of your companionship, which is what the jumping was all about in the first place.

A bit of spritz

The spritzer technique works for some dogs. Fill a spray bottle with water. When your puppy starts to jump, tell him "Off" and squirt him with a gentle spritz of water (not in his eyes!). (You can also add a bit of lemon juice or vinegar.) Now turn your back and ignore him for a for a minute or so. Do not praise the puppy afterward. Keep the bottle near the front door or wherever jumping most often occurs.

Try this for several days until the puppy shows some improvement in jumping situations. Once he demonstrates a little self-control, skip the spray and add the Sit command as soon as you think he's tempted to jump up. Follow with the Sit-praise technique as described above.

Try a shaker can

Some owners have success using a shaker can as a jump deterrent. Keep one by the front door and rattle it loudly as soon as he begins to jump. Say "Off!" and then praise him when all four feet hit the ground (that is assuming he stops jumping!). Next, give a Sit command and more praise because he's sitting nicely.

Shake hands

There's yet one more jumping correction if you're caught off-guard outdoors and don't have a leash, spritzer bottle, or shaker can handy. (Face it: You can't be prepared *all* the time!) When he jumps up and you suddenly realize that you have no counter-conditioner available, quickly grasp his paws and hold them in the air. Don't squeeze; just grip them firmly, not painfully, and without moving or uttering a word. Eventually, he'll wonder how to get out of this predicament, and he'll start to whine or struggle. Wait a few more seconds and then let go and order him to "Sit" if he has learned that command.

These are jumping no-nos:

>> **Do not bang him in the chest with your knee.** That can harm your puppy or adult dog, and he'll only learn to be afraid of you. Some dogs also view the knee as a game and become even more excited, which is exactly what you're trying to avoid.

>> **Do not step on his back toes with your foot.** It's a clumsy maneuver that may injure his feet if you press on them and hurt both of you if you fail and fall down, as some folks do. And he will only learn to shy away from you rather than *not* jump up.

JUMPING CORRECTIONS FOR THE KIDS

Training kids to not encourage jumping up is usually like putting water in a sieve. Little folks with their quick movements and squeaky voices stir up memories of the whelping box, and your puppy will instinctively chase or jump on children. In many families, there's usually one child a dog senses he can dominate, and that one becomes his equal, like his littermate. Those situations always call for parental intervention.

Set aside some time during the puppy's play period to work with the child and puppy together to teach the puppy not to jump on his favorite target. With your puppy on a leash or long line and one end attached to your waist or belt to make sure that you have control, have the child move about nearby. When your puppy starts to jump or give chase, tug quickly on the leash, and speak your firmest "Off," then "Sit," and then praise. If he repeats the jump a second time, follow the "Off" and give another leash pop, then release with praise when he finally settles down.

You'll need to repeat this exercise several days in a row (more than once a day if possible), then once a week for a while until you get a solid take. That takes a heap of dedication, but if your child is typical, he'll be running away and screaming every time the puppy jumps, and the puppy will think it's a game and give chase. It will be easier to take corrective measures than play referee every time. Fortunately, the kids grow taller and bigger and less enticing for the pup. But do you want to wait that long? Kid-proofing takes time, but in the long run you will save precious time extricating your child from puppy misbehavior.

Checking Out Counters

Once your puppy has a little leg under him, he will discover there's a whole new world "up there." Tables, counters, dressers . . . gosh, what fun! Your dinner and cosmetics are now at risk. Start preventive measures early if he shows interest in the joys of counter theft.

TIP

Use the old "set up the dog" routine: Place a tempting plate of something yummy near the counter's edge. When pup strolls past, he'll use his golden nose power to investigate the goodie. You know what he's up to! When he wanders close and starts to sniff, give him a stern "Aaahh, aaahh!" and then (hopefully) watch him slink away. Use those mind-reading techniques often while he's young and impressionable so he'll grow up to believe you're always one step ahead of him.

If your dog succeeds in stealing tonight's main course, or you discover that he's been inspecting counters in your absence, you'll have to set him up for self-correction. Make a couple of shaker cans and fasten them together with a length of thread taped to the tops. Tie another thread from the cans to a food lure that is secured to the counter so it won't fall down with the cans. Place the entire booby trap where the dog can grab it, then hide from view. A clattering pile of shaker cans should convince him that the sky has fallen, and he won't try it again. Be quick to pick up any edible food before he can recover from the shock and get rewarded anyway!

NO BEGGING!

Begging is so easy to prevent that I say "shame on you" if your Golden does it. If you never feed your dog from the table or from your plate during or immediately after a meal, he'll never learn to expect it. Isn't that simple? And no handouts when you're preparing meals or snacking in the kitchen or anywhere else. Hang tough with your kids on this issue, too.

A very young puppy should be crated when the family eats. An older pup who has had some training should do a Down-Stay on his dog mat or away from the table when you eat. You thus eliminate temptation and add one more reminder that you run the ship. (For more, see "Establishing Yourself as Alpha Dog," later in this chapter.)

On and Off Furniture

If you hate dog hair on your clothes or in your face when you sleep, promise your-self you will not allow your Golden on your bed or furniture. It only takes one time, one little cuddle on the couch or easy chair, and he will believe it's okay all the time. Remember that reinforcement stuff?

If you've laid down firm rules about the furniture and you notice your puppy is tempted to join you on the couch, keep his leash or short collar tab on his collar. When he makes his move, snap his lead and tell him "No!" Repeat several times to reinforce your message.

If you're desperate to sit and snuggle with your puppy while you read or watch TV, just slide down onto the floor beside the couch and enjoy those moments at his level.

You can also offer your Golden his own easy chair and allow him on only that piece of furniture. Just invite him up, and he'll remember. If he tries to climb on some-thing else, snap his lead and take him over to "his" chair and tell him "Up." It's tough sharing your chair with a dog who takes up more room than you do! (Kind of worth it, though!)

Golden Diggers

Some dogs dig, while others never do. Digging holes is a naturally doggie thing to do, but it can drive an avid gardener to the compost pile. If your yard looks like a mini-minefield thanks to your digging Golden, try to identify the reason for his behavior (if you can) before you despair and pour a concrete lawn. Here are some reasons dogs dig:

>> **Boredom.** Digging is most often the result of boredom. You own this Golden for companionship. He's figured that out, too. Companions forge their bond through regular play and exercise together. Without that kind of stimulation, your Golden may turn to digging or other creative forms of destructive behavior to alleviate his boredom or malaise.

>> **Other misbehavior.** Perhaps his digging is an extension of indoor misbehav-ior. Any mishaps in the house of late? If so, treat the indoor problem first, and then look to resolve the outdoor situation.

>> **Cooling off.** If you think he's digging because he's hot and wants a cool, damp earth spa to lay his body in during summer weather, fill a small child's swimming pool or move him to a cooler location indoors. Of course, when he's outdoors, you must do the obvious and make sure that he has access to shade and cool drinking water throughout the day.

>> **Nails need a trim.** Are his nails trimmed and short? Long, unclipped nails automatically lend themselves to soil-tilling habits. If you don't clip his nails, ask your vet to show you how or have a groomer do it for you (see Chapter 13).

>> **Romance.** Is he digging under fences in search of romance and wild females? Beef up that fence and arrange to have him neutered at the appropriate age (see Chapter 10).

TIP

To stop the digging, you can also booby trap the hole with buried chicken wire, hot pepper, or even the dog's own feces, so he'll scratch into them and become disgusted with his digging site. Puppies are more prone to dig, but take heart! They usually outgrow the habit.

REMEMBER

As with most things doggie, the best solution is prevention. If you can't supervise him, keep him indoors and out of your garden. If your dog could talk, he'd tell you that digging is a natural and self-rewarding behavior and only *you* find it offensive.

Eating Feces

Eating feces is a common problem that usually occurs at some time during many a dog's life. It's called *coprophagia*, and although it's disgusting, it happens in the best of canine families. In the wild, canine scavengers scrounge for their meals and find partially digested food in another animal's feces, yucky as that may be to humans.

Closer to home, your puppy's mom, for example, cleaned up after all her pups because her instincts compelled her to remove evidence of their presence from possible predators. Remember, she didn't know this was the 21st century.

Amid these and other theories that focus on dietary deficiencies, research has failed to produce a single reliable explanation or underlying cause for canine fecal ingestion. It's important to nip the habit in the bud, since ingesting and even sniffing stools that may be infected with parasites will lead to intestinal problems.

TIP

Try a few yard tricks to discourage the habit:

» The first, easiest, most obvious, and perhaps most important tip is to pick up the stools at once. He can't eat what isn't there, and he will probably outgrow the habit.

» You can mine the stools with a few drops of Tabasco hot sauce when the dog isn't looking. Once he eats it, he should decide it's pretty awful stuff.

» Try adding a bit of commercially available products called For-Bid and Distaste to his food, which are supposed to reduce fecal palatability. This is not recommended for young dogs and should be a last resort after strict yard sanitation.

The upside is that puppies who eat their stools seldom continue this practice into adulthood. The flip side is that if they eat another dog's stools, they could become infested with whatever parasites that animal may harbor. So it's worth the effort to eradicate the habit. (Improves dog kissing, too!)

Running Away

Unfortunately, there are no quick fixes for the dog who bolts, whether it's through the open front door or from the yard into the street. I could write volumes on boundary training outdoors and proofing your dog to Come, Sit, Stay, and Down under the most attractive of distractions. But the fact remains — your wonderful Golden buddy is still a dog. He's a creature of unpredictable instincts that can and usually will surface when you least expect them.

Boundary training will not contain your dog forever. The only guarantee in dog life is that your perfectly behaved 2-4, -6-, or 8-year-old dog *will* one day chase a single rabbit, pursue a wayward squirrel, or dash through the open door because he sees something only he finds incredibly tempting. When that happens, there are no second chances. Ask anyone who has ever lost their beloved and "obedient" Golden under a set of truck tires.

Keep him on a leash. Fence your yard and lock the gate. Build a dog run or install invisible fencing. Do not take chances, and don't trust your 5-year-old kid to walk him. This bundle of gold is a precious resource you can't afford to risk.

Vigilance does not end there. Do not assume because your dog is in a fenced yard he is safe from human predators. Stories abound in every state about clever dog thieves who snatched a friendly dog in the blink of an eye. Unsupervised time outside can be an invitation to heartbreak, so always keep an eye on your dog.

Avoiding Separation Anxiety

You can avoid the demon of separation distress and anxiety. If you condition your puppy to being left alone in his crate (briefly) from his first days at home, he will automatically learn that your comings and goings are part of his everyday routine, and he won't become upset by that. That also further ensures that he won't develop the problem when he's older.

TIP

Always keep your departures and returns low key. Don't shower him with big displays of attention or affectionate good-byes when you leave the house or come back home. That can create separation distress where none exists! Bear in mind that the dog is a pack animal, and like Adam, was not meant to be alone.

Incremental absences

Start by teaching him to stay in his crate while you're at home, working in another room, or in the yard. If he's a crate guy (and he should be), he'll just curl up in his den and take a nap. (See Chapter 7 for more on crate training.)

Vary the length of time that you're away, 10 minutes one day, a half–hour the next.

If you feel (or hear!) that he becomes agitated as soon as you leave, do lots of practice runs. Calmly put on your coat, pick up your car keys, step out the door and close it, come immediately back in, release him from his crate, and give a quiet "Down" command. When he's down and quiet, calmly praise him. Do this for a week or two and gradually increase and vary the time you stand outside the door.

WARNING

Do *not* offer sympathy or sweet talk like "Oooohh, did my big baby miss his momma?" Also, never punish him for his anxiety. Both techniques will make it worse.

Tasty rewards

To make your departure less stressful for your Golden (and only if he's stressed!), try a little peanut butter. Spread a small dab on a Nylabone or press it inside a sterilized hard bone and give it to him just before you leave the house. You can freeze the stuffed bone to make it last longer. It will create a pleasant association with your leaving, and will keep him happily occupied while you're gone. He should always have a good chewie or two for solitary munching.

Background noise and music

Leave the radio on while you're gone (soothing music, please, no heavy metal or hard rock) to keep him company and muffle any outside sounds that might agitate him. A television also works, and of course a night light if you're out after dark.

Enhance his environment

If your dog is uncrated while you're gone (surely not a puppy, though) and you see signs of stress due to your absence, you might try a little "environmental enrichment" to cheer him up. This lifestyle concept is used in zoos and animal parks, and it may work wonders for your nonstop Golden. Zoo exhibits today have moats and caves and climbing structures to entertain their charges. Modern zookeepers deliberately hide the animals' food in cracks, crevices, trees, and even plastic containers!

Of course, you can't replicate in-the-wild inside your home, and it would be dumb to put his food bowl in a tree. But you can modify these simple methods and offer your dog your own version of environmental enrichment.

A window to the world

The simplest extra is to allow access to a windowsill so that he can survey his "territory" while you're gone.

Be careful about this. You should only give windowsills to well-mannered dogs who have earned full house privileges. Some dogs go bonkers when they see the mailman or another animal outside. You don't need scarred up windowsills or a broken window. Do a few test runs and observe his behavior from a hiding place indoors or outside to see whether he can handle it.

Self-propelled toys

You can provide challenging and stimulating doggie activities with self-propelled "Boomer Balls" that move about randomly and challenge a dog's curiosity and predatory instincts.

If he's a chow hound, try leaving him a sustained-release food device. One commercial gadget called the Buster Cube holds food kibbles or freeze-dried liver. The multichambered cube releases food tidbits one or two pieces at a time as the dog pushes or rolls it with his nose or paw.

TIP

Make sure that he's in a room or area where he won't topple the furniture when the chase is on.

Exercise

Exercise, the great canine cure-all, also helps with separation anxiety. A dog who is tired mentally and physically is more likely to fall asleep once he accepts your absence. An exercised dog is more content; he's had his bonding time and feels secure again.

Thunderphobia and Noise Sensitivity

Every Fourth of July and New Year's Eve, the sound of fireworks sends thousands of dogs into panic mode. They hide in closets or dark corners; pace and claw at doors and windows; pant, whine, and bark; and basically go nuts. Worst of all, outside dogs will scale the fence or break through their electric fencing and risk getting lost or hit by a car, which, unfortunately, happened to a friend's dog, who ended up dead in a roadside ditch.

Dogs also become anxious when they see a lightning bolt or hear the heavy pounding of rain against the house. (Mine do!) They can also detect changes in the barometric pressure that signals an oncoming storm. One of my old Goldens would jump in my lap on a sunny day a half-hour before a summer storm came roaring through.

Even if your Golden doesn't show signs of anxiety during those noisy times like fireworks and thunderstorms, take precautions to ward off any behavior that could, and probably will, develop. This is especially important with a puppy.

Never allow him outdoors during a noisy celebration. Stay with him in an interior room, without windows if possible, pet him (no big hugs or kisses), and talk in a calm and normal voice so you don't reinforce the behavior. Turn on the TV or radio to help block the noise. Check the weather forecast for predicted changes so you can be home if possible. Years ago, one of my Goldens was crated while I wasn't home, and a surprise summer storm passed through. He was so terrified, he actually broke through the crate door, breaking a couple of teeth in the process. From that time forward, he always came with me for errands . . . just in case!

You can try some counter-conditioning to help him overcome those fears. The protocol is a long and delicate process, but worth the effort because of the potential risk and danger to the dog, as described above.

Make a recording of the offending noise. Then expose him to the noise by playing it softly at a low level that won't upset him. If he appears tense or uneasy, reduce the sound level until he is calm and relaxed. Conduct the sessions during meal times and petting sessions to create a positive association. Begin with short sessions, but increase the volume at each one over whatever period of time it takes to relax him with each increased noise volume. Continue very gradually until the dog shows no fear of the noise.

TIP

You can purchase a tape recording made for the very purpose of counter-conditioning your dog to thunder and other loud noises such as gunfire, traffic, sirens, and crowd noises. The recording comes with instructions.

An anxiety wrap-vest called a Thunder Shirt works with some noise-phobic dogs. Inspired by research conducted by livestock behavioral expert and autism-awareness advocate Temple Grandin, the vest uses pressure to calm the animal. The wrap distributes pressure over the back and sides of his chest, resembling a hug. One published study reported that a large percentage of dogs showed improvement after prolonged use of anxiety wraps. There were no adverse side effects for dogs who did not respond positively.

Using tranquilizers is not a healthy option and does not provide a long-term solution to the problem. Sound sensitivity usually gets worse with age, so treat the signs as soon as they appear. In extreme cases, however, you can discuss the use of tranquilizers with your vet.

Food Guarding

Food guarding doesn't happen overnight. Your puppy will give you warning signs, and if you ignore them, he'll get wolf-like and protect his toys as well as his food. Look back in time. Does he occasionally stop chewing when you approach him while he's eating, maybe just keep his head tucked in the bowl and kind of freeze in place without munching? Does he ever, even once, grumble at the kids or you during his meal? That's a growl, plain and simple, and it's not necessary or acceptable.

Reprogram his meal time. Start by placing his food bowl in an open area. If he eats in a corner, it will encourage him to expect privacy and will allow him to exert control over his personal space when he's eating.

Divide his kibble into small amounts so that you have to pick up his bowl to refill it a few times during each meal. After a few days, leave his food bowl down and squat down to add the small portions as he finishes each one. Occasionally, toss a goodie like a cube of cheese or baloney into the bowl while he eats.

WARNING

When food guarding occurs, you can bet your food budget there are other problems in your dog relationship. Somewhere along the chow line he has acquired the upper paw. He's probably also possessive of his toys or a favorite bone and you just haven't noticed. Go back to the basics (that's obedience training, but you already knew that) to remind him you're the one who buys the dog food and his toys. Make him Sit before he gets his food pan; put him on a Down-Stay for an hour once a day. No on-demand petting or treating. As with meals, he has to Sit or Down submissively before he gets his TLC. Don't worry — he won't mind that. He needs a leader, not a lover.

If you have a multi-dog family and a food-guarding issue, determine if it is a dog and not a people problem. Your dog may be protecting his food from his housemates. Simple solution: Just separate them during meal time. You can't change the hierarchy of the dogs, but you must make sure you are at the top of the entire pack!

Play in his toy box and practice there as well. Tell him to "Sit," remove his toy, and give him a tidbit or another toy in return. If he growls or refuses to release, snap on his leash at once and reinforce the Sit or Down, and give no more tidbits when he does. Quiet praise, that's all. When you fail to stay in charge, he'll be first in line to take your place!

Establishing Yourself as Alpha Dog

In order to be an effective golden leader, the alpha person, or top dog, you have to act the part. (Faking it won't do — your dog is smarter than you are.) Leaders do more than just give orders. Your everyday interactions can reinforce your alpha position to your dog. If you recall that what is clear to you is not always clear to the dog, you'll know the reverse is also true, and that even your very subtle behaviors will be obvious to him. These simple daily maneuvers (as described in "Exercise Your Leadership," later in the chapter) will remind your Golden — the insecure dog as well as the one who's got an eyeball on your job — that you're the Big Kahuna.

REMEMBER

Your golden goal is a happy and successful life together. To that end, always remember that dogs are groupies by heredity. In order to feel secure, they have to understand the hierarchy of their pack. If a wolf or other pack animal doesn't know who's in charge or he senses a weak leader, he'll try to assume that position for himself because every pack requires a leader (*alpha dog*) in order to survive. This top-dog business is a survival instinct that goes back to the time of Noah. Someone has to set the rules or havoc reigns (or "Havoc" runs away, or bites).

Dogs are not unhappy or disgruntled with this totem-pole arrangement. The truth is, they feel safe and protected knowing that they have a leader who is strong, protects the pack from bad guys, and keeps the other family members in their place. And as social creatures, they are happy knowing they have pleased their leader.

REMEMBER

Dogs like and need a strong but gentle leader; it defines their world and gives them parameters to follow. Leadership is the best gift you can give your dog. In wild dog packs, everything happens after the leader, the alpha dog, has eaten, been there-done that, or gives permission.

Given that your Golden's pack instincts are so deep and primitive, you should have no trouble achieving leadership status if you master good communication skills.

Recognizing Real Aggression

Not all puppies come with the potential for aggression. But within every dog pack, there's a broad spectrum of personalities, even in a breed like the Golden Retriever, which is famous for its sweetheart temperament.

While play-biting is normal puppy behavior, other symbolic behaviors are definite warning signs that canine aggression lurks inside your puppy's head:

>> **Snatching or guarding of toys.** Beware of the puppy who growls or curls a lip when you take his toys away or who snatches them up when you approach.

>> **Chronic refusal to let go.** Puppies or dogs who won't release their grip on toys are subtly moving toward an aggressive position.

>> **Growling.** While some dogs are naturally vocal, there is a detectable difference in their message. Never underestimate growling or allow it for any reason.

>> **Refusal to obey known commands, lie down on command, or give up a sleeping area.** He's testing you. Put on his leash and start from scratch.

>> **Stops eating when you approach his food dish.** Food guarding (see "Food Guarding," above) is a prelude to a dog bite.

>> **Mounts your children or another family member.** Mounting is not a sexual gesture. It's an act of dominance, with the dog demonstrating his alpha status. It is *not* cool to dismiss it as a macho, studly act. Tell him "Off!" in a stern voice and offer alternative behavior, a Sit or Down, and then quiet praise. Some experts suggest you distract the dog by spraying him with water or a water-vinegar mix immediately when the dog begins to mount (never spray it in the eyes). The key word here is *immediate*.

Getting rough with your dog or puppy will not control or eliminate aggressive behavior. (In fact, getting rough is unacceptable for any reason.) It will only heighten his defense response and increase his aggression. *Training* is the key, and the earlier the better. The leash and collar are your best tools, but you also need a good understanding of canine psychology, and some assistance from a qualified trainer who will work with you and your dog. It's not hopeless.

People often overlook or dismiss the preceding signals because the behavior may look like playful or innocent exuberance. And most often the aggression doesn't become an in-your-face problem until the onset of puberty. It's also more common in male dogs when the male hormone testosterone starts to flow.

Unfortunately, children are often the first to confront canine play aggression because of their small size and their own high-energy activities. If you see signs of aggression during play, immediately stop the game. You effectively penalize your dog or puppy by depriving him of his favorite playmate — you or the kids. Repeated displays of aggressive behavior may be evidence of a serious problem that warrants the attention of a qualified animal behaviorist.

Setting the ground rules

Because play and aggression seem to be opposite behaviors, dog owners are shocked when their otherwise sweet Golden gets a bit testy or threatening during play time. (Hmmm, did he *really* mean to be so nasty? The answer is — yes!) Aggressive "play" like wrestling, tug-of-war, or rough physical play almost always escalates into the real thing (because your Golden is, after all, a dog). Once again, obedience is your best insurance against such a happening.

You can (and should) avoid canine "play aggression" by incorporating some simple ground rules into your most common and everyday interactions with your Golden:

>> **Avoid games that involve direct physical contact, such as tug-of-war and wrestling, which are dominance-related activities.** Don't create situations that put you at odds or in conflict with your dog. It will just confuse him and dilute the effectiveness of your training.

>> **Practice the Come and Down commands every day by incorporating them into all of your interactions with your dog, including play.** (This is only after your dog has mastered those commands — see Chapter 9.) One helpful reminder is to do them during television commercials. Promise yourself and your puppy at least one long Down-Stay during every TV evening. These exercises preserve your dog's opinion of you as the head honcho of his pack. It is not mean — your dog will actually love you more.

>> **When playing with your dog, periodically assert control by stopping the game and commanding him into a Sit-Stay or Down-Stay.** Don't be grouchy about it — make it fun. Use a pleasant, firm voice and always praise him for his compliance.

>> **If your game involves a play object like a ball, tell your dog to "Give" or "Drop it."** If he frequently does not sit or drop his toy, review your training methods and look carefully for other signs that he may be testing you (see the next section) or trying to move into a leadership position. (Understand that these are unconscious canine maneuvers. Your dog will sense your weakness, and his ancient instincts will push him to push you.)

>> **Just like a child, your Golden doesn't need a buddy (or littermate), he needs a parent (leader).** All humans should be alpha in your dog's perception, but you have to be the boss first before he will identify other people in that role.

>> **Establish your leadership through positively reinforced obedience training.** For the average dog owner, dog leadership does not come naturally (we prefer to cuddle, not scold). Most people have to work at it, and that means training classes with an experienced instructor.

>> **Make sure that your children also observe the rules on play aggression.** Unfortunately, children are often the first to confront canine play aggression because of their small size and squeaky voices and their tendency to be more physical in play.

REMEMBER

Living successfully with a puppy, even a Golden one, requires a new awareness of your family dynamics. Be alert for signs that your puppy is testing other family members, especially the children. Dogs instantly recognize little people as vulnerable, and they instinctively move to dominate them.

Signs of aggression

Aggression is the number-one problem in canine behavior today, with dogs surrendered to animal shelters because of unacceptable behavior, including aggression. And, sad to say, Goldens are no exception. Your Golden must respect every family member and use his good manners with outsiders as well as family members, or he will become an insurance liability and you can end up in court.

This quickie quiz will tell you if your Golden is entering the danger zone:

>> **Does your dog frequently bite or nip at hands and feet?** Nip that habit in the bud fast. It won't go away by itself.

>> **Can you approach your dog or touch him when he's eating?** Can you put your hand into his food dish? Does he growl or stop eating when you go near his food bowl? If he stops chewing and just stands there like a stone, he'll soon progress to growling — bet on it.

>> **Will your dog get off the furniture or bed when you request it?** If he refuses, will he allow you to forcibly remove him? Does he growl or show his teeth if you try?

>> **Can you take a toy, a bone, food, or any forbidden object out of your dog's mouth without a struggle?** Does he growl, curl his lips (he is not smiling), or snatch it up when you approach?

>> **Will your dog allow you to touch all of his body parts without a struggle?** Can you hold his paws, examine his ears and teeth, or check his belly and his private parts? Does he growl or show his teeth at any time?

>> **Can each of your family members do all of these maneuvers without threat?** He should welcome friendly touching by everyone he lives with and loves.

WARNING

If you or your dog fail even one single question, you have a serious problem that will not go away on its own. Rough treatment is not an acceptable solution. Your dog will simply cave in to his canine instincts and respond more aggressively. You need professional help now. Find a qualified obedience trainer or behavior specialist.

Exercise your leadership

It's imperative when dealing with a dominant or aggressive dog that you become his leader in no uncertain terms. Use these symbolic (to your dog) practices every day to remind your Golden you're the top dog in the house. Remember the big P in Practice, and you'll soon do these things automatically:

>> **Always enter or leave first when you go inside or outside.** When you leave the house or open the yard gate or your car door, insist that your dog wait while you go in first. (It's part of his obedience training anyway.) That tells him the territory belongs to you, not him. This same principle applies indoors as well. Never step over or around your dog when you walk through a doorway or down a hall. Gently order him to move.

In my own Golden family, two dogs are rather insecure by nature and will leap up if I as much as step in their direction. My "middle-of-the-roader" will first check out what I want him to do, and my two extremely confident — and dominant — Goldens don't budge an inch unless I tell them to! Fortunately, their early in-depth training established who was top dog in this house.

» **Eat your own meals before you feed your dog.** Your dog should not eat before you do. In the wild, the alpha dog chows down first, and lesser pack members wait in the background for the leftovers. If your dog's meals are scheduled around your own breakfast and supper times, be sure that you feed him after you have eaten. Put him on a Down-Stay or in his crate or on his dog bed. Your Golden's canine mentality will get the message. (Of course, no begging at the table! That's also bottom-line good manners.)

» **Make him earn his meals.** Require that he sit before you offer him his food dish. Ditto for his treats — make him obey some command, Sit or Down or Speak, before he gets a goodie. The plus here is that you're also giving him more opportunities to succeed and demonstrate what he knows, which will build his confidence and your leadership at the same time.

» **Do not pet your dog when he nudges you with his nose or paw (in dog language, ordering you to pet him) or "just because you love him."** As with food treats, petting must be earned by first obeying a command. Give a simple command and then pet upon his response. (If he fails to respond to your command, you now have *two* issues to work on!) This one is especially tough, as we unconsciously "pet on demand." You can count me among the guilty!

» **When you pet your dog, roll him over and rub his tummy.** Exposing his tummy is a submissive posture, but he'll enjoy it for the attention. This petting principle is not a "forever" rule, just one to be implemented during trouble-some behaviors or occasionally as a reminder of who's boss. However, never pet a dog who is growling or continue to pet a dog who growls for more.

» **Implement a 30-minute Down-Stay every day.** All dogs should be proficient in the Down command (see Chapter 9). It's one of your most important (and convenient) training tools. Incorporate it into your TV viewing time. Easy!

» **Give a command only once.** When you give a command, say it firmly only once and mean it. If he does not respond, help him to perform the behavior, but don't repeat the command. As insurance, never give a command you're not prepared to reinforce, and never give one if you think he won't or is unable to comply. It sets you both up for failure. If you're looking at chronic noncompliance, you already know what you have to work on.

Believe it or not, your Golden will actually feel more secure without those subtle power struggles and will be happier knowing you're the boss.

PROTECTING HER YOUNG

The one exception to most biting rules applies to dams with nursing pups. Even the sweetest bitch will protect her whelp if she perceives a threat. That threat may be unjustified, but you'll never convince her of that; these are her kids, and this is her job! Some bitches won't even allow certain family members near their babies, and maybe only Mom or Dad can enter the whelping room or touch the puppies.

However, most Golden mothers are of the sweet variety and will tolerate visitors if their security person is there to reassure her. But watch her eyes grow wide with apprehension. She's not too happy with strangers near her pups. It's always best to keep things private for the first 3 or 4 weeks, until the dam indicates she's ready to have company.

Aggression and euthanasia

Sadly, more than 50 percent of all puppies will not be in their original homes at the end of their first year. Behavioral problems are cited as the single most common reason for giving up a dog. Hopefully, many will be retrained and rehomed, but the remaining dogs may ultimately be euthanized.

Adult dogs are equally at risk. Aggression in adult dogs is the most serious behavior problem encountered by veterinarians and dog trainers. According to the Humane Society of the United States, more than 4.5 million dog bites occur annually. Even worse, it's estimated that several times that number go unreported every year.

The real heartbreak with most aggressive Goldens is that they are sweet and loving most of the time. Then, often for no apparent reason, they bite the hand outstretched to pet them. How often doesn't matter. Even one serious bite, even for some imagined provocation, is a serious problem. That single dog bite, any time or any place, can have far-reaching consequences. Whether your dog bites you, another family member, or a guest, a host of other problems may arise depending on the state and county of your residence: criminal citations, liability issues with insurance companies, civil suits, small to enormous expenses from emergency room fees to plastic surgery, and the ultimate heartbreak, euthanasia of the dog.

Be honest about this. If your dog is a threat to strangers or to your own family, you must take every step necessary to rehabilitate the animal. You'll need help from a professional. You also must be realistic and accept the fact that some Goldens (thankfully very few) cannot be rehabbed. If you love your Golden, let professionals deal with him before he hurts someone else, and you have to deal with more regrets.

If your Golden is aggressive for no apparent reason with other dogs, you have a different set of problems. Dog aggression is a serious issue, and one that may or may not resolve with age and/or maturity. If it's a personality conflict with a particular dog, their living arrangements must be adjusted to avoid confrontations. If it occurs with multiple dogs, you have to evaluate the frequency and severity of the behavior to determine the best course of action. Such dogs can live happily in single-dog households. Difficult decisions for sure, but ones that must be made.

The Part of Tens

Dig into the chapters in this part for fun games and tricks that both you and your Golden will enjoy and that will enhance life with your Golden.

Explore websites that offer more information about being a Golden Retriever owner, including rescue organizations and the latest information on diseases and research.

Discover your dog's versatility in the show ring, on and off the field, as a support dog, and more.

Learn simple ways to keep your Golden happy, healthy, and safe to live his best life.

Chapter 17

Ten Great Games to Play with Your Puppy

One of the great gifts of Golden adolescence is your puppy's joyful exuberance in everything he does. And lucky you — you get to be a part of it! An important part of the total Golden experience is having fun together. Puppy games not only enhance the bond between you and your pup, but they also tire him out, a luxury you'll treasure at the end of a busy puppy day. In this chapter, I share ten of my favorite puppy pastimes.

TIP Make sure that all your play-teaching sessions are fun and successful. Keep them short so that you don't tax his attention span. Take advantage of your puppy's dependence on you and his strong desire to be near you and play with you. His confidence will grow as fast as his little legs and body.

Follow Me

Your puppy must never discover that it's fun or okay to run away from you, indoors or out, even when you're playing. Teach him to run *after* you instead by inventing games that encourage that behavior. If he's a little slow, pretend that you're racing and simply run in place or take tiny steps so that he can catch you. Whoop and holler, act like an idiot, and tell him "Good boy, Come!" — what a great adventure to outflank your mom!

TIP

When your puppy runs away from you, don't run after him because he will consider that a game of chase. To trick him into coming back, kneel down on the ground and pretend you found a treasure. Talk excitedly to this invisible object, even scratch and paw at the ground. Your puppy will come over to investigate, and you can calmly snag his collar.

Puppy Catch

Two people sit on the floor across from each other, 10 or 15 feet apart, with one of them holding and petting the puppy. Have the other person call the puppy with a silly happy voice, "Puppy, Come, puppy, puppy, puppy!" Open your arms wide when you call and praise and hug the puppy when he comes.

You can incorporate a ball or toy into the game and toss the toy back and forth for him to retrieve. Let him fetch the toy, give him a treat to release it, and then toss the toy across to the other person. That person hugs and praises him when he gets the toy, gives a treat, and tosses it back to person No. 1.

Kiss Me, Kate

Kiss me on command is a snap to teach. (It isn't exercise, but it's something you'll both enjoy forever.) Puppies, especially Goldens, are automatic licking machines. Just tell him "Kiss, kiss, goood boy, kiss!" every time he licks you. He'll be more than happy to oblige. Puppy breath doesn't last very long, so make the most of this one while you can!

Hide and Seek

Play fun outdoor games like hide and seek. It will help teach the Come command as well as reinforce your protector-leadership position.

JUST FOR FUN

Wait until he sniffs the grass or gets distracted. Then slip behind a tree where he can't see you. Peek out to see when he discovers you're gone and comes running back to find you. As soon as he gets near, come out, clap your hands happily, and call him, "Puppy, Come!" Squat down with arms outstretched to hug him as he races toward you. Trust me, he will come running!

Fetch

Sit on the kitchen floor and toss a favorite toy for your puppy to chase and bring back. "Puppy, Fetch." Your word association games start now. As he's bringing back the toy, say "Puppy, Come!" When he returns with the toy, be sure to let him hold on to it for just a moment or two before you take it from him for two reasons.

>> He'll know he's being praised for bringing back the toy.

>> He won't get the idea that you'll take his toy away every time he brings it back.

TIP

To make sure your puppy won't fetch the toy and carry it off in another direction, start this game at the end of a long hallway, closing any doors to make the hall escape-proof. Then he'll have nowhere to go but to return to you.

When he gives up the toy, tell him "Drop" and use that Good Boy praise. If he doesn't release the toy, remove it gently from his mouth while saying "Drop." Throw the toy again with lots of happy talk and praise him as he races across the kitchen floor to take it. He is discovering that fetching is fun and coming back to you means praise and hugs. And he's learning his New Word game. You're already started on "Fetch," "Come," and "Drop."

Double Fetch

A second version of the retrieving game uses two toys. Give him the first toy and put the other one in your pocket. Praise him when he takes the first toy and, after a minute, show him the second one and flash it about excitedly. Toss it and when he runs to get it, pick up the first toy and repeat the toss rotation. You can add a third toy if you wish. Pick up the toys as he drops them, and continue to exchange toys and let him run around with them in this fashion several times. Remember to back up as you praise him to encourage him to come to you. Get creative and invent your own version of this game. Keep the sessions short and stop the game when his interest level is still high. And *always* stop if he slows down, gets tired, or loses interest.

WARNING

When playing with your puppy, don't do anything to confuse him or make him apprehensive. Kids, especially, often think it's fun to tease a puppy and show him a toy and then hide it or pretend to throw it. Please don't let that happen. Explain that it will make the puppy distrustful and resentful, and he won't want to play anymore.

Find Me

This is the indoor version of Hide and Seek. It's best to play it with a helper who can hold the puppy while you hide in another room.

Start by allowing the puppy to see you leave, then go into another room, behind a door or sofa, or into the bathroom and into the shower stall. Once you are in place, call the puppy by name or by making a silly sound, and have the other person release the puppy. Continue to call or make noise until he finds you. Then get all excited and praise, praise, praise, and give him a treat. Continue the game and hide in different rooms and places.

Once your puppy has mastered the Sit-Stay command (see Chapter 9), you can play this game without a helper. Put him on a Sit-Stay and hide, then call him or make noises so he can find you.

I play this with my adult dogs, and they always fall for my little tricks!

Find the Treat

This is another indoor game similar to Find Me, but it uses a treat or toy instead. I recommend a treat since it's easier for the puppy to sniff the treat. Begin with a handful of treats — cut-up carrots work well — and let him watch you place the treat under a corner of the rug or behind a chair. Let the puppy come along, then point to the treat and tell him, "Find It!" Continue by placing the treat in different easy-to-spot places, using the same technique.

As with the Find Me game, you will initially need someone to hold the puppy while you hide the treat. Progress to hiding it in harder places, then in other rooms, before sending him to find it from your starting point. Once he is solid on a Sit-Stay command, you can play the game as you did with Find Me.

Regardless of his success, he will love the attention, praise and activity. It's a win-win for both of you!

Kick the Bottle

This game is best played outdoors where there is plenty of space. Put a few coins in two or three empty plastic gallon or half-gallon milk jugs. Set them in the yard with your pup and give one of them a kick (lightly — we're not talking football here!) across the yard. When he runs to chase it, kick another jug in a different direction. Continue to switch jugs as he runs to chase them. This is a short-term game. His enthusiasm will wind down quickly, so end it while he's still having fun.

Stuff the Kong

Kong toys are the best dog toy ever invented! Stuff a Kong with a small amount of cheese, peanut butter, or other safe and tasty edible. Hide it as with Find the Treat, but let him have it when he finds it. He will not need you to enjoy the rest of this one! He'll have plenty of fun digging the stuffing out of the Kong.

WARNING

Never play tug-of-war with your puppy or adult Golden with his toys or any other object. Tug-of-war is a dominance game, and your dog should never enter any situation, even in play, where he is at opposition with his boss.

Chapter **18**

Ten Websites for the Golden Retriever Believer

The vastness of the Internet never ceases to amaze. Dog lovers in general, and Golden Retriever owners in particular, can surf the 'Net for information about everything doggie, from breed-specific information to general care, training, canine legislation, and more. You can even join chat rooms, where you can just brag about your special Golden. This chapter shares ten websites of particular interest to owners of companion Goldens as well as the die-hard Golden competitor.

WARNING

While you surf, beware of websites that promote various products along with information. Their intent may be to sell rather than to inform.

Golden Retriever Club of America (GRCA)

https://www.grca.org

The national breed club for the Golden Retriever offers an excellent website that provides a bountiful menu of Golden topics and selections. Books, general breed information, regional breed clubs, and local contacts . . . just about everything Golden is a mere click away.

Encyclopedia of Canine Veterinary Medical Information

https://www.einet.net/dir32171/Diseases_and_Disorders.htm

This site gives you a brief synopsis and explanation of almost every canine illness and disease, the symptoms, and commonly suggested treatments. Do not treat an illness before discussing with your veterinarian.

Golden Retriever Forum

https://www.goldenretrieverforum.com

This website includes a chat room as well as several other forums to explore. It also offers information on a wide variety of topics, both Golden and general canine.

Morris Animal Foundation

https://www.morrisanimalfoundation.org/golden-retriever-lifetime-study

The Golden Retriever Club of America (GRCA) partners with the Morris Animal Foundation in research on cancers and genetic diseases that plague the Golden breed. The Golden Retriever Lifetime Study is a three-year, one-million-dollar collaborative project, codenamed MADGiC (Making Advanced Discoveries in Golden Cancers). The goal is to examine and understand the genetic traits that cause or contribute to hemangiosarcoma and lymphosarcoma in Goldens. With the help of veterinarians and Golden owners, the study collects data on the nutritional, environmental, lifestyle, and genetic risk factors of 3,000 enrolled Golden Retrievers.

VetGen (Veterinary Genetic Services)

https://vetgen.com

VetGen is a website devoted to veterinary genetic disease control research and genetic disease detection services for all purebred animals. Breeders and dog owners combine VetGen resources with other DNA data to target and eliminate genetic disease in their preferred breeds.

American Kennel Club (AKC)

https://www.akc.org

AKC is a not-for-profit organization that maintains a purebred dog registry, sanctions dog events, and promotes responsible dog ownership. The AKC website offers a wealth of doggie information on health care, training, puppy selection, national breed club contacts, breeder referral by state and by national breed club, breed registration, and, of course, details on AKC-sanctioned events and programs.

Golden Retriever Foundation (GRF)

https://www.goldenretrieverfoundation.org/research.html

The GRF is a tax-exempt, non-profit, charitable organization established to fund projects that benefit the welfare of the breed. Through donations and grants, the GRF works with and contributes to the Morris Animal Foundation and the AKC Canine Health Foundation on cancer research and canine health issues. Several funds under the GRF umbrella use contributions to support cancer research, fund rescue group expenses, and support educational programs.

Dog Owner's Guide

http://canismajor.com/dog/guide.html

This collection of previously published articles (from the tabloid of the same name) brings you articles on a variety of dog-related issues of interest to pet owners as well as owners of show dogs.

Golden Retriever Rescue Organizations

https://www.officialgoldenretriever.com/blog/dogs-world/golden-retriever-rescue-organizations-united-states-america

This website directs you to several of the more prominent rescue groups in the United States. For information on rescue groups in every state, visit the GRCA website (see earlier in this chapter), which has information on over 100 rescue groups in the United States and Puerto Rico.

K9Data.com

https://www.k9data.com

This is an open database for Golden Retriever pedigrees. The information is entirely provided by the users, and the names of the dog owners are entered into the database. Each entry offers the dog's AKC registration, pedigree, and health information (OFA and/or other clearances).

IN THIS CHAPTER

» Shining in the ring and in the field

» Mastering basic puppy retrieving

» Exploring hunting and field trials

» Serving society

Chapter **19**

Ten Things in Your Golden Retriever's Bag of Tricks

Despite the Golden Retriever's ability to excel at almost every activity devised for dogs, about 95 percent of all Goldens serve as all-American family companions and bed-warmers. However, if you take a moment to investigate the breed's versatility, you'll be amazed, and maybe inspired, at what your Golden's relatives have accomplished. And who knows, you might be tempted to dip your dog's paws into something more challenging than a run around the park or fetching the Frisbee in the yard.

Blue Ribbon Performers: Conformation

If *conformation* sounds a little stuffy, just say "showing dogs." Dog shows are more than a Miss and Mr. Golden Retriever beauty contest. The dogs are judged on physical structure, gait (how they walk and trot), and their physical condition, including temperament and animation (alert, eager, etc.). These qualities are listed in the breed standard in Chapter 2. The winner is judged to be the best representative of the breed and awarded points that apply toward the future title of show champion. That title appears as a Ch. before his name on his pedigree.

Grooming and Gaiting

If you hope to show your Golden, you have to learn how to *gait* your dog, since that is an important element of judging. Proper gaiting, or how the dog moves, is determined in part by the dog's structure, with the hindquarters (rear end) the main engine that drives the dog. Of course, other parts of the dog's anatomy also contribute to proper movement. You can view examples of gaiting on YouTube videos, but it is best learned with the help of someone experienced in conformation.

Proper grooming is more than a brushing your Golden's lovely coat. This is an art, and one that will absolutely affect a judge's opinion of the dog. Grooming is best learned at the hands of an experienced Golden owner or a professional who would be willing to show you the ropes.

TIP

You can't teach gaiting by yourself. You need an experienced person to evaluate your dog and help you get started. If you purchased your puppy from a show breeder, work with her to decide if your pup has show potential. Try to find a Golden Retriever club in your area or join a local kennel club where you'll meet other people who show their own breeds in conformation. Attend dog shows and talk to Golden Retriever exhibitors. Your veterinarian can direct you to a breeder or a club so that you can meet other dog show fanciers. If your beloved Golden has no show potential and that is your dog goal, love him for all his other fine qualities, and consider purchasing your next Golden from a reliable breeder with a good track record in the show ring.

Obedience Competition: More Than Good Manners

The constant parade of Golden Retrievers performing on TV, in print ads, and on merchandise continues to amaze me. One thing is clear: This dog is not only photogenic, but also trainable. Given the breed's tractability and incredible desire to please, most Goldens excel at learning details, which makes them easy dogs to train. In the world of obedience competition, Golden Retrievers always number among the top performers in all categories. In fact, every year more Golden Retrievers become obedience trial champions (OTCh) than any other breed.

Obedience shows are another ring activity, only this time looks don't count. Your Golden will have to master several basic obedience routines (stuff he already learned in basic obedience class) and achieve qualifying scores (a minimum of 170 out of a possible 200 points) in three different obedience shows to earn a title that will appear after his name on his pedigree. It's easy, and it's fun for both of you!

Obedience titles are earned on three levels of competition, with each level presenting a greater degree of difficulty. In the Novice class, you earn a CD (Companion Dog) title, and in the Open class, you earn a CDX (Companion Dog Excellent). The Utility class offers a UD (Utility Dog) title.

REMEMBER

A dog has to come up through the ranks and earn his obedience titles from the bottom up. Each class offers placement awards of first through fourth place in addition to qualifying, so if your Golden performs his exercises to near perfection, he can earn a trophy, too.

If you'd like to dabble in obedience, find a training club or check with a local kennel club for classes in advanced obedience. The American Kennel Club (https://www.akc.org) will send you its booklet, *Rules and Regulations for Obedience Competition,* if you write to the Club. You should also invest in a book or two devoted to obedience training.

Hunting, Hunt Tests, Field Trials, and the WCX

Does your Golden go bonkers to retrieve, not just birds, but even nonbird objects? Do you plan to use him as a hunting partner? If you'd like to fulfill the heritage envisioned by Lord Tweedmouth (see "Golden myths and history" in Chapter 2), you have lots of choices.

Hunting

If your outdoor passion is waterfowl or upland game and your Golden is from hearty hunting stock, that Golden nose will lead you to many hours of pleasure in the field. Of course, you'll have to deal with a muddy dog, cockleburs, and other field debris in his Golden coat, but a game bag stuffed with birds is worth it.

TIP

Like all performance athletes, a good hunting dog needs fine-tuning before he becomes a trusted hunting companion. For best results, team up with other hunters or field trainers when your Golden is still young to build good retrieving habits early in the game. A well-trained hunting retriever will be the envy of your hunting buddies, but "well trained" is the key phrase here. If this is your first hunting experience or your first working retriever, find a professional trainer or people involved in the sport to learn the basic principles of field training. Your youngster has a lot to learn in order to become a good hunting partner. Beg, borrow, or buy a few books on training a retriever for the field.

Hunt tests

Hunt tests are designed for the noncompetitive sportsman who may or may not actually hunt, but wants to work with his retriever in the field. Sponsored by the American Kennel Club (AKC), the United Kennel Club (UKC), and/or the North American Hunting Retriever Association (NAHRA), hunt tests consist of three or more stakes, or levels, designed with graduated degrees of difficulty that test a retriever's natural abilities. The tests are pass-fail. Each dog is judged against a standard of performance and does not have to outperform another dog in order to qualify.

Launched in 1985, the AKC retriever hunting tests have grown into a major event in the world of sporting dogs. Retriever owners and their dogs (real-life hunting dogs as well as retrievers who just love birds, water, and retrieving) work with freshly shot game birds (ducks and pheasants) under simulated hunting conditions to prove the dogs' natural hunting ability. Dogs who complete the requirements as set forth by the AKC rules for hunting tests receive a corresponding title, which will appear after the dog's name on his pedigree.

A JH (Junior Hunter) title (the first testing level) requires four qualifying scores or legs. Dogs must complete two simple retrieves on land and two in water at short distances of under 100 yards. The SH (Senior Hunter) title requires five legs earned in land and water tests that include multiple retrieves with greater difficulty than the junior test. A Master Hunter (MH) title needs six legs to earn that title. A Master dog must complete multiple complex retrieving tasks on land and in water, and work under more difficult and challenging conditions.

At all three title levels, dogs are judged on their own performance and are not eliminated because another dog did a better job. Because the tests are noncompetitive, the atmosphere is more relaxed and friendly, and participants are more supportive of the other dogs entered in each stake. But as with actual hunting, you need to train your dog before you are ready to compete. Find a professional trainer or experienced retriever people to work with. You can find working retriever owners in retriever clubs or sportsman's clubs that cater to hunting enthusiasts. Write to the AKC for *Regulations and Guidelines for AKC Hunting Tests for Retrievers*.

Wait! There's more. The UKC and the NAHRA also offer a noncompetitive hunting test program complete with game birds, gun safety provisions, and titles for the dog. Rules and regulations are available from both organizations.

Field trials

Field trials are the grand-daddy of sporting retriever events and date back to 1931. Licensed by the AKC, field trials are a big step up from hunting tests, and showcase the superstars of the working retriever world. Competition is fierce, and only the best capture the wins, placements, and points required to earn the title of Field Champion (FC) or Amateur Field Champion (AFC). Field championships are the most prized of working titles, particularly because this is an all-breed sport with Labradors, Goldens, and Chesapeakes competing on the same playing field.

Labradors routinely dominate field trials, with dozens of Labs earning titles annually compared to one or two Golden Retrievers. But it should be noted (in all fairness) that few Goldens run the field trial circuit, so the imbalance may be one of numbers rather than pure talent. However, if you think your Golden has the makings of a trial dog, be prepared for years of grueling training and competition.

Field trials differ from hunting tests because dogs are eliminated on the basis of their performance when compared to that of other competing dogs. Dogs are tested on both land and in water under more rigid circumstances than in hunt tests. The tests are designed on four ascending levels of difficulty to challenge both younger and more experienced dogs. The vast majority of the dogs entered have some degree of professional training, so a novice owner-handler is at a huge disadvantage.

WARNING

I hate to sound discouraging, but this is an expensive and highly competitive sport that requires enormous dedication to training and a thick hide to endure inevitable failures. With 50 to 100 dogs competing in most stakes, and only four placements awarded, it's no wonder this is often called a loser's game. If you decide to try it, start with the best-caliber Golden you can afford, purchased from a reliable breeder with field trial experience (as proven by the accomplishments of the breeder and the parents of the pups).

For the AKC *Field Trial Rules and Standard Procedure* manual, write directly to the AKC. As with hunt tests and hunting, training books and videos abound, and you'll be smarter and more successful if you read a few.

Working certificate tests

Finally, a field event devoted just to Golden Retrievers. *Working certificate tests* are very basic, noncompetitive field tests sponsored by the Golden Retriever Club of America (GRCA) to encourage and evaluate the instincts and natural abilities of Goldens in the field. The dogs are tested both on land and in water against a set standard of performance, and they are not expected to perform anywhere near the level of the field trial or hunt test retriever.

Designed with two levels of difficulty, the WC (Working Certificate) requires a short (35 to 50 yards) double retrieve on land and two shorter single retrieves in the water. The WCX (Working Certificate Excellent) consists of a longer triple retrieve on land, a double retrieve in water, with a few additional requirements to demonstrate trainability in the dog. The tests are sponsored by GRCA member clubs across the country and open to all AKC-registered Goldens. Most clubs hold practice training sessions before the tests to offer assistance to newcomers and club members.

So, if your Golden is a retrieve-a-holic or if he loves to hunt a little or a lot, these tests are excellent forums where you and your Golden can show off and have a grand time doing what he loves best. Complete rules and regulations are available from the GRCA secretary or from any area Golden Retriever Club.

If any or all of these events tweak your interest, you can start your puppy field training right in your own backyard. Eventually, you'll have to move on to more challenging areas, but basic puppy work is fun backyard stuff.

Retrieving

Tennis ball, Frisbee, retrieving bumper, fallen branches — if your Golden is like mine, he will retrieve them all, and retrieve, and retrieve, until he drops! This dog knows that "retriever" is the better half of his name!

TIP

Whether you plan a serious retrieving future for your Golden or just hope to have a little fun, the right start in retrieving basics will help you both enjoy his natural ability. The most important element in his retrieving life is his inherent enthusiasm for the job he was originally bred to do. Your job is to build on that enthusiasm with encouragement and success. The right start is especially important if you plan to train your Golden for hunting, hunting tests, or field trials. He'll need a good foundation in basic retrieving skills. (Yes, he already knows how to retrieve, but he has to learn to do it *your* way.)

Here are some ways to build your puppy's retrieving foundation:

>> **Use a soft retrieving bumper.** Start your 7- or 8-week-old puppy on a soft puppy bumper made from an old white sock (because white is highly visible) stuffed with any soft material. A soft paint roller is another good choice. Use your "bumper" for retrieving only, never for play time or any other purpose. If you have a pigeon wing, fasten it to the sock with tape.

>> **Work indoors first.** This is kind of an extension of his puppy-toy-retrieving games. A good place to begin is indoors in a long hallway. Close any doors so that there's no escape route and he has nowhere to run except back to you. Be sure the bumper is conspicuous on the flooring surface.

>> **Rev his retrieving engine.** Flash the bumper under his nose to get him excited and then toss it just a few feet in front of him. Throw straight ahead at his eye level, sort of a skimmer throw, because a 7- or 8-week-old puppy has very limited range of vision and can't follow objects that move rapidly up, down, or sideways. Use your Fetch command and give lots of praise when he retrieves. Encourage his return and praise him once again *while he still has the bumper in his mouth*. (If you take the bumper immediately, he'll associate coming back with you taking the bumper away and will learn not to come back.) Remove it gently while giving more praise and toss it again.

>> **Do three retrieves and stop.** Start with three short, easy retrieves a day in the same lesson, *never* more, and fewer if his enthusiasm fades. Always stop when he's still eager to retrieve again. The biggest mistake most people make is offering too many retrieves until the pup or dog gets bored and tired of the game.

>> **Move the game outdoors.** Once he gets the idea, move your lessons outdoors on short-cut grass and start with two or three retrieves of 20 or 30 yards, less if he can't follow where you toss it. Increase the distance gradually as he succeeds.

>> **Use a long line for control.** At some point during this scenario, he's going to take off with that bumper and head for the far corner of the yard. ("This is *my* bumper!") No problem. Attach your 30-foot-long line to his collar. The moment he picks up his bumper, call him with a Come command and give a gentle tug to remind him to return. (Don't reel him in like a fish. If he still resists, use a series of gentle tugs, only at those moments when he's back-pedaling or stops moving toward you.) Run backward as you're calling him excitedly to entice him back to you. Most Retriever puppy owners quickly learn to act wild and crazy to keep their puppies motivated!

>> **Add a thrower.** Once your puppy is returning without too much resistance, you can add a thrower to these sessions. As with all dog lessons, when you add any new element to a lesson, back up a step (in this case, shorten the

distance of the throw). Still working on mowed grass, the thrower stands 20 or 30 yards away while you hold your pup. The thrower calls "Hup, hup" while you tell your pup to "Mark." Once the pup's attention is focused on the thrower, nod your head to signal for the throw with more "Hups." (No huge throws for little pups.) Release the puppy while the bumper is in mid-air and don't forget to act wild and foolish again on his return. If he has trouble finding the bumper or going the entire distance, shorten the throws until he is successful. Success is the main ingredient in his basic training.

>> **Train in different places.** Work with your puppy in different places. Stay on cut grass, but vary the location of your training lessons. With each location change, you will be adding new distractions, so shorten up your throws each time until he's focused on his work. He has to learn to concentrate on his tasks in unfamiliar settings.

>> **Train with people who know more than you do.** Beyond this point, if you want to pursue field work with your Golden, you'll need a good book or two on training Retriever puppies for hunting and an experienced training partner. If your Golden puppy's a retrieve-a-holic, scour gun dog books and magazines and join a retriever club or hunting club (it doesn't have to be just Goldens) to find someone to train with.

Swimming

No doubt about it, Golden Retrievers are actually furry fish, or at least they *should* be. They love the water — lakes, ponds, puddles — and the muddier, the better. If you're into swimming and wet dogs, you've chosen the right breed. Swimming comes naturally to Golden puppies, although some may take a little longer to get beyond the puppy-paddle stage.

When introducing your Golden puppy (or Golden of any age) to water for the first time, observe these rules:

>> **Never force or throw your puppy or dog into the water.** Your Golden must go in the water on his own. You can lure, entice, cajole, and beg, but never, ever force.

>> **Don't start with cold water.** Would you bathe a baby in cold water? Positive association applies most naturally to water, too.

>> **Make his first swim pleasant.** A Golden's introduction to water should always be a positive experience. Start with a beach or pond with a shallow shoreline, warm water, and a warm day. Some Golden puppies take one look

at water and dive in headfirst without a second thought. Most will puppy-paddle at first, but a few will take off swimming like a porpoise.

>> **Go swimming with your pup.** Put on your aqua shoes and wade in with your puppy. Toss a toy and use lots of encouraging praise. Start in water up to his elbows or belly, and as he shows confidence, toss the toy a little farther each time. If he gets nervous or refuses, back off and stay in shallow water for a while. Never scold or force. Use your three Ps again — Praise, Patience, and Practice!

Tracking: Using That Golden Nose

Tracking is a distant relative of obedience trials, only the dog works independently and follows his nose to prove his scenting ability. The dog must follow a *track*, a path walked by a stranger, across complex terrain that includes twists and turns, fences, hedgerows, and other hazards.

Two AKC titles are offered, and the tests are sponsored by AKC-licensed dog clubs. To earn a TD (Tracking Dog) title, the dog must complete a 400- to 500-yard track. The TDX (Tracking Dog Excellent) faces a more complex track of 800 to 1,000 yards. Tracking buffs hail this sport as exciting and exhilarating for themselves as well as their dogs! Complete rules are available in the Tracking Regulations from the AKC.

TIP

Dogs have an estimated 220 million "smell cells" in their noses compared to the 5 million in the human nose. And their sense of smell is said to be up to several million times more sensitive. No wonder your Golden can dig up hidden treasures in your backyard!

Agility

Is your Golden a Frisbee fanatic? Does he climb the kids' slide at the park? Can he leap tall buildings in a single bound, or at least jump on his doghouse? Then he might be a natural for agility.

In agility events, the dogs race through a complex course of obstacles to jump over, crawl under or into, cross over, straddle, or weave through. They are judged on speed and accuracy, earning both qualifying scores and placements for their performance. The sport is open to all breeds of dogs, but athletic Goldens usually excel. Agility enthusiasts have a favorite saying, "Try it, you'll like it!"

Agility clubs are turning up in most major cities, so if you're interested, check with your vet, a local kennel club, or write to the national agility organization listed with the AKC. *The Rules and Regulations for Agility Trials* are also available through the AKC.

Golden Assistance Partners

Take a healthy dose of all the Golden Retriever activities previously described in this chapter, add the Golden's great willingness to please, and you have the ultimate public servant — and he'll never dip his paws into campaign funds!

» **Assistance dogs:** As skilled assistance dogs for the physically disabled, Golden Retrievers pull wheelchairs, pick up books and pencils, turn on lights, open refrigerator doors, and complete dozens of other daily tasks for their disabled person. Goldens easily master complex tasks and minute details and are especially adept at sensing their owner's needs and wishes. Assistance-dog owners state emphatically that their dog has made the difference between merely existing and living a quality life.

» **Guide dogs for the blind:** Golden Retrievers, Labrador Retrievers, and German Shepherds are the three breeds most widely used as guide dogs for the blind. A guide dog's primary responsibility is what the name implies — to guide his owner in public in heavy crowds, public transportation, traffic, and other busy areas. Guide dogs are raised the same way as assistance dogs — by volunteer puppy-raisers until they are 12 months to 18 months of age, when they enter formal training. Dogs who complete the program are matched to the physical and mental characteristics of the blind recipient.

» **Hearing dogs:** Hearing dogs are canine alarm systems for their deaf owners. A hearing dog will alert his owner to as many as a dozen different sounds, including a door bell, an alarm clock, a telephone, a smoke alarm, a baby's cry, or a window surreptitiously opened by an intruder. Companion Goldens can easily be trained for this task if their owner suddenly becomes deaf. Some assistance-dog providers also train hearing dogs or can refer you to an organization that does.

» **Drug dogs:** From airports to seaports to border patrols, Golden Retriever drug detection dogs patrol their beats in search of illegal narcotics and other contraband substances. Thanks to their superior scenting ability, they can sniff out everything from marijuana and cocaine to cash and alcohol. If there's a downside to a Golden's service in the drug force, it's his huggability and happy personality, which can present a nonthreatening figure to the criminal. Nevertheless, tons of Golden supersleuths work for the U.S. Customs Service and other law enforcement agencies as part of the nation's growing army of drug detection dogs.

» **Arson dogs:** Arson detection dogs are trained to sniff out gasoline, kerosene, and other types of accelerants that can be used to start a fire. In this area of law enforcement, even modern science has difficulty competing with the Golden nose. Arson officials have recorded cases of canines locating a fire site under inches of ice and water and in places where lab technology failed to find accelerants. In Iowa, a state court set a nationwide legal precedent when it ruled that an arson dog's nose work was admissible evidence in a criminal proceeding. Fortunately, a Golden just thinks he's having fun sniffing around a fire scene.

» **Search and Rescue Goldens:** You've seen them on TV, dogs searching through rubble after an earthquake or a bombing, looking for survivors buried under concrete and debris. Known as *Search and Rescue (SAR) dogs*, they work for no reward other than the pleasure of the work itself, finding a human being, then being rewarded with their favorite toy or object. SAR Goldens also assist local law enforcement agencies searching for children and people who are lost or victims of suspected crimes.

For more information on canine search and rescue operations, contact the National Association of Search and Rescue (NASAR), P.O. Box 3709, Fairfax, VA 22038.

» **Therapists in Golden armor:** Too bad doctors can't invent a Golden Retriever pill. The breed is arguably more therapeutic for the physically disabled and emotionally disturbed than any medication in the marketplace. Take two brown eyes, soft silky fur, a wildly wagging tail, and a dog who senses what you need at any given moment in a crisis, stir well, pet, and you have a Golden Retriever Doctor Feelgood.

Goldens are active in nursing homes, hospitals, children's wards, prisons, and schools. They work with all ages and all human conditions and make each and every one feel better about themselves or their predicament. To paraphrase a famous cowboy, "Happy tails to youuuuu. . ."

The Golden Trickster

Beyond the Golden's talents in every area of canine sport and activity, he also can master all the usual doggie tricks, like give paw, shake hands, roll over, play dead, speak, spin, sit pretty, and stand on your hind legs and dance. And of course, kiss. A tutorial on each of these tricks is beyond the scope of this book. But you can find websites, books, and YouTube videos on how to teach your Golden how to be cute "like all those other breeds."

Chapter **20**

Ten Ways to Help Your Golden Live a Longer and More Golden Life

The average Golden Retriever lives for 10 to 13 years. That's way too short for Golden lovers, or any dog lover for that matter. Don't we all wish we could create a world where our dogs lived as long as we do? But even though Mother Nature is in charge, there are some important things you can do to maximize your Golden's health, which will translate into a longer life.

In this chapter, I share ten valuable suggestions that will help your dog live a healthier, and therefore longer, life. Actually, they are more than suggestions; they are cardinal rules that you should follow if you care about the well-being of your precious Golden friend. If I sound like a fanatic on this subject, it's because I *am*.

Keep Your Golden Lean

Obesity is a serious canine health problem that affects your dog's longevity. Indeed, just an extra ten pounds can shorten your Golden's life. The excess weight strains every major body system and predisposes a dog to joint disorders, hypertension, and congestive heart failure. My goodness, your dog deserves a better fate than that!

Many veterinarians state that at least 50 percent of all the dogs they see are overweight. Most of their clients don't realize that their dogs are fat or that the excess weight can cause such devastating problems.

TIP

How do you tell whether your dog is "just right?" When the standing dog is viewed from above, he should have a distinct waist, a narrowing between his rib cage and his rump. You can also do a rib cage test: Place your hands on each side of his ribs and press very gently. You should be able to feel his ribs beneath a layer of muscle with your palms. If you have to press hard to find those ribs, or if they aren't there at all, then you know what you have to do. His diet starts today!

Check first with your vet to determine your Golden's optimum weight. If he's over by five pounds or more, consider what you have been feeding him and whether it's the correct food for his age, weight, and lifestyle. Incorporate more exercise into his daily routine. Whatever he's been doing, he'll need to do it more often, as long as your vet agrees that it's healthy and okay. Skip those table scraps if they are part of the problem. A raw carrot won't hurt your Golden, but a pile of mashed potatoes? That's another story!

Practice Dental Hygiene

The message here is simple: Clean your Golden's teeth, and he will live longer! A survey conducted at one Veterinarian Congress in Vancouver, B.C., determined that dog owners can extend their dog's life by simply providing routine dental care. Other studies show that 80 percent of dogs show signs of oral disease by age 3. Scary, isn't it?

Why is dental care so important? Plaque and tartar buildup on his teeth will cause periodontal disease. Bacteria then enters the he bloodstream through the damaged gums and attack the kidneys, liver, heart, and lungs. Result: early death. As an example, kidney failure, a common cause of death in senior dogs, often starts at a damaged gum line. It would happen to you, too, if you didn't brush your teeth!

The American Veterinary Dental Association reminds you that you are your dog's dentist *and his toothbrush*. Start when he's a baby and get him used to having your fingers in his mouth (also great for bite control!). No matter what your dog's age, it's never too late to start. Although daily brushing is best, twice weekly or even weekly brushing might be a more reachable goal. Find the nitty-gritty on how to brush his teeth in Chapter 11. Just make sure you do it.

Exercise

Your Golden will stay healthy — and better yet, content — with a generous dose of daily exercise. Remember, your dog is an athlete who needs to run, play, swim, and do busy, active things. Regular exercise will strengthen all his body parts, muscles as well as heart and lungs. I firmly believe that our daily 2-mile walk has given my Goldens extra vitality as well as extra years. My vet agrees; she is always amazed at their muscle tone and vigor. My 15-year-old Golden did her double-mile trek daily with the rest of our Golden pack until the day before she died; in fact, she couldn't *wait* to hit the trail.

Spay Your Female Golden

Have your Golden girlfriend spayed. This one surgical procedure will totally remove the possibility of certain cancers in the female dog.

Statistics show that spay surgery offers reduced risk of breast and uterine cancers, pyometra, false pregnancy, uterine torsion, and vaginal and uterine prolapse. Your personal benefits include no messy estrus fluids dripping all over your house and no undesirable suitors hanging around the yard.

Neuter Your Male Golden

The stats are just as good for male dogs. Neutering will totally eliminate the risk of many cancers that affect male dogs, and decrease the risk of several others. Neutered dogs enjoy zero to reduced risk of testicular cancer prostate problems, anal tumors, hernias, and testicular infections.

Your personal benefits include absolute birth control for life, relief from hormone-driven urges such as aggression toward other males, territorialism on his home turf, neighborhood wanderlust, marking with urine at home and in new places, overt dominant behavior, sexual behaviors such as mounting (your leg!) and arousal, and your own frustration during his hormonal surges when male dogs resist doing what they are told. Altered dogs also are less likely to bite or exhibit temperament problems that could affect your family and neighbors. Your insurance company will love it, too!

REMEMBER

There is no downside to spay/neuter surgery. It will not affect your Golden's true personality, and your Golden will still be the silly, affectionate beast you know and love. And he'll live longer, too. Gosh, what more could you ask?

Know How to Take Emergency Action

Become an emergency expert so that you can recognize and handle canine accidents and emergencies. Because my dogs can't talk, I have to be their eyes and ears and always be observant and prepared. In many emergencies, just an extra few minutes could save a life.

Be a Teacher

You already know your Golden does not come preprogrammed or pretrained. It's your job to teach him correct behavior and good manners just as you did with your children, or as your parents did with you. He will be a joy to live with and a welcome addition to the neighborhood as he learns how to be a well-behaved member of human society. Ill-behaved dogs of any breed are at greater risk for accidental death and euthanization.

Socialize

A puppy needs to learn about the world beyond his own backyard if he is to mature into a stable, well-behaved adult. He can't do it alone; you have to be his travel agent. Unsocialized puppies grow up fearful and are candidates for animal shelters, and you know what happens to them.

Expand Your Dog World

The more "dog people" you know, the more dog information you will absorb. (Of course, you'll have to sort the good from the incorrect or useless.) Start with your veterinarian. Ask lots of questions about *everything* connected your dog's well-being. A curious, compliant dog owner is a vet's best client!

Join a dog club, or better yet, join a Golden Retriever breed club. You'll meet breed aficionados and ordinary Golden owners who are crazy about their dogs and love to "talk dogs" and share brags and doggie information. You'll be surprised at how dog-smart they are. You can be, too!

Visit dog events, obedience trials, conformations shows, or outdoor events like hunt tests (find them through the Internet). Introduce yourself and ask questions. You already know these folks love to talk about their dogs! It's easy to develop friendships that will help you become a smarter dog caregiver.

Become a Canine Nutritionist

WARNING

I'm talking more than dog food here. There are so many people foods that are dangerous to fatal for dogs, that it's hard to keep up with all the new, and potentially bad, stuff on the market. Most people know that chocolate is very bad for dogs and other pets. (You did, right?) The amount and type is proportionate to the dog's size. Just one ounce of chocolate per pound of your dog's body weight is poisonous. The toxic component in chocolate is theobromine, which the dog processes very slowly, allowing it to build to toxic levels in his system. The AKC has an excellent website, https://www.akc.org/expert-advice/health/what-to-do-if-your-dog-ate-chocolate/, that gives complete information on treating a chocolate emergency.

Grapes, raisins, onions, avocado, citrus, and macadamia nuts are also highly toxic for dogs and other pets, and can be fatal if ingested. The ASPCA has an excellent website that details foods that are dangerous or fatal to dogs and other pets: https://www.aspca.org/pet-care/animal-poison-control/people-foods-avoid-feeding-your-pets.

The toxic and fatal ingredient I find most disturbing is xylitol. It's in more and more products today as the food industry adds it instead of sugar. It's now even in certain peanut butters, so be sure to read labels before giving any peanut butter to your dog. One sad story tells of a German Shorthaired Pointer who chewed up a plastic can of sugar-free gum containing xylitol and died a few hours later. Read labels, be aware! It's a dangerous food world out there.

Index

choosing
  puppies, 43–52
  release word, 108
  shampoos, 188
  veterinarians, 139–141
cigarettes, 64
cleaning
  supplies for, 63
  teeth, 183–185
clipping nails, 76–77
CML (canine malignant
  lymphoma), 66
coat
  about, 23
  healthy body signs and, 147
  in senior dogs, 193
coccidia, 169–170
coins, 63
collar tab, 58
collars
  about, 57
  chain training, 120–121
  choke training, 120–121
  Elizabethan, 159
  flea, 172
  head, 122
  prong, 121–122
color
  of dogs, 9, 23–24
  of eyes, 21
combs, flea, 173
Come command, 112–114
Come-Along, 58
commands
  Come, 112–114
  for crate, 83
  Down, 116–117
  Down-Stay, 117–118
  Drop It, 118
  Enough, 119–120
  Give, 118
  leave It, 118

Off, 119
Outside, 89
Sit, 114–115
Sit-Stay, 117–118
volume of voice for, 82
Wait, 115–116
communication
  consistency of, 93
  correcting behaviors, 94–95
  puppy kindergarten class,
    95–100
  puppy preschool, 92
  voice, 94
Companion Dog Excellent
  (CDX), 38
Companion Dog (CD) title,
  38, 241
competition pup tests, 49–51
confidence, building, 78
confidence and courage test,
  49–50
conformation, 239–240
conformation ring, 18
consistency, importance of, 93
cooling off, digging for, 213
core vaccines, 143–145
correcting behaviors, 94–95
costs
  food, 15
  of grooming, 11
  miscellaneous, 15
  obedience classes, 15
  pet food, 125–126
  spay/neuter, 138
  veterinary expenses, 14
coughing, 194
counter surfing, 211
cow hocks, 22
CPR, 155
CPV (canine parvovirus), 143
cradling test, 47, 48
crate training
  about, 81, 83

accidents and, 84
adult dogs, 84
curtain for, 85–86
overuse, 86–87
size of crate, 84–85
traveling and, 84
crates, 62
croup, 21
curtain, for crates, 85–86
cyanobacteria, 187

D

dam
  defined, 37
  health of, 39–41
  temperament of, 41
DCM (Dilated
  Cardiomyopathy), 205
dehydration, 155
demodectic mange, 177
dental floss, 63
desire to retrieve test, 50
dewclaws, 22
diaper pails, 64
diarrhea, 155–156
diets, exotic, 134. see also food
digging, 212–213
Dilated Cardiomyopathy
  (DCM), 205
dips, flea, 172
discipline, punishment vs., 94–95
disease, hereditary
  about, 199
  cataracts, 201
  Dilated Cardiomyopathy
    (DCM), 205
  elbow dysplasia (ED), 200–201
  epilepsy, 202–203
  eye disease, 201–202
  eyelash problems, 202
  eyelid problems, 202
  hip dysplasia (HD), 199–200

About the Author

If there is one thing that defines Nona's life, it's this: She could not live without her Goldens. For the past 40 years, they have been her best friends and the inspiration for her books. They have also blessed her with friends from all corners of the dog world: breeders, veterinarians, dog writers, professional trainers, great training partners, and so many good dog friends who adore all furry creatures great and small.

Nona's special love has always been working with her Goldens in the field, and she has trained them for field trials and hunt tests as well as for obedience competition. She has trained several of her dogs to the Master Hunter level and Qualified All-Age status in the field, and many others to obedience and other working titles. Nona has also judged field events and enjoys nothing more than watching a stylish retriever doing what he loves best.

Several of her Goldens have worked as furry therapists at local nursing homes. Each monthly visit proved that friendly paws and wagging tails are the world's best tonic for the sick and lonely.

Nona studied journalism at Truman State University and began writing to help make the dog community a better place to live. She has written over two dozen dog books, and this is her sixth book about her beloved Golden Retrievers. Her very first Golden book captured the coveted Dog Writer's Association of America Best Breed Book of the Year award in 1993.

Her passion for her dogs colors everything she does, especially her books and writing projects.

If she can teach, motivate, or inspire her readers to do it right or better, the world will be a happier, safer place for dogs. And that will make her dog life even more golden than it already is.

Dedication

For China, Arrow, Apache, Ginnie, Doc, Ms. Schatzie, Sugar, Geronimo, and goofy Windy, and all my Goldens at the Rainbow Bridge.

Author's Acknowledgments

My precious Geronimo — best friends forever. Miss you, my sweet buddy.

I have never written a dog book on my own. So many people (including the four-footed variety) make each venture possible. Thank you to my publisher, Katie Mohr, for inviting me to revisit this important work and believing that my contribution has value; I cannot thank you enough! And to my editor, Lynn Northrup, your patience with my technical limitations and my clumsy learning process was so much appreciated. My OCD about canine information often tests my OWN patience! I thank you for your keen eye and helpful (and necessary!) "golden" tips! And to my good friend, Glenda Brown, a huge thank you for tackling the review process. Your oversight gave me confidence that this work will help make present and future Golden owners enjoy a more Golden life with their fur kids. And a final hurrah to Chris Gonnerman, my computer guru, who saved my computer and this book not once, but twice!

A very special thanks to my human family, who always grant me extra space when I am obsessing over another dog book project.

And, of course, I can't forget my Golden family — past and present training partners, hiking pals, and couch cushion buds, who have blessed my life for the past 40 years. You are the inspiration behind every single word.

Publisher's Acknowledgments

Associate Publisher: Katie Mohr

Editor: Lynn Northrup

Production Editor: Siddique Shaik

Cover Image: © cmannphoto/Getty Images